LEAVES FROM THE NOTE-BOOKS

OF

LADY DOROTHY NEVILL

MACMILLAN AND CO., Limited
LONDON · BOMBAY · CALCUTTA
MELBOURNE

THE MACMILLAN COMPANY
NEW YORK · BOSTON · CHICAGO
ATLANTA · SAN FRANCISCO

THE MACMILLAN CO. OF CANADA, Ltd.
TORONTO

Leaves from the Note-Books

of

Lady Dorothy Nevill

EDITED BY

RALPH NEVILL

MACMILLAN AND CO., LIMITED
ST. MARTIN'S STREET, LONDON
1907

First Edition October 1907
Reprinted November 1907

PREFACE

WHEN, some time ago, a collection of my mother's reminiscences was given to the public, we received a large number of suggestions that a second similar volume would be certain of the same cordial welcome as was extended to the first. The following pages, containing memories and observations extending over a long period of years, are the result of these kindly exhortations.

The task of arrangement and of selection from my mother's scrap-books and note-books has been carried out by me under her supervision; and I have also included as many recollections, hitherto unpublished, as her very excellent memory was able to furnish. Of the many anecdotes which are given, the majority, it is hoped, are here told for the first time in print; most of them, indeed, recount personal experiences of her own or of some of the well-known people with whom during a long life it has been her privilege to meet. In preparing the volume valuable assistance, which it is our desire here gratefully to acknowledge, has been rendered by many well-wishers, some of them old friends, some of them unknown to us except by their encouraging and helpful letters.

It may be added that my only aim in the pages which follow has been to arrange a mass of material —some of it no doubt old, but a great deal, I hope, new—in such a form as may interest and amuse the reader and thus serve to occupy a few leisure hours. If failure be the result, the blame must be laid entirely at my door; while should the book in any measure achieve its aim, the whole credit belongs properly to my mother.

RALPH NEVILL.

CONTENTS

I

XI

XII

XIII

XIV

CONTENTS

PHOTOGRAVURE PLATES

I

IT has always been a passion with me to collect odds and ends of every sort and put them into scrap-books and note-books. Consequently I now have many volumes filled with old squibs, cuttings, photographs, scraps of verse, menus of banquets, and other trifles which, together with notes scribbled at the side, recall many pleasant and amusing days now long vanished into the past. In many of my books, I must confess, the contents are arranged in the most haphazard fashion, which now and then produces some rather amusing contrasts; for instance, opening one at hazard I came upon an old broadside of 1832 entitled "The Great Battle for Reform," side by side with a picture post-card dealing with the Suffragette agitation,—a combination which brought into my mind the following little anecdote. Long before

1   B

the days of advanced female politicians, in the year
1832, an elderly couple, peacefully sleeping in their
four-poster, were one morning roughly aroused at an
early hour by their excited maid-servant who, bursting into the bedroom, bawled out, "It's passed! It's
passed!" Extremely annoyed, the old lady called
out from inside the bed-curtains, "What's passed,
you fool?" "The Reform Bill," shouted the girl,
"and we're all equal now"; after which she
marched out of the room, purposely leaving the
door wide open to show her equality.

I possess many mementoes of old elections;
amongst them an election favour or ribband on
which is embroidered "Disraeli," a souvenir sent
me by Lord Beaconsfield in the early days of his
political career.

Mr. Bernal Osborne, amongst others, also used
to remember my passion for collecting, and, consequently, I have a good many old election addresses
and squibs which are now beginning to possess
some slight antiquarian interest.

In 1868, at Nottingham, there was a tremendous
electoral struggle, in which no less than five candidates took part. Mr. Bernal Osborne, who eventually found himself at the bottom of the poll, was
one of these, and sent me a curious little paper
which was published during the progress of what
was a very acrimonious contest. This was an
ephemeral sheet, called *The Nottingham Lamb*, a
copy of which I still retain, issued apparently for
the sole purpose of chaffing all five candidates.

As has been said, Mr. Osborne was defeated at this election; he did not indeed succeed in again entering the House of Commons till 1870, when he was returned for Waterford, the Irish constituency which, after his Nottingham defeat, he had unsuccessfully wooed in 1869. Subsequent to this election party feeling ran so high that Mr. Osborne had to be smuggled out of the town in a covered car, some of his opponent's supporters having announced their intention of lynching him. A few days afterwards he wrote to a friend: "I am slowly recovering from the success of an Irish election." Mr. Bernal Osborne, as is well known, possessed the derisive faculty in an abnormal degree, and this he could not help exercising everywhere, even in the House of Commons. He was, indeed, the hero of many amusing incidents which convulsed that august assembly, and even to-day tales are told of his readiness in banter and repartee. I do not, however, know whether the following little story is generally known.

Mr. Osborne had a great friend, an Irishman, and also a Member of Parliament, though of quite opposite political views. This gentleman, whose name was Tom Corrigan, was not by any means a teetotaller; indeed, malicious people said that he never addressed the House except when under the inspiration of sherry. On a certain night "Tom" chanced to follow Bernal Osborne in a debate upon some Irish question or other, and at once began: "What does my honourable friend know of Ireland? I answer, nothing, or less than nothing. We all know the lines of the poet—

A little learning is a dangerous thing " . . .

"Go on, Tom," interjected his friend across the House; "go on, and quote the next line!"

"And why should I be after quoting the next line, Mr. Speaker, sorr?"

"Because, Tom," again interrupted Bernal Osborne, "the next line should particularly suit you, for it runs: 'Drink deep,' Tom, 'Drink deep.'"

Mr. Osborne was always very severe upon those who spoke above their own capacity and other people's comprehension. His favourite butts in the House of Commons, indeed, were those pompous and Pharisaical members whose *doctrinaire* views he was ever ready to deride.

Amongst the political squibs in my scrap-book there is one directed against the over-taxation which in long-past days certainly did press very heavily upon the people of England. Exceedingly well written, it is, I believe, an extract from an article by Sydney Smith, published in the *Edinburgh Review* about 1820. In the form of what we should to-day call a political leaflet, it is rendered all the more effective by the manner in which the words are arranged, and also by the very adroit use made of capital letters :—

TAXES

upon every Article which enters into the Mouth, or covers the
Back, or is placed under the Foot;

TAXES

upon every thing which is pleasant to See, Hear, Feel, Smell,
and Taste;

TAXES

upon Warmth, Light, and Locomotion;

TAXES

on every thing on Earth and the Waters under the Earth;
on every thing that comes from abroad, or is grown at home;

TAXES

on the raw Material;

TAXES

on every value that is added to it by the industry of Man;

TAXES

on the SAUCE which pampers Man's appetite, and the DRUG that
restores him to health; on the ERMINE which decorates the
JUDGE, and the ROPE which hangs the CRIMINAL; on the
BRASS NAILS of the COFFIN, and the RIBBANDS of the BRIDE.

AT BED or AT BOARD, COUCHANT or LEVANT,

WE MUST PAY.

The School Boy whips his TAXED Top;
The Beardless Youth manages his TAXED Horse with a TAXED
Bridle on a TAXED Road; and the dying Englishman,
pouring his Medicine which has paid 7 PER CENT,
into a Spoon which has paid 30 PER CENT,
throws himself back upon his
CHINTZ BED which has paid 22 PER CENT,
MAKES HIS WILL,
and expires in the arms of an Apothecary who has paid
£100
for the privilege of putting him to death.

HIS WHOLE PROPERTY IS THEN TAXED FROM
2 to 10 PER CENT;

Besides the Probate, large Fees are demanded for burying
him in the Chancel;
his virtues are handed down to posterity on TAXED MARBLE;
and he is then gathered to his Fathers to be

TAXED

NO MORE.

The old broadsides are now represented by the
leaflets and posters which so plentifully abound
uring modern elections. Within the last thirty
years election posters have assumed many different
developments, though, as a rule, it must be said
that they are lacking in the incisive if rather brutal
force which characterised the cartoons and caricatures of other days. The attempt once made by
the late Mr. Lowe, afterwards Lord Sherbrooke,
to put a tax upon lucifer matches, called forth, I
remember, a perfect flood of ephemeral literature,
as well as a quantity of derisive illustrations, which
no doubt played some part in causing the abandon-
ment of what was regarded as a very unpopular
tax. A terra-cotta statuette of Mr. Lowe standing
upon a match-box is one of my treasures, and
another is a match-box crowned with the bust of
the politician in question.

Mr. Gladstone—his pastime of tree-felling, his
habit of sending post-cards, and his collars—afforded
the caricaturist a very congenial subject to work
upon. I still have a very malicious cartoon entitled "Khartoum v. Criterion," in which the

Grand Old Man is pictured holding his sides with laughter in a box at the play, whilst above is shown the death of General Gordon at Khartoum. As a matter of fact, by no possibility could Mr. Gladstone have known that the very evening on which he was going to the Criterion, Gordon was being done to death in the far-off Soudan ; and whatever may have been his faults, callousness or inhumanity was most certainly not numbered amongst them.

A political caricaturist of modern days, whose works I collect, is Sir F. Carruthers Gould. His wit, indeed, always of the most good-natured description, is one of the most valuable assets of the Liberal party, whilst the very moderation of his sarcasm, combined with an almost preter- natural aptitude for hitting off a situation, makes the work of this talented caricaturist tell in a quite unusual degree.

The best amateur caricaturist I ever knew was the late Sir Frank Lockwood, who used every year to send his friends some whimsical design of his own composition. Among the New Year's cards which he sent me — souvenirs I still cherish — the best of a clever series is, I think, the one I received at the end of 1893. In this Old Father Time is pictured as a butler holding out a cham- pagne bottle labelled 1894, whilst another, 1893 *sec*, lies empty on the ground. Underneath is written, " A fine wine, and not so dry as the last." On another, Time—as a sportsman carrying a dead pheasant, 1895—is shown keenly eyeing an astonished young bird (1896) perched upon a milestone, the while he murmurs, "I'll have a shot at you next, my little man." Sir Frank Lockwood was a great loss to all his friends, for a more agreeable, clever, and cheery companion never lived.

Looking over an old scrap-book of mine I came upon some Italian caricatures of the carnival at Rome in the old days, when the Pope was still an independent sovereign. These had been collected when I was travelling in Italy with my mother about the year 1842. The carnival, I remember, was not particularly gay. There were immense crowds, and a perpetual rain of confetti and dead battered flowers, which increased to a perfect storm when our carriage passed any house inhabited by our friends. The people of Rome, however, enjoyed it all immensely, and a young lady said to me, "If Paradise be half as delightful as the carnival, what can be so happy?" Some English people, however, said it was more like Purgatory!

During our travels at that time, when going by sea on a Tuscan vessel from Genoa to Naples, we met Lord Vernon, who was our fellow-passenger as far as Leghorn. He talked a great deal about Dante, the study of whose works was his hobby, and also gave us a very lively description of his interview with the Pope.

His Holiness, he said, after some very complimentary remarks, had inquired of him how he

translated the passage at the beginning of Canto
vii. of the "Inferno"—

> "Papé Satan, Papé Satan, aleppé." [1]

The difficulty, Lord Vernon told us, was overcome
by his telling the Pope that a great diversity of
opinion existed as to the passage in question, and
he would therefore be especially grateful to his
Holiness if he, the highest authority possible, would
tell him what the exact meaning of it might be. The
Pope, however, who was just as quick at parrying
home-thrusts as Lord Vernon, changed the subject,
and pounced upon another passage, describing the
effect of sunshine upon a rock, which he said he
had been able to verify one day near his convent
when he was a Carmelite monk. Lord Vernon
then said to him, "Your Holiness's observation
is most valuable, and, with permission, I will
put it in a note to the translation I am making."
"No, no!" exclaimed the Pope; "non bisogna
mai nominare il Papa,"—"There is no need whatever to mention the Pope at all."

Anything which recalls the past becomes of interest as time goes on, and some of the mementoes
of other days which I have carefully preserved
bring vividly back to one's mind scenes now almost
historical, as well as the people who figured in
them.

Programmes of public meetings and menus of

---

[1] This is a line of exceedingly obscure meaning. Pollock in a note
translates it, "Ho, Satan! Ho, Satan! my Alpha or Chief!"

banquets are amongst the trifles which I have
collected and kept, and of these I have a considerable number. The menus I sought for with the
greatest eagerness were those of public lunches
or dinners attended by some great orator or politician, and when I got them I generally managed also
to obtain the signature of the guest or guests of
the evening, which naturally adds very greatly
to their interest. Of these souvenirs recalling
great social functions of the past, I have in
particular a quantity of the time of the Jubilee
of 1887, which has now become almost an historic
memory. Besides their interest as souvenirs, these
menus may one day be interesting as illustrating
the way in which the people of our time dined. As
a matter of fact, there has been very little change
in the number and nature of the dishes served at
public dinners and banquets during the last thirty-
five years, as can be seen from some menus I still
retain as a remembrance of the entertainments
given to the late Shah of Persia (that is the one
before the last), on his first visit to this country
in 1873.

Other relics which I treasure are certain old cards
of invitation to parties, weddings, and other social
functions, which recall to my mind friends for the
most part, alas, long since passed away.

There was a good deal of robust joviality about
the weddings of old days, and the bride and bridegroom always drove away in a chariot drawn by
postillions resplendent in blue jackets and white

breeches, and wearing enormous white favours at their breasts. These, as a rule, were mounted on what were generally known as "Newman's Greys" —horses supplied by Newman, the job-master. A team of four was by no means uncommon, and very smart and appropriate such an equipage looked. What astonishment would it not create at a wedding to-day! But the post-boys and postillions of my youth in their quaint attire, together with "Newman's Greys," have long ago journeyed their last great stage and left no successors behind them. Their calling has now long been obsolete, and were they once more to reappear they would attract about as much attention as men in armour. Lord Lonsdale (I believe, almost alone) still makes use of postillions, who in yellow jackets and white beaver hats strike a picturesque note at Ascot and some other race-meetings which he attends in old-fashioned style.

I remember some amusing stories told in connection with marriages of the past. There was, for instance, the old peer who, though very proud of his family, tempered his pride with a considerable sense of humour. One day he was very much surprised to be told by his sister that she had conceived a great affection for a well-known though somewhat eccentric savant who, although generally esteemed, was of very humble Semitic extraction.

Not quite determined as to what course of action he should take, he sent for the prospective bridegroom with the intention of talking matters over, and after some conversation said,—

" And now, sir, I should like to know something about your family ? "

" I think it will be sufficient," was the reply, "to say that I descend from the illustrious blood of Abraham, Isaac, and Jacob."

" Oh," said the peer, " of course our family has nothing to compare with that! Therefore, if my sister really likes you, you had better take her."

The bridegroom became a Christian ; but his brother - in - law always expressed very sceptical views as to this conversion, and would often say, " Christian — fine Christian, indeed — why, the fellow has phylacteries sewn into the ends of his trousers." Nevertheless the marriage did not turn out at all badly, and proved anything but an unhappy one.

Another rather amusing story is the one told about an East Anglian clergyman of the past who was one day considerably embarrassed at receiving a visit from a lady parishioner who, on entering the room, at once said that she had come to ask his opinion, as her spiritual guide, upon a subject about which she felt quite unable to make up her mind—did he think that it could ever, under any circumstances, be right for a woman to propose to a man ?

Much taken aback, the poor rector replied that he certainly thought there might be circumstances which would make such a proposal justifiable ; upon which, without the slightest hesitation, the lady exclaimed, as Nathan said unto David, " *Thou* art the man ! " And, seeing no possibility of escape, he was.

Norfolk in past times produced many strange types. I remember an old parson who lived near my brother's place—a landowner as well as a clergyman, and one who farmed his own land, thus being what was known as a " Squarson." One Sunday his parishioners found affixed to the church door a notice which said, " In consequence of domestic affliction there will be no service to-day." Everybody being naturally much concerned, sympathetic inquiries were at once made, when it was ascertained that the domestic affliction was an accident which had happened to a fine bullock, in consequence of which it had been destroyed, after which the rector had decided personally to superintend its being cut up. Another old parson, at one of whose churches service was usually a mere form on account of the lack of worshippers, found himself deprived of the services of his ancient clerk, who was well used to his ways. On his arrival at the church the following Sunday the new one set vigorously to work at ringing the solitary bell, an innovation which was anything but to the rector's liking, as he quickly showed by shouting, " What on earth are you doing, you fool, you ? Don't you know that if you go on ringing like that some one is sure to come ? "

My brother himself was something of a character,

and could give an apt enough reply when he chose. Two old ladies, cousins of ours, once pestered him to let them see his country retreat, where he lived a very solitary existence. Thinking at last to end their importunities, he wrote saying that they might come and stay for a few days, in reply to which he was informed that they hoped he would see that some one was present as chaperon, as it would be hardly proper for them to be all alone with him. Further correspondence (and their visit also, I must add) was, however, checked by the brief note which he returned, in which he said that as, according to computation, their ages and his own amounted to about two hundred years, he thought that the voice of scandal was not much to be feared.

People of original character and brilliant intellect were undoubtedly more frequently to be met with some thirty or forty years ago than is now the case, when almost every one seems to be cast in a mould of a more or less mediocre kind.

There was, for instance, Mrs. Norton (who is still remembered on account of her remarkable cleverness and graceful gift of versification), and her sister, the beautiful Duchess of Somerset, who had been Queen of Beauty at the Eglinton Tournament. I knew the latter very well, a most original woman, possessed of a great deal of the Sheridan cleverness and wit. Meeting her one day at an exhibition of pictures, one of the principal features of which was a portrait of Mr. Gladstone, she led me up to it and, pointing to the picture, a most execrable piece of painting, said, " At last we Conservatives are avenged." At one time she was very much taken with the idea of utilising guinea-pigs as a new sort of dish, declaring that they were most excellent when cooked, and actually induced me to try them. I must candidly admit that they really were not at all bad ; she got me a little cookery book entirely filled with recipes for preparing the curious little creatures for the table.

There does not now exist, I fancy, any brilliant little circle of people such as in the 'sixties started that curious sheet the *Owl*, though from time to time attempts at something of the sort have been made. There was, for instance, the little coterie the members of which called themselves "the Souls."

These, I believe, had more or less regular meetings for mental communion and improvement, and at one time they attracted a good deal of attention. There were certainly several clever people amongst them, as well as some exceedingly attractive and good-looking ladies, whose mental aspirations (so they declared) lay in the direction of a higher intellectual life than the one led by ordinary mortals.

The late Sir William Harcourt, whose keen and incisive wit was ever very quick at summing up things at a true valuation, is said, when asked what he thought of "the Souls," to have replied, "All I know about 'the Souls' is that some of them have very beautiful bodies."

I often regret that I did not keep a complete set of the *Owl*; it was a very clever little publication, and for a time created a considerable sensation in London society. Originally started by Mr. Evelyn Ashley, Mr. James Stuart Wortley, and the present Lord Glenesk, it was published in a small shop in Catherine Street, the first number consisting of but a single page containing some clever political comments, a little light and satirical verse, as well as a good deal of amusing chit-chat. The price was high, sixpence, for it was in no way intended for the general public, being indeed, at its inception, sent gratuitously to many of the best known people in London. Its success, however, was so enormous that the scope of the paper was very considerably enlarged, many celebrated people becoming contributors, including Laurence Oliphant, and an *Owl* dinner being held every Monday, at which the forthcoming number of the paper was discussed. By the public the *Owl* was regarded more as an aristocratic literary plaything than as anything else, but whenever it appeared (for it was published or not according to the inclinations of its editors) every copy would be sure to be snapped up. The political information, in particular, contributed by those in the best position to know, was especially good, and it used to be said, indeed, that the *Times* itself was occasionally anything but averse to drawing upon the notes printed on the *Owl's* front sheet, which invariably contained a good deal of novel and accurate information as to forthcoming events, both in the parliamentary and diplomatic worlds.

Lord Wharncliffe used frequently to entertain the staff of the *Owl* at dinner at Wharncliffe House, occasionally contributing acrostics (for which he had a natural bent) to the columns of the paper, whilst Lady Wharncliffe would sometimes send notes as to any current event which might be of interest to the fashionable world.

In the copy of the *Owl* published on June 22, 1864, is an amusing account of a meeting of the staff held at the Star and Garter, Richmond; it is entitled "The Owls in the Ivy Bush." On this occasion there were present the Hon. Mrs. Norton, the Bishop of Oxford (Wilberforce), Lord Houghton, Mr. Bernal Osborne, Laurence Oliphant, Sir William (then Mr.) Vernon Harcourt, Abraham Hayward, and some others. A very brilliant assemblage of wit and intellect, which, I fear, the London society of to-day (or rather what passes for London society) would be totally unable to equal.

Some of the jokes and scraps of verse which appeared in different numbers of the *Owl* were exceedingly brilliant and amusing, whilst fads and fancies of the day were dealt with in a very humorous fashion.

The following lines, for instance, were published in the *Owl* at the time when Mr. Banting's system of reducing fat was a general subject of discussion :—

c

"Banting in Infernis

Here lies the bones of him whose strife
Was how to drop the staff of life :
Falstaff he was ; survivors he has shown 'em
How "nil" to leave "de mortuis nisi bonum."

In another number is a witty riddle also dealing
with the eminent upholsterer in whose instructions
for producing a reduction of weight the fat people
of 1864 placed so much trust :—

"Why is Lord Palmerston like Mr. Banting ?"
"Because his present measures are far smaller than
the clothes (close) of last session would warrant."

My cousin, Sir Henry Drummond Wolff, is
one of the few survivors of that brilliant band who
were contributors to the *Owl,* and no doubt will
have much that is amusing and interesting to say
about it in the volume of Memoirs which he has
at last been persuaded to prepare for publication.
Unrivalled as a *raconteur,* Sir Henry was a constant
guest at my luncheon-table in the 'eighties, when
almost every Sunday three-fourths of the Fourth
Party, that is to say, Lord Randolph Churchill, Mr.,
now Sir John, Gorst, and Sir Henry used to give me
the pleasure of their company, to the delight of
all who chanced to be present.

Those were the early days of the Primrose
League, the immediate success of which put us
all in very good spirits. A little later on, at
the time when the League as a political force was
beginning to make its influence felt, the late
Comte de Paris became much interested in its

methods, conceiving the idea that some organisa-
tion of a similar kind might be formed to promote
Orleanist interests in France. He questioned me
a good deal about the League, I remember, and I
referred him to my daughter, who, ever an ardent
worker on the Conservative side, thoroughly understood its machinery. As a result of his inquiries,
a French "White Rose League" was soon afterwards formed, the badges being in the form of a
gilt rose, specimens of which we received and
still retain. France, however, manifested little
enthusiasm at this attempt to breathe new life
into Royalist circles, and after a short time nothing
more was heard of the White Rose League,
which soon relapsed into an obscurity from which
indeed it can hardly be said to have ever really
emerged.

The originator of the Primrose League, as is
well known, was Sir Henry Drummond Wolff,
who from the first received enthusiastic encouragement from Lord Randolph Churchill, then a
brilliant pillar of the Conservative party, and full
of political energy and intellectual strength. An
audacious conversationalist when in a good mood,
few were able to excel him in quickness and facility
of expression, whilst he would at times exhibit a
gaiety which was very contagious. Nevertheless
Lord Randolph would never allow the tone of the
conversation thus engendered to degenerate into
familiarity, and would be quick to resent any
approach to it. He always seemed to me as being

a man who was secretly conscious that he must make his mark quickly. Who can tell that some foreboding of his premature end did not loom before him? Socially his personality was a very striking one, and that personality he managed to impress upon the electorate within a very short time of his entry upon a political career. He realised, as it were, I think, that advertisement (I am not speaking in a sense derogatory to his memory) was necessary in a democratic age, and well advertised he was. The newspapers were filled with his portraits and doings, whilst his twirling moustache proved a never-ending subject of amusement to the carica-turists. Theatres and music halls rang with references to " Randy-Pandy," who at one time was certainly the best known figure in England. Then came the fall, brought on, I believe, by his con-viction that the Conservative Government were absolutely unable to do without him. Bismarck it was, I think, who said, " no man is indispensable, every man can be replaced," or words to that effect, but Lord Randolph held a different opinion.

Considering himself absolutely necessary to the very existence of the Conservative party, the selection of Mr. Goschen to fill his place came upon him as a complete surprise, for he had left that politician quite out of the calculations which he had made.

Lord Randolph's exclamation on learning that his resignation as Chancellor of the Exchequer had been accepted is well known to everybody, but the words "I forgot Goschen" were not the only ones which were used by him.

Mr. Walter Long (who may now be called the chief hope of the Conservative party) chanced to be present when Lord Randolph received the first intimation of what was practically his political doom, and the following is the true version of what occurred.

Mr. Long was that day in the smoking-room of the Carlton Club, sitting with Lord Randolph, when the latter, who had just heard the news that Lord Goschen (then, of course, Mr. Goschen, and not an M.P.) had accepted the Chancellorship of the Exchequer, exclaimed: "All great men make mistakes. Napoleon forgot Blücher, I forgot Goschen."

I may add that it is with Mr. Long's consent that I publish the true version of a somewhat dramatic historical episode.

II

Society—Conversation and the lack of it—Miss Gordon Cumming and
Munro of Novar—The Duke of Wellington's hatred of publicity
—Sir Robert Peel's wedding at Apsley House—Mr. Delane—An
eccentric patron—A curate's wit—The Stock Exchange and the
West End—Prince Edward of Saxe-Weimar's drive home—
American influence—Lions—Mr. Watts and the crinolette—
Matchmaking—Lady Beaconsfield—Some anecdotes—Lord Henry
Lennox and the Duchess of Cleveland—Maria, Marchioness of
Ailesbury—Frances, Lady Waldegrave.

SOCIETY in old days cannot in any way be compared with the motley crowd which calls itself
society to-day. A witty Frenchman of the
eighteenth century once said that in perusing the
memoirs of the time of Louis XIV. one discovered, even in the bad company of that age,
something which was lacking in the good of his
own day—a remark which with but slight alteration might, with justice, I think, be applied to the
society of to-day as compared with that of fifty or
sixty years ago. To-day it would be difficult to
discover accurately who is in or who out of society,
or, for the matter of that, whether society itself
exists—though, of course, many little coteries of
people think that they, and they only, are the
leaders of the fashionable world.

In old days society was led by certain recognised rulers who framed its ordinances, against
which there was no appeal; whilst it was entertained by men whose capacity for wit and brilliant
conversation was universally admitted—individuals,
indeed, who ruled with almost undisputed sway
and retained their power even when age had
somewhat dulled their wits. Society was quite
content to listen, and it was not considered good
manners to resent being told things one knew
perfectly well even by people who did not sometimes know them at all. Now, however, everybody
chatters; it is not talkers that are wanted, far
from it; but listening is almost a lost art. The
general tone of modern conversation is, without
doubt, much lower than it was in the days of the
great talkers of the past—inane flippancy being
treated in much too lenient a manner. The general
impression given by those who habitually indulge
in it always seems to me to be that they are not
quite sure that they are ladies and gentlemen, and
are therefore perpetually engaged in trying to
laugh it off.

On the other hand, the conversational autocrats
of other days were far too dictatorial, and, in many
cases, undoubtedly checked general conversation
owing to a secret fear of incurring their displeasure and evoking some verbal castigation not
at all conducive to social enjoyment.

The professional conversationalist, who in former
days did really exist, has now long since passed

away. To-day he would be voted a bore, for his social qualifications were not such as would render him popular in the modern world, in which every one likes to share in the conversation, which for the most part deals with trivialities.

The great talkers of old days, bold of speech and ruthlessly outspoken at times, were especially deft in making use of banter, a weapon of which, when necessary, they availed themselves with terrible effect. This banter, let it be understood, was quite a different thing from the chaff of to-day, which in most cases is little more than silly comment on personal peculiarities, or criticism of a very primitive and obvious kind which sometimes sinks to the level of childish teasing. A good maxim which should never be forgotten is that to chaff any one up to such a point that the victim loses his temper, places the assailant in a very awkward and uncomfortable position, whilst demonstrating his complete mental inefficiency in that particular line in which he has been attempting to indulge.

It should never be forgotten that one angry or even irritated individual will completely spoil a dinner-party. The difference between a clever talker and one who delights in saying things which embarrass and annoy is much the same as that which exists between a first-class fencer and a bungling assassin.

In these days, when the art of conversation is little understood, it is no infrequent thing to encounter hosts and hostesses who wilfully check conversation by remarks, in many cases well meant, such as, "Now we will talk of something else," "Don't you think we have heard enough about that?" and other verbal stupidities which affect the good talker like an icy blast.

The necessity for such crude methods can never really exist, for it is perfectly easy to lead a conversation away from one topic to another by almost imperceptible gradations which do not entail that awful silence which is the solemn requiem of social enjoyment. After a pause of this kind general conversation is difficult to revive, and then it is that a bold and even an assertive talker is especially valuable in order to put every one at their ease. In connection with this subject I cannot help telling a little story which will exemplify what I mean.

Miss Gordon Cumming, a lady noted for her independence of speech, would at times make very apposite and amusing remarks. Years ago there was a certain Scotch gentleman, Munro of Novar, who was well known for his carelessness as to dress, which indeed amounted almost to eccentricity. He was, by the way, the possessor of a very fine collection of pictures, which were sold in order to help the Turks in their struggle against Russia in 1878, by his successor and heir, Mr. Butler Johnston, M.P., who was a warm and generous supporter of the Ottoman Empire. This gentleman, I remember, created a great sensation by making a most admirable speech in the House of Commons, which at the time caused people to predict a great political future for him. His health, however, broke down and nothing more was heard of him, for, becoming an invalid, he withdrew from public life and died not very long afterwards of consumption. Munro of Novar was, as I have said, very unconventional in his attire, and usually managed to display a considerable amount of shirt between the ending of his waistcoat and the beginning of his trousers. This snowy space was one evening especially noticeable. During dinner, for some reason or other, an awful pause in the conversation, amounting practically to a dead silence, occurred, when Miss Gordon Cumming, raising her voice, suddenly remarked, "I beg to call the attention of the company to the very lucid interval between Novar's waistcoat and his trousers." This utterance, naturally provoking uproarious laughter, caused the chieftain in question to make the necessary adjustment in his dress, and put every one into a good humour.

The general level of conversation in the so-called society of modern days must, of necessity, be low, for society, or what passes for it, is now very large, whilst wealth is more welcome than intellect. Good conversation, therefore, is practically non-existent. The majority of people, indeed, would, I think, quite frankly admit their incompetence in this respect, perhaps adding that serious conversation is a bore, which is true enough when an attempt is made to indulge in it by those who have never learned anything and never wish to learn. To such the world appears much as it does to that species of lizard which, from having lived for ages in dark caves, has no power of sight.

In former days the love of publicity, which is such a conspicuous feature of modern life, had little or no existence, and people, for the most part, disliked the chronicling of their doings by the Press—an aversion which can hardly be said to flourish at the present time. The second Duke of Wellington, in particular, was especially averse to attracting public notice of this kind, and was once very angry at a full account of a social function which had taken place at Apsley House appearing in a daily newspaper—one, I may add, of the very highest class.

When the late Sir Robert Peel was married to Lady Emily Hay (the Duchess's sister), the wedding breakfast took place at Apsley House, to which, as usual, no Press representatives had been invited. What was the Duke's horror, therefore, to read the next day in his morning newspaper, a full account of the proceedings, together with a report of such speeches as had been delivered! He was absolutely furious, and knowing that I was a friend of the proprietor of the paper, came round to see me, in a towering rage, to try to get me to discover the culprit. "I am sure," said he, "one of these newspaper fellows smuggled himself in and lay under the table whilst the breakfast was going on." In spite, however, of my strenuous efforts, the miscreant was never discovered, much to the annoyance of the Duke, who for years would never speak to the owner of the paper—a dear friend of mine, who happily is still alive.

Some time after this the latter told me that, to avoid any other incident of this kind occurring, he had given strict orders that no report of any social festivities whatever should appear unless accompanied by the written permission of the hosts, and I rather fancy that the rule in question still holds good.

At that time, of course, the Press was not regarded quite in the same light as it is to-day, and the majority of its representatives were viewed with a good deal of suspicion. Mr. Delane, however, was an exception to this, and was everywhere warmly welcomed in society. I often went down to parties which he gave for Ascot races at a house which I believe is now tenanted by the Jockey Club, and also used to see a certain amount of him in London. Well do I remember his once saying to me in connection with some troubles which he was describing: "Ah! you have no worries; your path is strewn with rose-leaves, and those carefully ironed out."

The fear of public opinion which now exists had little influence upon certain people in old days. There were many who held very tenaciously to the doctrine that with their own they could do absolutely what they liked. Such a one was the peer who, when thwarted, would occasionally display an almost injudicious independence of action which gave rise to many stories, of which the following is one. He had several livings in his gift, but having become a Catholic found that owing to his change of faith the law prohibited him from presenting any one to them. This, for some reason or other, particularly annoyed him, and he determined to have the matter thoroughly investigated, when he found that this prohibition only applied to Catholics : a Buddhist, Mahometan, or even an avowed Agnostic could present—a Catholic patron alone could not do so. More angry than ever at this discovery, he then conceived the idea of advertising these livings for sale, giving especial instructions that a proviso should be inserted that "no Christian need apply," the consequence of which was that, as he used gleefully to narrate, he eventually sold the rights of presentation to a Jew.

Whilst on the subject of presentations to livings, I remember an old story of a bishop and his chaplain which may possibly bear repetition.

A bishop was once having a discussion with his chaplain as to the exact nature of wit, and defied him to explain it. The chaplain in reply said, "Your Lordship will see that I can easily do that. The rectory of —— is vacant, give it to me. That will be wit." "If you can prove it," answered the bishop, "the living shall be yours." "It would be a good thing well applied," rejoined the chaplain, and by his nimbleness of mind gained the coveted appointment.

It was in the 'seventies that two new and powerful forces began to make their influence felt in society, for about that time Americans—of whom formerly comparatively little had been seen—began to come to London in considerable numbers, and then began those Anglo-American marriages which are now quite common. About this time also the Stock Exchange began to make itself felt as a social power outside the City, whilst several young men —pioneers of that vast body who now every morning migrate from the West End to their various offices—declared their intention of adopting the City as a regular career. Before that time hardly any one in the West End of London understood anything about stocks and shares. Whether, on the whole, London society has gained much by this departure seems a somewhat doubtful question. Many younger sons, it is true, have found a means of making a livelihood; but, on the other hand, many elder ones have, in consequence of unsuccessful speculations, been compelled to look about for one. Directly the City mania obtained a firm grip upon what was practically virgin soil, people began to make much of every one whom they thought capable of pointing out an easy path to wealth; and many shrewd business men, who hitherto had never dreamt of forcing the strongly

guarded portals of society, were not slow in taking
advantage of such a state of affairs. In almost
every case they obtained more than they gave,
and the ample hospitality which they dispensed
brought in a rich harvest of speculators, who,
with childlike confidence, eagerly rushed into any
and every venture. They fondly dreamt that
with the advice of their new-found advisers wealth
beyond the dreams of avarice was now really
within their grasp ; but the hopes of only a very
few were realised, and the large majority burnt
their fingers very severely by over-indulgence in
speculation.

At the time when rich aliens were first beginning to be admitted into society a little incident
was the cause of much amusement to the late
Prince Edward of Saxe-Weimar. One wet evening during the season Prince Edward, coming out
from the opera and just about to step into his
carriage, spied a foreigner of very humble extraction, who had amassed a considerable fortune in
the City and was noted for his hospitality, vainly
searching for his brougham. The poor man was
in a state of despair bordering on distraction, and
as the financier in question lived, like Prince
Edward, in Portland Place, the latter, who was the
kindest of men, very courteously offered him a lift
home.

The offer was accepted with many expressions of
the most profuse thanks ; but as the carriage rolled
on Prince Edward gradually began to be somewhat

alarmed at the behaviour of his companion, who
began carrying on a long conversation with himself
of a solemn and prayer-like nature.   Listening more
attentively, the Prince at last was able to make
some meaning out of the broken sentences, which,
uttered in a sort of Dutch-English, produced a sort
of weird, wailing effect.

" A broud tay indeed," the man was saying, "a
broud tay for me and mine.   Oh dat my boor
mother had been sbared to see me dis night, triving
side by side with a Brince of the blood!"

Now, I fancy, Anglicised foreign financiers take
these sort of things more or less as a matter of
course.   No one, indeed, is at all surprised at meeting people of uncertain nationality, one or two
at least being certain to be included in every
fashionable party.   To do these individuals justice,
most of them, after a mysterious process of Angli-
cisation, become public-spirited men, whilst the
great majority yield to no one in vaunting the
superiority of the Englishman over the foreigner.

At the same time, with the influx of the rich
foreign element into English society has come a
new conception of life altogether, and wealth as
the ultimate end of existence has been placed upon
a pinnacle which it never occupied before.   In one
respect, however, there can be no doubt but that
the new English have deserved well of their newly
adopted country : this is in their magnificent gifts
and bequests to hospitals and charities, acts of
generosity which must silence much criticism.

On the whole, I think the influx of the American element into English society has done good rather than harm, whilst there are many old families which, both in mind and pocket, have been completely revivified by prudent marriages with American brides. At the present day, so close has the union between ourselves and the United States become that Americans are hardly looked upon as foreigners at all, so many people having American relatives ; but in old days things were quite different, and we rather dreaded the social influence of a people whom we did not know. Bright and vivacious, it may with justice be said that it is by the American girl that we have been conquered, for she it is in reality who has brought about the excellent understanding which now exists with the great people beyond the Atlantic.

In the late 'seventies and early 'eighties society was very fond of "lions"—a taste which, I fancy, has rather decreased during recent years. People vied with one another in getting celebrities of different kinds to come to their lunches, dinners, and parties, and I fear that I must plead guilty to having joined in the prevailing craze, which, as a matter of fact, was no new one as regards myself, for I have always liked to meet out-of-the-way or remarkable people. On one occasion, however, I received what I must confess was a well-merited reproof. I had arranged a luncheon-party, one of the guests being a well-known lady—well-known on account of her beauty, —and it suddenly struck me that my old friend

D

Mr. Watts, a great admirer of perfection in the human form divine, might like to meet her. So I sent him an invitation, to which the following was the reply :—

LITTLE HOLLAND HOUSE,
28th March 1884.

DEAR LADY DOROTHY—Many thousand thanks. I am pleased to meet remarkable people, especially those from whom I can profit, and I delight in beauty, but I have little interest in those who become famous from accident, so I should prefer to come and *see you* and a few old (or new) friends such as I had the pleasure of finding at your house the day when I enjoyed myself very much. The amusement you so kindly offer me in this case would be in the indulgence of curiosity, not a nice feeling to be encouraged towards any one who wears a crinolette ; so please give me another opportunity of so pleasantly paying my respects to you,—And believe me to be, dear Lady Dorothy, yours sincerely,

G. F. WATTS.

Possessing a mind which was essentially of a very high and elevated type, Mr. Watts could not bear the thought of a lady being, as he thought, " trotted out " as a curiosity, which I fancy my letter had led him to believe was the object of the lunch, though, of course, such was not really the case. The reference to the crinolette—that monstrosity which seemed to be designed in emulation of the Hottentot form—sounds strange to modern ears. It is to be hoped that this artificial protuberance—hideous, uncomfortable, and supremely ridiculous—has now for ever disappeared.

The crinoline, a much worse monstrosity, once nearly cost me my life owing to the one I wore catching fire. It was, of course, nothing but a revival of the hooped petticoat of the eighteenth century, and was introduced, as far as I remember, by the Empress Eugénie. The name originated, I think, from the *crin* or horsehair of which the crinoline was made; though it is also said to have arisen from a milliner who invented it and was called Madame Crinoline; but such a story is, I think, based upon no solid foundation.

Matchmaking mammas, perhaps, existed in greater numbers formerly than to-day, when young ladies are so advanced that they are well able to do their own matchmaking.

Many were the stories told of a certain lady who, clever, shrewd, and good-natured withal, yet made little secret of her intense desire to marry off her daughters, a feat which she duly succeeded in performing. Once at a ball given in a very beautiful mansion, at which, however, the decorations were more select than the company, a gentleman whom she knew came up to her and said, "Ah, Lady ——, what a beautiful house this is." "It is, indeed," was her reply; "but remember my daughters don't dance with the house." On one occasion, however, it was declared her matchmaking schemes had been thoroughly baffled by a certain young peer who, rich and extremely nervous, seemed likely to succumb easily before her attacks. His very nervousness, however, proved his salvation. The lady one evening met him at a party, and, dragging the unfortunate youth into an adjoining boudoir, opened fire with, "I must tell you that I have frequently remarked your attentions to . . ."; but she was not allowed to proceed further, for, breaking into her speech with a sudden and extremely nervous rush, her would-be victim, with the words "Pardon me, but I promised my dear mother never to flirt with a married woman," made for the door, and thus unwittingly escaped from confirming the proposal which he had never made.

In after-years, when all her daughters were satisfactorily married, this lady used to say, "Only give a sensible woman three wet days in a country house, and she'll marry her daughters to any one."

Formerly, of course, English society was not nearly so cosmopolitan as it is to-day, and there were many people quite ignorant of foreign manners and customs, which were looked upon with a certain amount of contempt.

The late Lord Clarendon used to tell a story about Lady Beaconsfield. Her husband had introduced her to a distinguished Frenchman, and the latter, wishing to be very civil to the Prime Minister's wife, made an attempt to kiss her hand as she advanced to shake hands with him, upon which, not caring for this foreign mode of salutation, she drew her hand away, at the same time saying, "Monsieur, ce n'est pas propre."

This rather amusing incident has, I fancy, been more than once described as having happened to other ladies, but as a matter of fact Lady Beaconsfield was really the perpetrator of the blunder in question.

In former days there was generally some one person in London society who was credited with saying the most ridiculous things and making absurd mistakes in conversation. Mrs. Hudson, the wife of the famous railway king, was, I believe, the Mrs. Malaprop of her day, but I never met her. Another lady, however, who flourished during the 'seventies and 'eighties, when she entertained very largely, undoubtedly did occasionally say things which were ludicrous in the extreme, and in consequence caused other similar things which she had not said to be attributed to her. It was positively asserted, for instance (and perhaps with truth), that at the beginning of one season she had made the somewhat startling announcement that she was going to give two big balls— one for the *beau-monde*, the other for the *demi-monde*, by which somewhat doubtful appellation she merely meant to indicate the people who were not quite at the very top of the social tree. Many stories also used to be told of what this poor lady had said at a dinner at the British Embassy in Paris. Seated next to a Frenchman, who was freely talking in his own language on a subject which she deemed better unheard by the footman behind her chair, she is supposed to have pointed at the servant, who she knew understood French, whilst she murmured in a low voice, "Prenez garde, le derrière de ma chaise comprend le français."

Another lady, newly admitted into society, having sent a card to Lord Cassillis (whose name is pronounced "Cassells") for a ball she was giving, was afterwards very indignant at some one remarking, "Cassillis seems getting on very well with your daughter," and at once went round the ballroom saying, "I never asked that publisher to come at all."

Then there was the gushing lady who, after a dinner-party where the Chinese Ambassador and his wife were amongst the guests, found herself, as she thought, sitting next the Ambassadress, over whose gorgeous robes she went into an ecstasy of admiration, at first evoking nothing but a mysterious smile from the object of her praise. When, however, she proceeded to even greater lengths in the way of caressing gush, the supposed Ambassadress at last significantly placed a finger upon her lips, and, pointing with the other hand to where another quaint Chinese figure was sitting, quietly murmured, "Takee care, my wife velly jealous."

The old Duchess of Cleveland—not the one who lived at Battle Abbey; she had been Lady William Paulet—was a great character in her way, very stiff and precise in her manner of talking, as well as abominating all familiarity, such as calling people by their Christian names. Lord Henry Lennox, I recollect, used to delight in irritating the old Duchess by making use of slang expressions, which never failed to call forth from her the remark, "May I inquire, Lord Henry, whether, when you have completely mastered the language of the servants' hall, you mean to adopt its manners as well?"

Another lady, whose straight upstanding figure, deep voice, and striking appearance can never be forgotten by those who knew her, was Maria, Marchioness of Ailesbury, who, to the end of her life, sported a mass of corkscrew ringlets, which fell in abundant masses around her somewhat aquiline and commanding profile. In great request in society, she frankly declared that she would go to no country house unless she could stay a fortnight, as otherwise "it would not pay her." She lunched and dined out to such an extent that it was currently, and, I believe, truthfully, reported that she herself kept no cook. Her only extravagance was engaging tall footmen—any man about six feet high who attracted her attention being promptly engaged, no matter what his character might be. These footmen she herself used to put through a sort of military drill, with a view to imparting to their actions that grace and dignity to which she attached so much importance.

Frances, Lady Waldegrave, who was the daughter of old Braham, the singer, was a woman of very determined character, and not a bit ashamed of her origin. She would often jokingly say, when present at a party at which any curious or unknown people were amongst the guests, "I am sure every one will say they are some of my vulgar relatives." It is rather a strange thing that in days when society was still somewhat aristocratic and exclusive, Lady Waldegrave and Lady Molesworth, both with no pretensions to good birth, should have been rivals in leading it.

Lady Waldegrave expended huge sums on the decoration, or rather destruction, of Strawberry Hill, which she filled with heavy gilt furniture literally crowned with coronets. She also employed a very indifferent painter to paint pictures of her friends. These works of art were totally out of place at Strawberry Hill, where they produced the worst effect imaginable. Art indeed was not at a very high level during the Victorian era, for though there were some good artists, there were many very bad ones as well.

III

THE country houses in England may be said to be a unique national possession, for in no other land does the same sort of mansion exist—that is to say, a more or less commodious dwelling for the most part of considerable antiquity, surrounded by an estate which affords, or rather did afford, the owner sufficient and congenial occupation in the form of sport. France has her historic châteaux, and before the Revolution had a certain number of country houses with parks approximating somewhat to those existing in the England of to-day ; but few have survived the great upheaval of 1789, and little land remains attached to most of those that have.

The old houses and stately mansions of England form a valuable artistic possession, and many of them have been utilised as the scene of their work

by our authors and novelists. Who can forget
Brambletye House and the Mistletoe Bough of
Harrison Ainsworth ? Thackeray also drew his
picture of the palace of the Marquis of Carabas
from some stately, though it must be admitted,
cheerless country mansion ; whilst, as the following letter shows, the grounds of Bulstrode furnished
Lord Beaconsfield with his description of Armine
in *Henrietta Temple* :—

HUGHENDEN MANOR, *April* 17, 1865.

DEAR DOROTHY—We came down here with our own
horses ; the first time for many years. How delightful after
railroads ! We baited at Gerrard's Cross, twenty miles from
town, and then strolled into Bulstrode Park to see the new
house the Duke of Somerset is building in that long-neglected
but enchanting spot. There, though they told us we should
find nobody but the clerk of the works, we found the Duke
and Duchess, who had come down for a couple of hours by
rail from Slough, and so they lionised us over all their new
creation, which is a happy and successful one—a Tudor pile,
very seemly and convenient, and built amid the old pleasance
which I described thirty years ago in *Henrietta Temple* ; for
Bulstrode, then mansionless and deserted, was the origin of
Armine. Excuse this egotism, the characteristic of scribblers
even when they had left off work. Adieu, dear Dorothy.

D.

In the days when landlords were able to live
upon their estates and were content with a more
or less simple country life, enlivened only by an
occasional party of their friends, the country house
was no inconsiderable political force. The views
of its possessor, indeed, greatly influenced the
neighbourhood, whilst as a rule a fairly contented

tenantry followed their landlord—Whig or Tory—
and voted according to his lead; besides this they
took a genuine interest in everything which concerned him or his family. To-day this has ceased
to be, for the rich city men or American millionaires
are but seldom in touch with those living around
their mansions, hired either for sport or pleasure.
The modern standpoint as regards country life is
well demonstrated by the remark of a lady whose
husband had bought a country house, and was told
that some pleasant people lived in the country-side
near by. "Pleasant or not, it matters little to
us," was the retort; "we shan't see anything of
them,—we shall get our friends down from London
with the fish." Nor is such a standpoint to be
wondered at when it is remembered how little a
permanent resident in the country can be in touch
with those whose whole life is a rush for pleasure
and amusement, a habit of which they not unnaturally cannot divest themselves even when far away
from town. Formerly country-house life was very
quiet, perhaps even humdrum, but within the last
thirty or forty years it has undergone a complete
transformation.

In old days the possessors were wont to reside
upon their estates for the greater portion of the
year, whilst the people who hire country houses
merely run down for week-ends in the summer and
shooting parties in the winter.

The modern practice of letting one's country
house would have appalled the landed proprietors

of other days when such a thing was yet undreamt
of. There was then, of course, a real bond of connection (very often one of respectful sympathy)
between a landlord and his tenants, which, except
on a very few estates, has now quite ceased to
exist.

At present the majority of country squires are
far too poor to resist letting their places, which
are naturally regarded much in the light of a commercial asset, their sale-value for the most part
consisting in their capacity for affording some city
magnate or American millionaire the shooting or
hunting necessary to amuse him in the intervals of
a life of business and speculation. Country life, or
rather short spells of it, has now become a sort of
luxury of the rich ; but few of any considerable
means care to reside for long periods in the country,
as was the case in old days when people regularly
settled down there.

In the late Lord Bath's time I used to go a
great deal to Longleat, the beautiful palace—
for it is little less—built by Sir John Thynne,
the favourite of Somerset, some of whose letters
beginning "Edward, Protector by the Grace of
God," are still preserved in the house. The fourth
Lord Bath was very much interested in politics,
and many interesting people used to assemble
under his hospitable roof. I well remember being
at Longleat on the occasion of an election at
which the present Lord Bath was standing as a
candidate. His successful election was greatly

assisted, every one in the house believed, by a canvasser of a race which has always been prominently to the front in political matters—a donkey —over whose back two panniers were slung, in each of which reclined one of Lord Weymouth's children, whilst the legend, "Vote for Papa," was prominently displayed.

Lady Bath and her husband were the very perfection of what a host and hostess should be, and besides the social pleasures of these visits there was always the beautiful park to drive about in, a veritable feast to the eye in itself, especially the picturesque spot very appropriately known as "Heaven's Gate."

It was only the other day that I was once more at Hinchingbrooke, the lovely old place where many years ago I used to go and stay with a most delightful friend of mine — the mother of the present Lord Sandwich. Besides being a charming conversationalist, she had a most unusually lovely voice—indeed the famous Costa used to say that he had hardly ever heard a finer. The house is a wonderful old place, filled with magnificent pictures, whilst there is a quantity of marvellous old letters and manuscripts in the library. I remember going there to meet the present Duchess of Devonshire just about the time that she made her first appearance in England. She was then in the full radiance of youth and beauty, creating a sensation wherever she went.

Another country place of which I have many

pleasant memories is Goodwood House. Especially
well do I remember the elaborate and splendid
festivities which took place at the coming of age
of the present Duke of Richmond, on which occasion the old English custom of roasting an entire
ox was observed. The rejoicings lasted an entire
week.

It was no uncommon thing before the days of
easy railway travelling for a friend of the family to
reside almost permanently in a country house. I
remember such a one at my father's house in
Norfolk—Colonel Nelthorpe by name—an old
bachelor who might well have stepped out of one
of Fielding's novels. This old colonel had a room
known as Colonel Nelthorpe's room, and a stall for
his horse in the stables, both of which were always
kept vacant and ready in view of his arrival during
such brief periods as he might choose not to reside
at Wolterton. His servant, whom he addressed
in tones such as we might fancy Squire Western
would have employed, he called " Wulliam," and to
" Wulliam " went the whole of Colonel Nelthorpe's
not inconsiderable fortune, a bequest which somewhat staggered my poor mother, who, though as
a rule a most unworldly woman, had in this instance
conceived an idea that the old colonel would be
sure to leave his fortune to her two little girls
(my sister and myself), for whom she declared he
had always shown a distinct partiality. When we
were alone with this old veteran in the country all
the tit-bits were for him ; but her attentions were

lavished in vain, for, as I have said, nothing came to us, and all went to " Wulliam."

My father's friendship with Colonel Nelthorpe (one of the ugliest men, by the way, I ever remember) had been in a great measure caused by their being jointly associated for a very long time in the command of the West Norfolk Regiment of Militia, now the 4th Battalion Norfolk Regiment.

My father commanded this battalion for years, whilst Colonel Nelthorpe was its lieutenant-colonel right up to his death, at a great age, in 1854, having served in that capacity for about forty years.   In 1815 he had commanded a detachment of the regiment which had been sent to Ireland, and the year before he died, at the age of eighty-two, he took part in the annual training, on which occasion, the Peace Society having circulated much anti-military literature, the militiamen were openly reproached, hooted, and ridiculed in the streets of Norwich. It was to this battalion of militia that Captain Borrow, the father of the celebrated author of *Lavengro*, acted as adjutant for forty-two years, whilst one of George Borrow's brothers, who died in Mexico, also served in it as a lieutenant.

Colonel Nelthorpe belonged to another age, and my father also had a wide experience of a world the ways of which are now almost totally forgotten. As a very young man, in the first years of the nineteenth century, he had met Casanova at Vienna, where he had a prolonged interview with him—an interview which impressed him unfavourably and gave him but an unpleasant opinion of that prince of adventurers, whom he declared to be testy and disagreeable. In justice to Casanova, however, it must be added that my father would fly into a rage upon the slightest opportunity, and in addition nurtured a supreme contempt for all foreigners. The meeting, therefore, between the diminutive and irritable English peer and the gigantic Venetian (who, in his last years, as is well known, was in the habit of constantly getting into tempers on account of imaginary insults) could hardly have been expected to pass off in perfect peace.

The sight of a foreigner, indeed, as a rule sent my father into a rage, for he seemed almost to resent the presence on earth of any other nationality except the British. Notwithstanding this, however, he for some years had a Russian valet—an importation from St. Petersburg, where he had been *chargé d'affaires* three years before the battle of Waterloo. This valet, of colossal height and formidable appearance, was by nature the mildest of men, as was shown by the sweet and almost caressing smile which he would oppose to the storms of abuse which were wont to rage around him when anything had gone wrong. Never, perhaps, were his looks sweeter than when, as a finale to a tirade of unusual vehemence, my father would say, "Let it happen again, and as sure as I stand here I will throw you out of the window."

My father was well known as a character in that part of Norfolk in which he lived, and his friend, old Lady Suffield, known as the "Double Dow," who resided not far away, was another. This old lady had most aristocratic ideas,—quite those of another age, indeed, for she simply could not bear to think of people of inferior birth being allowed to break down the social barriers, which, according to her, should rigidly fence in the aristocracy, and more especially the person of herself.

On one occasion, when present at an assembly at the county town (Aylsham), she was horrified to discover that two local men, sons of a successful miller and merchant in that place, had obtained admission, and it was not long before she gave a very pointed demonstration of her resentment by exclaiming in a loud voice, "It is most unpleasant here. I can hardly see across the room for the flour dust."

She herself at her advent into this world had been the victim of great resentment on the part of her father, the Earl of Buckinghamshire, who, when he was apprised of her birth by his butler, is said to have somewhat gloomily replied, "Then you had better go and drag the baby through the horse-pond." He was, it must be added, not unnaturally very much annoyed at the birth of a girl, instead of a male heir who should succeed to his estates.

Old Lady Suffield, besides presenting my father with her picture by Sir Thomas Lawrence, also gave him a mat or rug which she herself had worked. In old days ladies spent a good deal of time in

E

making carpets and the like. At Wolterton was a carpet, cross-stitch, worked all in one piece, by my great-grandmother, Lady Walpole; whilst a tablecloth and twelve dinner napkins were reverently preserved on account of having been spun by her.

Needlework carpets were much valued by the families to whom they belonged. There is still, I believe, at Croome a portion of such a carpet which once covered the floor of a boudoir in the family mansion in Piccadilly, now long since passed into other hands; whilst at Apethorpe, in Northamptonshire, there used to be a very large needlework carpet which had been presented to that Lord Westmoreland who was Ambassador in Vienna, having been worked by the ladies of that city by way of especial compliment.

The "Double Dow" and her ways carried one right back to the eighteenth century, to which she in reality belonged, having been married in 1792. Nevertheless she lived well into comparatively modern days, dying only in 1850.

Living at Blickling in stately splendour, old Lady Suffield always drove up to London, despising the railroad as being a vulgar innovation. In my youth the post-chaise still flourished, and my father constantly travelled in one.

Well do I remember seeing Lord George Bentinck waiting for him in a post-chaise standing outside our house in London. He had come to fetch my father, as they were both going to drive down to Newmarket together. This, I think, was

the only occasion on which I got a good look at
this handsome pillar of the Turf, as he was in those
days, and the two things I remember about him were
his voluminous cravat and the delicate moulding of
his hands, one of which (the very perfection of
form, I thought) rested on the ledge of the open
window of the chaise.

In 1846 a great dinner was given to Lord George
at Lynn, at which my father, who was then High
Steward of the town, presided. Mr. Disraeli was
present, and made a speech which received a most
enthusiastic reception.

Two great friends of my father were Admiral
Rous and George Payne, both staunch supporters
of the Turf, and therefore in complete sympathy
with his desire to win the Derby.

Admiral Rous, who died in June 1877, had left
the Navy some forty years before, principally, I
believe, on account of the scant recognition which
a considerable feat of seamanship performed by
him, under the very greatest difficulties, had
received from the authorities at Whitehall.

Setting sail from Quebec in command of the
Pique, his ship struck upon a reef off the coast
of Labrador, and was only got off in a terribly
damaged condition, the rudder being practically
torn away. Notwithstanding this, Captain Rous
ran three thousand miles to Spithead in twenty
days, the vessel making about two feet of water an
hour the whole time, which entailed tremendous
exertions at the pumps on the part of the crew,

who would undoubtedly have abandoned hope
had it not been for the indomitable spirit of their
commander.

Admiral Rous was a great opponent of high
betting, which he always declared meant ruin to
the Turf. Like many of his contemporaries he
hated tobacco, the smoking of which he considered
almost an ungentlemanly act. Besides being
devoted to racing, the old Admiral would never
acquiesce in the modern view of cock-fighting,
which he defended to the end in the most uncompromising manner. To-day the race of men of
whom he was a type has totally disappeared, for
modern England does not breed them; but whether
such a state of affairs is for the country's good
seems to me a very doubtful question. Bluff and
straightforward, totally devoid of superficial senti-
mentality, such men expressed the very spirit
which has made that British Empire which a
feebler and more sentimental generation, prone
to much prattle of humanitarian and socialistic
fads, would seem desirous of destroying.

George Payne, who lived not far away from us
in Queen Street, Mayfair, was another man whose
whole existence may be said to have centred in the
Turf, though, unlike Admiral Rous, the attraction
with him lay a good deal in the betting. Nevertheless, unflinchingly honourable and high-minded,
Mr. Payne was a great deal more than a mere
gambler.

Many are the stories that have been told of his

distaste for going to church; yet at heart he was anything but an irreligious man, as the following anecdote will show. The late Lord Alexander Gordon Lennox was one night returning from some party with Mr. Payne; it was very late, and both were very tired. Reaching the latter's house, Lord Alexander said, "Now, old fellow, you will be in bed in five minutes"; to which the answer was "No." "Why," continued the original speaker, "whatever are you going to do?" To which George Payne replied, "I am going to say my prayers. I always have a bucket of cold water in my room, and if I am very tired, put my head in it to waken me up to say my prayers."

Lord Alexander also used to say that George Payne would never stand any young fellow saying anything against religion at the club, but would at once flare out at the offender.

There are, indeed, many people like George Payne, who, whilst they may not be regular churchgoers, are yet at heart religious in the best sense of the word. A certain gallant officer, for instance, who commanded a battalion of the Guards, though not very fond of going to church, used, when in the country, to make a practice of going for a long walk alone, during which he would indulge in meditation. On one occasion he was attacked by some one who, in the course of his oration, said, "Why, one would think you soldiers had no souls to save!" The author of this somewhat impertinent homily was, however, completely routed by the good-humoured answer which the Colonel in question made. He calmly looked the lecturer in the face, and merely remarked, "Mayn't a man save his soul by the way he likes best?"

As a matter of fact Satan is willing enough to let men go to church on Sunday provided they work for him the rest of the week, as I fear many outwardly religious people do!

In his career upon the Turf George Payne was peculiarly unfortunate from a financial point of view; as is well known, he completely dissipated two fortunes. By no means really astute, he would back a number of horses in a race in the—usually delusive—hope of making sure of the winner, a mania which cost him much.

It used to be computed by those well able to judge that Mr. Payne had spent a fortune alone in the hire of chaises and horses in the time previous to the introduction of railways, for it was his practice to spare no expense in order to get from one place to the other with the greatest speed possible.

My father himself was never particularly successful at racing, though he won the Two Thousand Guineas and once ran second for the Derby. When he did win a race, however, every one on the estate knew it, for he would at once set to work upon his favourite project of enlarging the lake in the Park. On the other hand, whenever fortune chanced to show herself in an especially unkind mood, which was very often the case, all the men employed at this work would be at once dismissed, whilst the most rigid economy would prevail till such time as another horse managed to get first past the post.

By no means an uncultivated man, fond of pictures and of art generally, racing and its attendant betting was, nevertheless, my father's master passion. To him Newmarket was a very Mecca and, wherever he chanced to be, at home or abroad, the loadstone towards which his thoughts were perpetually directed.

The old Duchess of Cleveland (mother of Lord Rosebery), a lady dowered with no mean intellectual gifts, lived to a very great age, being well over ninety at her death. She was possessed of a considerable sense of humour, and used to tell several entertaining stories of the many visitors who were always coming over from Hastings to see Battle Abbey. When the Duke of Cleveland first took possession, he naturally acceded to the request of the Hastings Corporation that the Abbey ruins should be open to the public once every week, and on the first public day eight hundred people arrived, swarmed all over the place, and were only prevented from entering the Duchess's own boudoir by the determined attitude which she assumed, advancing against the intruders with the fury of her eye rendered doubly formidable by the huge pair of spectacles which she habitually wore. The notes she used to receive from visitors were sometimes very curious ; one individual, for instance, wrote saying that he considered he had a right to go over the Abbey at all times, as one of his ancestors had fought at Hastings, and he himself had been christened "Norman"!   Another, a lady, wanted to know if anything very pretty had been found at the spot where Harold fell, as in Rome she had seen such lovely ornaments found in the tombs there.   This rather reminds me of another lady whom I once heard saying that her favourite study was the history of the Moors in Mexico, and the relics they had left behind there.

People used to be very fond of boasting to the Duke and Duchess of their Norman descent, amongst others Mrs. Grote, who, when at Battle in 1867 with her aunt and the celebrated historian, declared that she was a lineal descendant of Harold's younger brother, "Earl Leofwine,"—a name which in the course of time had been transformed into Lewin.

At one time, over the fireplace in the Abbots' Hall was a stuffed black horse, which used to be pointed out to visitors as the identical animal which had carried William the Conqueror at the battle of Hastings.   In reality the horse in question had never carried any one more celebrated than Sir Godfrey Webster, and then only at a review.

The arrangements at Battle Abbey in the time of the Duke and Duchess did not err in the direction of excess of comfort.   The Duke was inclined to economy, and the Duchess, an extremely clever woman, was so much immersed in various intellectual interests, mostly of an archæological kind, that she did not trouble to give much attention to household management. Matters were allowed to take their own course more or less, with the result that on one occasion the French Ambassador, on his way from the station to the Abbey, was delayed by the breaking of the carriage pole, which collapsed owing to extreme and untended old age. It was, certainly, no place for sybarites, who generally agreed with the quotation from the Litany which a witty and luxurious member of the Foreign Office once wrote in the visitors' book—

From Battle, murder, and sudden death, Good Lord deliver us.

At the same time great care was devoted to the remains of the old buildings, which, wherever possible, were as judiciously restored as the taste of that day permitted.

There is something singularly attractive in the country-side around Battle Abbey, by reason of its having been the site of that great struggle which really created England—the battle of Hastings. It was on Caldbeck Hill, on the evening of the 14th of October 1066, that the Norman trumpets blared forth their pæan of victory.

The right of power, as an old historian says, had been tried by the great assize of God's judgment in battle. England had been beaten, but by the very fact of her defeat was to develop into a greater England than ever any of Harold's Saxon thanes would have dreamed possible.

Here on this hill Duke William, having caused

his standard to be set up, stood amongst his Barons and Knights "solemnly rendering thanks to the King of Glory, through whom he had the victory— mourning also frequently for the dead." An appropriate place, indeed, would this be for a statue to the great Norman whose memory as the real maker of England deserves a recognition which it has never obtained. Underneath might well be inscribed the words which he addressed after the battle to his faithful old follower, Walter Giffard, Lord of Longueville, near Dieppe—

I thank God we have done well hitherto, and if such be God's will, we will go on and do well henceforward.

IV

BATTLE ABBEY was purchased by the Duke of
Cleveland, then Sir Harry Vane, in 1857, but
within the last few years it has once more become
the property of the Webster family, the present
Sir Augustus Webster, with admirable devotion
to the traditions of his line, having repurchased it
when it was put up for sale.

At Battle Abbey once lived the celebrated
Lady Holland, who, as Elizabeth Vassall, daughter
of a rich Jamaica planter, became the wife of
Sir Godfrey Webster, the fourth baronet. As a
matter of fact, young Lady Webster was prevented from living in the Abbey itself by Sir
Godfrey's mother, the Dowager, being made to
reside with her husband in a little house close
by; and with the intention of driving away her
mother-in-law, the bride, it is said, attempted to

frighten the old lady by arranging ghostly mani-
festations and sounds in the Abbey. These, however, proved of no avail, and merely increased
the quarrel between the old and the young Lady
Webster. In the end, indeed, matters reached such
a pitch that Sir Godfrey took his wife abroad, with
the result that at Florence she met Henry Fox,
third Lord Holland and the nephew of Charles
James Fox, with whom she eventually eloped.

Old Lady Holland at one time held a sort of
"court" at Holland House. Owing to her elope-
ment, as may well be understood, she was never
received at St. James's; nevertheless, she was made
a great deal of by the leading ladies of the Whig
party, who used to crowd to her evening receptions,
and her youthful escapade was in latter years
almost totally forgotten or overlooked. I well
remember being taken to see her, and, on the
occasion of these visits, though imbued with great
awe, I did not find her the terrible old woman of
whose sternness I had heard so much; she was, as
a matter of fact, very nice to me. The old Duchess
of Cleveland used, very amusingly, to tell how, as
a girl, she once paid a visit to Holland House, and
was treated with the greatest sternness by its
mistress, who cross-examined her (so she would
declare) exactly as if she had come straight out
of a charity school, and expressed the strongest
disapproval on learning that her young visitor was
allowed a sitting-room as well as a bedroom in her
father's house. "I think it the greatest of mis-

takes," said Lady Holland, "to allow girls so many luxuries—unless you marry well you will feel the difference." In after-years the Minerva of Holland House sent a message to the Duchess to come and see her "as an old acquaintance," but the latter, mindful of the snubs she had received as a young girl, bluntly refused to go. To me, as I have said, Lady Holland was most affable; my sister and myself, however, it should be added, had gone to see her at her special request, my brother being just engaged to marry Lady Holland's granddaughter, Miss Pellew, whose mother, Harriet, was the daughter born of her first marriage with Sir Godfrey Webster. In order to prevent her child from being claimed by its father after her divorce, Lady Webster, as Lady Holland then was, had caused it to be hidden away; she then pretended it was dead, and actually had a funeral service performed over the body of a kid, after which Harriet Webster returned to her mother's house as an adopted child. The sham burial is alluded to by Byron, who wrote:—

> Have you heard what a lady in Italy did,
> When to spite a cross husband she buried a kid?

Many were the stories of her dictatorial ways and passion for interfering with and upsetting everybody. At times, indeed, she was positively insolent. She was declared, for instance, on one occasion when a very shy young man was sitting next her at dinner, to have plunged her hand into his pocket, drawn out his handkerchief, and, with a sniff of disgust, given it to the servant behind her chair, with the words, "Take that to the wash!" In Count D'Orsay, however, Lady Holland met her match, for, seated next him at dinner during the early days of his residence in England, she kept letting her napkin slip from her lap, expecting that the awestruck young foreigner would continue to keep picking it up, as a commanding motion of the hand on each occasion directly indicated. Polite at first, he soon wearied of what he discerned to be no accident but a mere piece of impertinence, which was effectually checked by the words, "Should I not do better, Madam, to sit under the table in order to keep passing you your napkin more quickly?" Lady Holland's passage-of-arms with the Belgian minister, M. Van de Weyer, is probably better known. With characteristic bad taste she jeered him about the Belgians, saying, "Les Belges! Qu'est ce que les Belges? I never heard of them." "Madam," was his grave reply, "it was some one called Julius Cæsar, a pretty clever fellow, as you may have heard, who called them by that name."

Lady Holland could not brook the slightest opposition to her wishes, and would ever attempt to overcome any obstacles which might stand in the way of her will. On one occasion, whilst at Tunbridge Wells, she heard that no stranger was ever allowed to visit Eridge Castle—which, I believe, up to my cousin's father's day was actually the case.

Accordingly, she never rested till she obtained leave to inspect it, and when this was accorded, marched through the place in triumph with a large party, in which her maid was even included. Her behaviour, indeed, even when staying at other people's houses, was dictatorial in the extreme. Once, when at Brocket on a self-given invitation to a party with old Lord Melbourne, she completely upset the household and installed herself exactly as if she were at home. Her room, as it happened, chanced to be on the first floor, the windows completely surrounded by the magnificent flowers of a splendid magnolia. Lady Holland, however, did not appreciate their scent, which, as she afterwards casually told Lord Melbourne, was too strong; and, without asking permission, ordered every blossom to be cut off within twenty-four hours of her arrival.

In spite of these very unlovable traits of character old Lady Holland, I believe, had many good points, the chief of which was that she never bore malice against those who refused to submit to her iron rule. Indeed, the contrary rather was the case, and those who firmly stood up to her in no way fell into her bad graces. A staunch and faithful friend, she was long remembered with gratitude and regret by those who had known her well, and, in spite of all her faults and her dictatorial ways, she contrived to make Holland House the resort of the most cultivated, learned, and clever society of her day.

Although Lady Holland did not owe her position as presiding genius at Holland House to any especial distinction as a brilliant conversationalist or wit, she occasionally made some very trenchant and clever criticisms. Of two old people (a devoted couple who, it was notorious, had been lovers for many years whilst the wife's first husband was yet alive) she said: "Is it not pretty to watch them—they almost make adultery respectable!"

Lord Holland—a mere cypher in the household —was a man of great geniality and charm, and no doubt this largely contributed to the attraction of his wife's parties. He, poor man, would as soon have thought of asking any one to dinner without first consulting her as of attempting to fly. This, perhaps, was no bad thing, for he was so good-natured that had he been allowed to invite people as the fancy seized him, Holland House would have been perpetually suffering from a very invasion; as it was, the dinners there were far too crowded, many of the guests having to find places at a side-table. Lady Holland, who liked to do out-of-the-way things, very often chose to dine about two hours earlier than any one else, alleging her weak health as an excuse, but, as Talleyrand said, there was probably another reason—to upset everybody; this she loved to do, not from caprice, but in order to show her power.

Wielding great social influence, though of a totally different kind from that exercised by Lady

Holland, Lady Palmerston is still remembered by those who knew her as the most admirable hostess possible to conceive. At Cambridge House in old days she used to give the most charming parties imaginable—indeed, I liked them best of all those which I remember. There is no doubt that her tact and her advice were often of great political service to her husband.

Lord Palmerston himself was a most adroit man of the world, and besides this there was in his character a certain not unpleasant mixture of French levity combined with English familiarity. His social qualities served him in excellent stead in his political life, for he had a manner of speaking to people, even to those he did not know, which conveyed the impression that their name, constituency, and even their family were perfectly well known to him. By these tactics, and also by asking the wives of M.P.'s to his parties, he was able to do a great deal in the way of retarding the passage of any measures which, for a time at least, he might not be anxious to see pressed forward.

Mr. Bernal Osborne was often a terrible thorn in the flesh to Lord Palmerston, although nominally a strong supporter of that statesman, under whom he served as Secretary of the Admiralty in 1857. Towards the close of his tenure of this office Mr. Osborne, however, became very dissatisfied, and used to complain that his post had been reduced to something very like a mere head-clerkship, his duties being limited to registering

F

minutes of the Board by day and furnishing silent
notes by night. Mr. Osborne, of course, was by
nature opposed to control of any sort, and being,
above all, a political free - lance, the holding of
office in any form was quite unsuitable to his
disposition, interfering as it did with those on-
slaughts for which he was so well known in the
House of Commons. Later on in life he became
a trifle more restrained in his utterances, age
causing him to regard everything with more
patience. His long experience of politics, he once
said, had sobered him so much that he could spy
good qualities in every one—even in bishops.

Lord Palmerston was a politician in whom the
country, as a whole, reposed the utmost confidence.
Though a Liberal, he was a regular John Bull, and
neither "retrenchment" nor "reform" was, I
think, particularly dear to him; whilst, as was
well known, any slight to England would be met
with very spirited remonstrances during his tenure
of office. There were those indeed who assailed
his Government as not being Liberal at all.
Bernal Osborne, for instance, roundly attacked
the Army Estimates in 1860, when he was particularly severe upon Aldershot, which he described
as "an indifferent preparatory school for forming
indifferent generals." Later on, when the House had
gone into Committee, Osborne declared that Lord
Palmerston (who had characterised his assailant's
remarks as light and violent) was suffering from
the effects of the Mansion House dinner, combined

with the larger doses of colchicum taken to combat them. Lord Palmerston received this attack in a perfectly bland manner, merely retorting that colchicum was sedative rather than exciting, and consequently more suitable to the Honourable Member than to himself. On another occasion Mr. Osborne applied to Lord Palmerston the lines—

He frolics with the burden of four score,

adding that the Prime Minister's fault, nevertheless, was not age but youth, as was shown by his extravagance—a youthful folly. "He is indeed," added he, "never satisfied unless he is squandering the public money." This was a pleasantry which Lord Palmerston did not relish at all, and, it was said, never forgot.

Mr. Cobden disliked Lord Palmerston as a politician, and would often say to me, "Whatever I may do the old rascal will always insist upon calling me his honourable friend." As a matter of fact, Lord Palmerston once offered the great Free Trader a baronetcy, an offer which was without hesitation declined.

Lord John Russell was a totally different man, both in manner and appearance, from Lord Palmerston—short, stumpy, and not at all good-looking. I only recollect having met him once, on which occasion, I must say, he was most agreeable. This was at a time when he had taken Tennyson's house near us in the country. A great friend of

Lord John's happening to be one of our guests, it was suggested that we should all go over in a party, which we did, and were most kindly received. I especially remember some one pointing out to me a writing-table in the library with two enormous stains of ink splashed on each side of the blotting-book. "They are rather remarkable ink-stains," said my guide; "the Poet Laureate made one, and the Prime Minister has made the other."

Bernal Osborne was always giving Lord John nicknames in the House of Commons. One of these was "a political Mrs. Harris," another "Dr. Sagrado." His Irish policy in particular provoked some extremely sarcastic attacks from Mr. Osborne, who once declared that it differed as little from that of the Conservatives as Tweedledum differed from Tweedledee. "Drainage seemed to him the only thing upon which the Liberal Cabinet was agreed — a set of Commissioners of Sewers was what it really was."

As a girl I was much at Lady Jersey's house in Berkeley Square, having been a great friend of her daughter's. The great lady of her day, she wielded considerable social influence, which she used, whenever possible, in favour of Lord Beaconsfield, then plain Benjamin Disraeli, and not particularly favoured by society in general. As a matter of fact, Mr. Disraeli had rendered Lady Jersey an important service, having taken great trouble to assist one of her relatives under peculiarly delicate circumstances.

This she never forgot, and did everything she could
to help him. Another great lady who also lent her
aid to the young politician was Lady Londonderry,
who used to hold a sort of court at Holdernesse
House (now Londonderry House). Here she
would receive her guests sitting on a daïs under a
canopy. To me she was always most affable, but
I could not with truth say that, as a general rule,
she took much trouble to entertain those who
came to her receptions; indeed, she exhibited great
hauteur, and sometimes took little notice of them.
Some great ladies in old days (but not the very
clever ones) gave themselves great airs; small
wonder, when they were brought up to think they
were the very salt of the earth. One there was
whose behaviour at her parties was so frigidly
condescending that people used to ask one another,
" Are you going to see Lady —— insult her guests
to-night ? "

Nevertheless, as I have said, Lady Londonderry
joined with Lady Jersey in doing everything possible to assist and push on Benjamin Disraeli, with
the result that their efforts were eventually crowned
with success. I remember Lady Chesterfield (who,
after Lady Beaconsfield's death, was a devoted
friend of the great statesman; indeed he wanted,
and I think actually proposed, to marry her) saying to me how strange that she should not have
known Dizzy in old days. But it was not so
strange after all; for at the beginning of his career
there were many who fought shy of him, and later

on certain people disliked his wife. Lady Beaconsfield was, however, a dear friend of mine, and I was
much grieved at her death. Her handwriting was, I
think I may say, the worst I ever saw, so different
from her husband's, which was firm, clear, and easy
to read. Nevertheless, she wrote bright little
letters, which gave one excitement as well as
pleasure, for to discover their meaning was much
like deciphering a cuneiform inscription. The
following is a specimen of her style :—

> GROSVENOR GATE,
> *May 9, 1859.*
>
> MY DEAR DOROTHY—I have a portrait same as yours.
> Under mine is written in old English letters : " Forti nihil
> difficile "—nothing difficult to the brave—which I put
> because it is Dizzy's motto, and I think he has earned it.
> At the back of the portrait—" Dizzy, 1859." It stands on
> my table in one of the new sort of frames. He will write
> his name on the portrait if you prefer it. Town is going to
> be very gay, at least the Palace. Comte Persigny comes here
> as Ambassador very soon, to our party's great dismay.
> Duc de Malakoff very sorry to go—kiss'd Lord Malmesbury
> on each cheek! When are you coming to town? Dizzy
> begs his love to you, and kind regards to Mr. Nevill.—
> Affectionately yours,   MARY ANNE DISRAELI.

She wrote to me frequently with regard to
politics, in which she took great interest :

> GROSVENOR GATE,
> *February 15, 1860.*
>
> DEAREST DOROTHY—I was so glad to see you bright and
> strong this morning, and I hope you will come to town very
> soon. You have no idea of the excitement about this
> unpopular budget—a great meeting at Lord Salisbury's—
> Lord Derby spoke beautifully.

The Government consider themselves in danger; your young friend, Dizzy, is in fine fighting form.

Most affectionately yours,

M. A. DISRAELI.

I have said that Lady Beaconsfield's handwriting was the worst I ever saw; but, on reflection, I think such a statement is inaccurate—my own is worse.

When I lived in the country, in Sussex, I used at one time to educate a few poor girls at a school which I had built for their benefit. When their education had gone on as far as seemed necessary, I used to try and find good places for them; many turned out treasures, a few did not do me much credit. One, a very nice girl, I thought was likely to suit the person to whom I sent her—a famous doctor. He asked her several questions which she answered satisfactorily, but when she produced her character, written by me, it was returned to her, after a brief perusal, with these ominous words: "I cannot take you now, for I am sure this letter must be a forgery—no lady could have written it." The poor girl came back to me crying, and not knowing quite what to do. By means, however, of a personal interview, I was able to convince the doctor that the letter was no forgery, and everything was put right.

At the dinners given by Lord and Lady Beaconsfield, the guests were for the most part either politicians, or people connected with politics, to which one might say the host devoted his whole life.

Most of these dinners, Lady Beaconsfield told me,
were furnished by a caterer at a fixed price of so
much per head, and I well remember her declaring how annoyed she was with my brother (who
always accepted every invitation, and invariably excused himself at the last moment on the
grounds of impending death) at his having, after
the most solemn assurances, played her his usual
trick. "He might," said she, "just as well have
made me throw a sovereign into the Thames," for
this was the price per head at which her contract
was made. They were not at all bad dinners from
a gastronomic point of view, though in these luxurious days I suspect they would not be thought very
much of. The Beaconsfields were in no way
luxurious people, nor did they care for art, which
did not then excite as much attention as to-day,
when every one appears to be more or less interested
in house decoration, collecting, and the like.

Mr. Disraeli's marriage to Mrs. Wyndham Lewis
was of great use to him in his political career, for,
his own means being anything but considerable, the
fortune which was thus at his disposal saved him
from much trouble and worry ; whilst Mrs. Disraeli,
being absolutely devoted to her husband, was
always delighted to assist him in every possible way.
I well remember, however, his being very much
annoyed at a remark made by Mr. Bernal Osborne,
which somehow got round to his ears. "After all,
Dizzy only likes his wife out of gratitude." As a
matter of fact this was far from being the case, for,

though fully appreciative of what he owed to his wife, the great statesman was also completely devoted to her.   As a proof of Dizzy's carelessness about money, and almost culpable lack of mercenary precaution, I may add that to the best of my belief (though he well knew that Lady Beaconsfield's fortune must return to her husband's family after her death) he never took the trouble to insure her life.   He was indeed absolutely devoid of all calculating financial instinct, though shrewd and clever enough in all matters which might in any way assist his political career.   I have already told how he contrived to secure Lady Jersey's support; in another way he managed to conciliate Lord Lyndhurst, for, recognising how valuable the latter's aid would be, Dizzy, who stood high in a certain lady's graces, forbore from paying his court to her on perceiving that he was regarded as an unwelcome intruder by his older rival.   By this self-sacrificing behaviour, he secured a most valuable political patron and ally.

Lord Beaconsfield's long friendship with me was in a great measure caused by his sincere affection and regard for my dear brother, the late Lord Orford, with whom he was ever on the most intimate terms, as the following graceful letter will show :—

2 WHITEHALL GARDENS, S.W.,
December 28, 1876.

MY DEAREST ORFORD—A little line to thank you for remembering me.   One likes to be remembered by those

whom one never forgets. I am here alone, at this dreary
season, in consequence of the confusion in those waters
where we once passed happy hours. I was going to pass my
Xmas at Weston with our friends the Bradfords, and then
to Trentham for a few days, when my Sovereign Lady
appealed to me not to leave her at this moment, and
declared it an act of high imprudence for myself and Derby
to leave town at this conjuncture.

Our friends, the Turks, are better diplomatists than
Europeans in general, and the affair will probably be longer
than the common mind imagines. It requires one's wits
about one. I feel as if sailing on a sea full of torpedoes.
My profound conviction is, that the Russians dread war, and
never contemplated it except with a crowd of allies. When
the pinch comes they find themselves quite isolated, and
Mephistopheles Bismarck scarcely suppresses his laughter
when he beholds that gentle Faust, the Emperor of Russia,
struggling in his toils. But to get them out of the scrape
with honour, *Hic labor, hoc opus est.* There must be a
golden bridge, and if necessary, it must even be gilt: every
possible facility—perfume on the violet.

I hope you are well and tolerably happy.—Remember
sometimes, your affectionate   BEACONSFIELD.

Lord Beaconsfield in his early political days,
it must be remembered, had many difficulties of
a widely different sort with which to contend.
In addition to the disadvantage of not being
favourably looked upon by many, some did not
scruple to call him a mere dandy who should
not be taken too seriously. Later on he had to
educate his party, being obliged, as was once
rather wittily said, "to drag an omnibus full of
country gentlemen uphill."

His Reform Bill of 1859 even excited a certain
amount of ridicule. I remember it being described

as " a piece of Downing Street millinery," whilst his
" Fancy Franchise," as it was called, was declared
to be "not at all the thing for the people of
England." A more serious criticism called it
" change without progress." It is very difficult to
say what Lord Beaconsfield's real view of politics
was, but my own impression is that he was deeply
attached to the traditions of government by aristocracy, the romantic side of which appealed to his
imagination and nature. At heart I think he
feared the eventual triumph of a sort of mob rule,
the coming of which it was ever his object to delay.
Undoubtedly in his last years he was extremely
pessimistic as to the future, having, rightly or
wrongly, no particular confidence in the political
sagacity of an English democracy, the judgment of
which he thought could be easily swayed by
unprincipled and specious agitators.

Always most guarded in his references to his
great opponent, Mr. Gladstone, and speaking very
little about him at any time, Lord Beaconsfield
without doubt entertained a real and sincere
distrust of him as a politician, quite apart from any
question of rivalry. There were times, I know,
when the Conservative leader was more than half
inclined to think that the Liberal policy was being
dictated by no sound mind, a conviction which is
fully supported by certain references to being
" governed by Colney Hatch," which Lord Beaconsfield made to a very dear relative of mine. Mr.
Gladstone, indeed, owing to his habit of saying

things which he afterwards declared were never
meant to convey the meaning which was naturally
to be drawn from them, caused many people who
were not under the spell of his marvellous fascination to wonder whether the Grand Old Man's intelligence had not become more or less unbalanced.
He had a habit of saying things which, taken
literally, meant much, but as a number of them
were often but pious opinions, it was better to
assume that they meant nothing at all. To take
Mr. Gladstone too seriously was sometimes very
dangerous, as I believe a foreign diplomatist of
singularly trustful nature once discovered. From
a conversation with the Grand Old Man the
secretary in question, then *chargé d'affaires*, formed
the impression that the evacuation of Egypt by
England was merely a question of a comparatively
short time. Was it not an act of justice dear to
Mr. Gladstone's heart? Bursting with joy at this
noble utterance, this somewhat ingenuous diplomat,
in spite of warnings from more worldly colleagues,
at once informed his Government of the glad
tidings, which Government, making serious inquiry
into the matter, of course discovered that England
had not the slightest intention of removing one
soldier from the land of the Pharaohs. The end of
the whole affair was that the unfortunate and con-
fiding diplomatist fell into great disgrace, and was
eventually practically obliged to abandon his career.

Bernal Osborne once nicknamed Mr. Gladstone
the " Milo " of politics, a name which certain

events at the end of the Grand Old Man's political
career rendered singularly appropriate. Milo of
Crotona, the Greek athlete famous for his strength,
perished, it is said, owing to his hands becoming
fixed in a cleft of a tree which he had endeavoured
to rend in twain. Mr. Gladstone's political life, or
at least tenure of political power, was ended by his
having become entangled in the Home Rule movement and by the efforts which he made to cleave
in two that Parliamentary bond which, in spite of
his endeavours, still holds England and Ireland
together.

Mr. Osborne himself held some very original
views as to the Irish question, being particularly
opposed to the system of government by a Viceroy,
which he deemed obsolete and demoralising, besides
tending to bring Royalty into contempt. Dublin
Castle, he declared, was regarded by both Conservatives and Liberals as a political club, of which
the Viceroy was merely a temporary manager, a
roi fainéant with no real power. The British
monarchy in Ireland, he once said, is in reality
embodied in the not very agreeable form of the
Judge at the Assizes, who puts on the black cap.
Mr. Osborne always maintained that occasional
visits from the Sovereign would effect a great deal
in conciliating the Irish people, by nature inclined
to poetry and sentiment.

V

AMONGST the odds and ends which I have pasted into different volumes I found the other day a memorandum, dated 28*ème Pluviôse, an* 4 *de la République,* addressed to the Minister of War and signed by Buonaparte, at that time General-in-Chief of the Army of the Interior. The memorandum in question deals with a request for increased pay made by certain officers, which General Buonaparte declares, on account of *la modicité de leur traitement,* to be *fondé et légitime.* The signature of the great captain is a very original one, the letters running very much together, and the whole ending with a double and determined flourish. Looking at it my mind wandered back to the days of my childhood when Napoleon was still remembered as having been a terrible and dangerous foe to this country.

It is difficult, indeed, for those of a later generation to realise the feelings of Englishmen of even
seventy years ago towards our neighbours—now
our friendly allies—across the Channel. To those
who had lived through the time of the Napoleonic
wars France was ever a rapacious and world-
enslaving country, only awaiting another Buonaparte to make a descent upon the shores of England.

To-day the name of the great Emperor, now
almost a mythical figure, arouses as much admiration here as across the Channel, but to those who
had actually experienced the feeling that a French
invasion was immediately imminent, the French
were brigands and Napoleon merely " Boney "—
feared, hated, and despised.

In the early years of the nineteenth century,
when all England was in daily anticipation of a
French invasion, Norwich was not behindhand in
publicly demonstrating its hatred of the Corsican
tyrant.

At a celebration of his defeat in 1813 an effigy
of Buonaparte was burned in the market-place,
whilst a year later another effigy, loaded with
fetters, was paraded in processions both at Yarmouth and Thetford. On the restoration of the
Bourbons there was a great demonstration in the
market-place at Norwich, the church bells being
rung and bonfires lit, whilst amidst uproarious
cheering the Chevalier de Bardelin, for some twenty
years an exile from France who had supported
himself by giving drawing and French lessons at

Thurgar's school, took his seat on the mail coach, free, as he said, once more to return to his beloved France. He received a real old English farewell, horses, guard, coachman, and passengers being decorated with the emblem of the Bourbons, the white cockade. Before he came to Norwich (where he was universally popular) the Chevalier de Bardelin had been a *garde du corps* of Louis XVI., in which capacity he acted at Versailles on that memorable day, October 6, 1789, when the mob from Paris nearly assassinated the King and Queen. In 1816 M. de Bardelin married a Norfolk lady, Miss Sutton, and until his death in 1852, at the age of eighty-five, he kept in constant communication with his Norwich friends, whom he always delighted to welcome on their visits to France. His daughter became the Baroness de Fabry.

As late as 1843 there died at Lynn a man who had been a schoolfellow of Napoleon, and who in the days of his boyhood was said to have taken part in many a rough and tumble with him. This was Mr. Peter Lewis Dacheux, who, having many years before immigrated into England, had, as a Roman Catholic priest, long attended to the religious wants of such of his co-religionists as resided in the old Norfolk town.

There are a good many relics of Napoleon in England. At Hertford House is the table on which was signed the Treaty of Tilsit, whilst in the library of Highclere Castle, the beautiful home of Lord Carnarvon, is shown the table and chair

used by the Emperor when putting his signature to
the act of abdication at Fontainebleau. On the right
arm of the chair is an " N," roughly cut as if with
a penknife, said to be the work of Napoleon himself, it having been a well-known habit of his to
cut almost mechanically an initial upon the arm of
his chair whilst pondering over the various schemes
which perpetually occupied his mind.

My father possessed a very fine bust of the
Emperor by Canova, but what has now become of
it I am quite unable to say. I also remember at
Wolterton a print of Napoleon, given to my uncle,
General Walpole, by the lovely Pauline Borghese
—this, fortunately, my nephew, the present Lord
Orford, still retains.

It is curious to read of the difference which
Napoleon showed in his treatment of Marie Louise
and Josephine. The former he sometimes allowed
to enter his *cabinet de travail*, whereas Josephine
would never have been permitted to set foot
in it. The Emperor in all probability allowed
his Austrian consort more latitude on account of
her royal birth, for of the two women Josephine
without question was the better loved of the
two.

Oddly enough, I can say that in a sort of way
I once saw the Empress Marie Louise. In 1843,
when travelling on the Continent with my parents,
we stopped an evening at Villach, a town in
Germany just on the Italian frontier. There was
at that time no railway, and the very evening we

arrived the ex-Empress Marie Louise was expected
at seven o'clock, having sent on orders for horses to
be in readiness. I remember that the postillions
in the courtyard were in a great state of excitement, being helped to don their state liveries by
the bustling damsels of the inn. Everybody,
indeed, was eagerly expectant, but all had to
wait till nine o'clock before Marie Louise arrived,
and when she did come all our hopes of seeing her were dashed to the ground, for it was
too dark to see much, except the four exceedingly dusty carriages which conveyed her and
her suite.

A certain number of the numerous portraits of
the Emperor were drawn from life whilst he was
at Mass. This was said to be the best time to
catch his expression. Couder sketched him thus
in 1811, and Girodet twice in 1812, whilst many
other portraits of him are known to have been
inspired during this religious function. During
Mass Napoleon stood, according to the military
custom, with his arms folded and his eyes glancing
in all directions. He made little pretence of
following the service or taking any especial interest
in it, never knelt, but stood, grave, serious, and
meditative. In front of him, at a *prie-dieu*, knelt
the Empress, to whom he would occasionally stoop
down and address a remark. On the whole his
attitude was in no way irreverent, and contrasted
very favourably with that which Louis XVI.
is reported to have adopted in the Chapel of

Versailles, where some English visitors were scandalised at seeing the King laughing and joking with the Comte d'Artois.

The Emperor's attendance at Mass was accompanied with considerable ceremonial. On each side of the altar in the chapel a grenadier stood on guard, whilst a roll of drums announced the entry of the Emperor and Josephine. The whole building glittered with the brilliant uniforms of the imperial household, whilst a certain portion was set aside for ladies-in-waiting and other friends of the Empress. Nevertheless, Napoleon would never allow any special passes of admission to be issued for his chapel, declaring that public worship should be free and for the people. Any charge for chairs in a building devoted to religious purposes seemed to him odious. "One ought not to deprive the poor," said he, "because they are poor, of that which is a consolation in their poverty."

When Napoleon re-established the Catholic religion in France, Girardin told him that he would find attendance at Mass a bore, and advised him to see that some excellent musicians and singers should always be present to mitigate the tedium of the ceremony. The Emperor took his advice and procured some of the best artistes that Paris could produce. These were well paid, dividing between them some six thousand pounds.

In matters of religion Napoleon betrayed the

genius of a consummate politician, as was shown by his conciliatory attitude when in Egypt towards Mahomedanism, which faith he ordered his troops to respect. As regards his own personal beliefs it would seem that at all events he was very far from being an unbeliever, his habit of crossing himself in moments of danger, for instance, going to prove this. One of the Emperor's favourite maxims, indeed, was, "The future is in the hand of God." By nature inclined to fatalism, he was also imbued with a good deal of native Corsican superstition. Friday in particular he ever considered a momentous day: on a Friday he entered the military school of Brienne, and on a Friday he left Saint Cloud to set out upon his disastrous Russian campaign.

The sound of church bells was always especially pleasing to Napoleon and produced a most extraordinary effect upon him. At Malmaison he would listen to the church bell of the village of Rueil with the greatest pleasure, breaking off from any conversation in which he might be engaged to do so. "Ah!" he would say, "that sound recalls to me my early days at Brienne; how happy I was in those days!"

Never, probably, did any man excite such hatred, and, on the other hand, arouse such devotion as the Emperor.

When travelling in the island of Elba in 1854, my cousin, Sir Henry Drummond Wolff (then Mr. Wolff), came across an octogenarian who had been

Napoleon's gardener, and had gone with him to the palace of La Malmaison. Monsieur Holard, as this old man was called, told Mr. Wolff that though he had for ever lost his benefactor his name was graven on his heart—he had indeed made desperate efforts to follow the Emperor to St. Helena, but, not being allowed to do so, found himself, by the irony of fate, gardener to the Duke of Wellington, then (1817) residing at Mont St. Martin in the department of the Aisne. He had been recommended to the Duke by Sir Neil Campbell, and at first had had some scruples as to the propriety of entering the service of his imperial master's conqueror. These, however, were overcome, and Monsieur Holard spoke gratefully of the kindness shown both to himself and his wife.

A great favourite with the Emperor, he told how, wishing to give his master a pleasant surprise, he rose one morning early, in order to arrange a number of small flower-pots in the cyphers of each member of the imperial family. Before his task was quite finished, however, Napoleon, ever an early riser, appeared on the scene and expressed his pleasure at such an ingenious device, adding, however, that one cypher had been forgotten—one which, as he said, should have been placed first— the cypher of Queen Hortense. But Holard was not to be found wanting, for, producing a quantity of pots filled with the flower called hortensia, he explained how at that very moment he was just about to arrange the missing cypher.

"Ah! Coquin," said his master, whilst he affectionately pulled the gardener's ear, "I have never found you fail yet."

The hortensia, as it is called in France and Germany, is the magnificent Chinese flower known in England as the hydrangea. The French sea-captain who brought home the plant from China in 1790 named it hortensia as a compliment to his wife, whose name was Hortense. It quickly became very popular in Europe, and was the "Lieblings blume" or favourite flower of Queen Louisa of Prussia and also of the great Goethe. When Mr. Wolff paid his visit to Elba, Claude Holard was, as has been said, an old man of eighty, but his mental faculties were in no wise impaired by age or by the many vicissitudes which had fallen to his lot, and he gave his visitor many details of his life, which had been anything but an uneventful one. Born at Metz in 1773, he became a soldier in the Austrian army at the early age of fifteen, saw service, and was taken prisoner by the forces of Dumouriez near Brussels. Allowed to return to his native place, he afterwards joined the army of the Ardennes, and was wounded at the battle of Fleurus whilst fighting under Jourdan. This wound ended his military career, and he became Syndic of Marine at the port of Breskens, a small town on the Scheldt opposite Flushing, and married, for his prosperity seemed now assured. A trading vessel, however, in which he had sunk his little fortune, was captured by the enemy, and this loss, in addition to the difficulty of collecting certain debts, eventually caused him to leave Breskens and make his way to Fontainebleau, there to lay before the Emperor the story of his misfortunes, which were much aggravated by the poor state of health into which he had fallen. Certain persons of influence interested themselves on his behalf, and he was nominated gardener to the Emperor's sister, Princess Elise of Piombino, afterwards Grand Duchess of Tuscany, in which capacity he served till 1814, when, being ordered to repair to Elba, he was made director of the imperial gardens, becoming, in due course, gardener of the palace of La Malmaison during the hundred days. After the Emperor's final defeat and fall, the poor man, as has been said, made every effort to be allowed to accompany his imperial master to St. Helena; but this was not to be, and then followed a long period filled with undeserved misfortune. It was in 1851 that Prince Demidoff engaged him once more as head gardener in the gardens of San Martino at Elba, the same post which the old man had occupied many years before under the great Emperor; and, though this relieved him of all fear of actual penury, Mr. Wolff was informed that he was much hampered and worried by many vexatious restrictions and regulations not at all to the taste of an old soldier of the Napoleonic times.

Whilst at Elba, Mr. Wolff was told several anecdotes about the Emperor, of which the following shows very clearly that the idea of a return to

France was ever present in the great captain's mind.

A balustrade being in course of erection in some part of the so-called palace of San Martino, one of the Emperor's suite declared the wood to be so bad and the bars so thin that the whole affair could not last for any time at all. "How long," asked his imperial master, "do you give it then— a year?" "Yes, sire," was the reply. "That will do," rejoined the Emperor, with a smile.

During his stay at Porto Ferrajo, Mr. Wolff had an opportunity of inspecting the books left behind by the Emperor. Amongst them he particularly noticed two French handbooks to the study of the English language, a rough cypher "N" being pasted on the back of each. Most of the leaves were uncut, but another linguistic guide showed signs of having been a good deal perused. This work, in which the original English was placed side by side with a French translation, was entitled *The Hundred Thoughts of a Young Lady* —"Cent pensées d'une Jeune Anglaise"—written by Mistress Gillet. Queer reading this must have been for the conqueror of Austerlitz!

Napoleon's flag at Elba, which is, I believe, still in existence—three golden bees on a red band running diagonally over a white ground—was a modification of an old Tuscan ensign, made by the ship's tailors of the *Undaunted*, the vessel which brought him to Elba.

Another smaller flag of the same sort, which

is said to have been the regimental banner of the Old Guard which accompanied the Emperor to the island, may be seen amidst other Napoleonic relics at the Invalides in Paris, where also is his cocked hat decorated with an Elban cockade.

During his visit to the island in 1854, Mr. Wolff had many conversations with persons who had been in close contact with Napoleon. He chanced to travel in company with a certain Monsieur Larabit, who, as a young officer of engineers, had superintended the repair and reconstruction of most of the defences of the island some forty years before, and who would often speak of the great interest taken by the Emperor in the completion of his palace (in reality little more than a country house) at San Martino; and also of the remark which he used to make, " Ce sera la maison d'un bon bourgeois riche de quinze mille livres de rente." With this old senator (as he had now become) Mr. Wolff witnessed the tunny fishing for which Elba is noted, at the same time hearing from the veteran's lips an account of how he had seen the Emperor on the 27th of June 1814 attempt to land one of these fish, and fail owing to lack of sufficient strength. As an instance of an extraordinary link between the present and the past, it may be mentioned that during his visit to Elba, Mr. Drummond Wolff was on one occasion rowed in a boat by a man whose father had for years been a prisoner in the hands of Algerian corsairs.

A striking instance of the almost mesmeric

power which the Emperor Napoleon undoubtedly possessed, is shown by the reconciliation which he effected with General Lecourbe, the story of which, I think, has never been told in English.

Holding command in the army of the Rhine under Moreau, General Lecourbe must certainly be mentioned in the foremost rank of those who contributed to the military glory of France; but, nevertheless, owing to his devotion to Moreau, whose cause, when brought to trial by the First Consul, he warmly espoused, his name was ruthlessly obliterated from the roll of the French army. He had offended Buonaparte, and for ten years remained in the obscurity of civil life.

In 1815, however, after the Emperor's return from Elba, generals of tried capacity had to be found, and Napoleon's thoughts flew to Lecourbe. Accordingly, an order from the Ministry of War commanded him to present himself at the Tuileries, to which a curt reply was returned to the effect that General Lecourbe, being no longer a soldier, could not recognise any order of the sort; if the Emperor wished to see him one of his aides-de-camp must convey the intimation. On the morrow arrived an officer with a personal invitation from His Imperial Majesty to come the next day to the Tuileries at eleven o'clock in the morning. "I will go," said the old warrior to a friend, "but I shall speak my mind—at last I shall be able to have it out with him." The interview, indeed, seemed likely to be a stormy one.

At eleven the next morning the General (not in uniform) awaited the Emperor in the hall next his breakfast-room, from which Napoleon soon emerged. Perceiving Lecourbe, he at once motioned him to approach, but before he was able to do so strode forward himself (a thing he never did for anybody), and then, drawing himself up, fixed the old soldier with his eagle gaze.

"General Lecourbe," said he in a resonant and penetrating voice, "your grievances against the Emperor Napoleon I confess are great, but they have not, I hope, obliterated all recollection of your old friend, General Buonaparte. He, remember, is still your friend; will you be his?"

At these words the veteran, already strangely moved by the mere appearance of the Emperor, completely lost his self-possession, whilst two big tears slowly rolled down his cheeks on to his grizzled moustache. Terribly embarrassed, he could hardly stammer out a few words of thanks, and his emotion rather increased than lessened when Napoleon said, "I was sure I should find again the comrade of other days!" Then, unbuckling his sword: "There will be work to do on the banks of the Rhine; you know the ground, and I can rely upon you?" "Yes, Sire, you may be sure of that." "Take then this sword, General, as a pledge of our reconciliation; there is no one able to use it better than yourself."

Upon this the old man, completely overcome, seized the hand of the Emperor in both of his own, and, rapturously kissing it, ejaculated : " Rely upon me, Sire ! Rely upon me ! "

That afternoon General Lecourbe's name appeared in the *Gazette* as commander of an important army corps.

On the other hand, there were men in whom the great Napoleon inspired the most bitter hatred. Such a one was the Prussian general, Field-Marshal von Kleist, to whom the Emperor sent the Legion of Honour. Baron von Kleist, however, declined to wear it, and, purchasing a toy bust of Napoleon, hung the decoration around its neck, always carrying the bust with him wherever he went. The Emperor heard of this contemptuous treatment and was greatly incensed thereby, declaring that he would shoot von Kleist if he could catch him, but this he never did. The Baron had conceived a violent antipathy for the Man of Destiny on account of his rough and indeed almost brutal treatment of the gentle Queen of Prussia (Königin Louise), always declaring, indeed, that it had been with the greatest difficulty that he had restrained himself from drawing a loaded pistol from his pocket and killing the Emperor during the progress of the interview between the two sovereigns, at which he had been present.

Baron von Kleist, when in command of a portion of the Prussian army in 1813, greatly contributed to the defeat of Napoleon at Leipzig. Disregarding the cautious orders of Prince Schwarzenberg, the Commander-in-chief, he marched by night across

the heights of Nollendorf, and after a fierce battle
completely defeated Marshal Vandamme, capturing
sixty thousand men—practically the whole left wing
of the French army.   For this brilliant military
feat he was made Graf von Nollendorf, and received
from his King a complete dinner-service of fine
Berlin china, included in which were several large
vases, bearing on the one side the arms of von
Kleist, and on the other the cross of Kulm, a
decoration especially instituted for those who had
taken part in the battle of that name.   This dinner-
service is still in the possession of the old soldier's
descendants.

It is believed that the only passport ever signed
by Napoleon for an Englishman to visit England
was one given to a Mr. Manning.   This gentleman,
whilst at Oxford, received what he considered to be
a very serious affront or injury from the authorities
of his college, and took the matter so much to
heart that he migrated to France, where he became
the intimate of many clever and learned Frenchmen, including Carnot and the Abbé Remusat.
Becoming interested in the East, Mr. Manning
afterwards set out on a long journey through
Thibet, China, and Japan, travelling, it must be
added, in native dress.   In after-years, owing to his
intimate acquaintance with the Chinese language,
he was prevailed upon to accompany an English
expedition to China, where, by a somewhat extraordinary chance, his vessel being shipwrecked, he
was picked up and taken to St. Helena.   Here, he

had an interview with Napoleon, during which, being asked by whom his French passport was signed, he tactfully replied, "Par l'Empereur," an answer which much pleased the illustrious captive, who, by the special order of Hudson Lowe, was not allowed to be addressed otherwise than as General Buonaparte.

It may not be generally known, perhaps, that from time to time assertions have been made— some of the most emphatic kind—that Napoleon once actually passed a considerable time in London. The date of his visit is said to have been 1791-92, and the place of his residence George Street, Strand. Whilst in all probability there is not the slightest foundation for such a story, it would be curious to know from what circumstance such a report arose.

About the time that I was a child there was written a poem, in which Napoleon and his old army were resuscitated, by the very clever and original pen of a young Hungarian poet, Baron von Sedlitz by name. This poem, called the " Mitternachtliche Heerschau," or " Midnight Review," is still, I fancy, very well known on the Continent, but the English translations seem to be now totally forgotten. One of these, by William Ball, was set to music and sung by the famous singer Braham (the father of Frances, Lady Waldegrave) about 1831. He was an old man at the time, but nevertheless is said to have rendered the words with such weird and striking effect as to

produce a very great impression upon his hearers.
The version in question, which has been reprinted in
Notes and Queries within comparatively recent years,
rather fails to convey the impressive simplicity of
effect attained by the original poem.   There are
lines, however, which are certainly striking :—

And at the midnight hour the chieftain leaves his grave,
Slowly he comes on his charger white amid his chosen brave ;
The ranks salute their silent lord, the stately march renew,
And now with clanging music pass before their master's view.

On their airy steeds on every side the thronging dead obey,
The blood-stained hosts of the battlefield in all their fierce array,
Ghastly beneath their glowing helms the grinning skulls appear,
And countless weapons high in air their bony hands uprear.

The weird scene which these verses describe has
been depicted by Raffet, in one of whose lithographs the spectre of the great Emperor is shown
passing a review of a phantom army.

Another translation of the " Midnight Review "
was written by Mr. Leitch Ritchie, a well-known
writer in his day, who at one time edited the *Era*,
and also did a good deal of work for publications
like the *Keepsake* and *Heath's Picturesque Annual*.
This version has not, to the best of my knowledge,
been reprinted since it first appeared in a quarterly
magazine (now somewhat difficult to obtain), about
seventy-seven years ago, which will be my excuse
for giving it here side by side with a French
version which, it may be added, the Government of
Charles X. sought to suppress.   Though no great
poetic genius is shown in Mr. Ritchie's lines,

avowedly a word for word translation, the writer may nevertheless be said to have caught something of the simple and impressive dignity which caused the German poem to create such a sensation when it first appeared, some six or seven years after the Emperor's death.

THE MIDNIGHT REVIEW

Nachts um die zwölfte Stunde
Verlasst der Tambour sein Grabe,
Macht mit der Trummel die Runde,
Geht ewig auf und ab.

A minuit, de sa tombe
Le tambour se lève et sort,
Fait sa tournée et marche
Battant la caisse bien fort.

At midnight, from his grave
The drummer woke and rose,
And beating loud the drum,
Forth on his round he goes.

De ses bras décharnés
Remue conjointement
Les baguettes, bat la retraite,
Réveil et roulement.

Stirred by his fleshless arms,
The drumsticks patly fall,
He beats the loud retreat,
Réveille, and roll-call.

La caisse sonne étrange,
Fortement elle retentit,
Dans leur fosse en ressuscitent
Les vieux soldats péris ;

So strangely rolls that drum,
So deep it echoes round !
Old soldiers in their graves
Start to live at the sound.

Et qui au fond du nord
Sous la glace enroidis,
Et qui trop chaudement gissent
Sous la terre d'Italie.

Both they in farthest north,
Stiff in the ice that lay,
And who too warm repose
Beneath Italian clay.

Et sous la bourbe du Nil
Et le sable de l'Arabie ;
Ils quittent leur sépulture,
Leurs armes ils ont saisi.

Below the mud of Nile,
And 'neath Arabian sand ;
Their burial-place they quit,
And soon to arms they stand.

Et à minuit, de sa tombe
Le trompette se lève et sort,
Monte à cheval et sonne
La trompe bruyant et fort.

And at midnight, from his grave
The trumpeter arose ;
And mounted on his horse,
A loud shrill blast he blows.

Alors sur chevaux aériens
Arrivent les cavaliers,
Vieux escadrons célèbres
Sanglants et balafrés.

On aery coursers then
The cavalry are seen,
Old squadrons erst renown'd,
Gory and gash'd, I ween.

Sous le casque, leurs crânes blanchâtres
Ricanent, et fièrement
Leurs mains osseuses soulèvent
Leurs glaives longs et tran-chants.

Beneath the casque their blanchèd skulls,
Smile grim, and proud their air
As in their bony hands
Their long sharp swords they bear.

Et à minuit, de sa tombe
Le chef se lève et sort ;
A pas lents il s'avance
Suivi de l'état-major.

And at midnight, from his tomb
The chief awoke and rose ;
And followed by his staff,
With slow steps on he goes.

Petit chapeau il porte,
Habit sans ornemens,
Petite épée pour arme
Au côte gauche lui pend.

A little hat he wears,
A coat quite plain has he,
A little sword for arms,
At his left side hangs free.

La lune à pale lueur
La vaste plaine éclaire ;
L'homme au petit chapeau
Des troupes revue va faire.

O'er the vast plain the moon
A paly lustre threw ;
The man with the little hat
The troops goes to review.

Les rangs présentent les armes,
Lors sur l'épaule les mettant,
Toute l'armée devant le chef
Défile tambour battant.

The ranks present their arms,
Deep roll the drums the while,
Recovering then, the troops
Before the chief defile.

On voit former un cercle
Des capitaines et généraux ;
Au plus voisin à l'oreille
Ce chef souffle un mot.

Captains and gen'rals round
In circle form'd appear ;
The chief to the first a word
Then whispers in his ear.

Ce mot va à la ronde,
Résonne le long de la Seine ;
Le mot donné est la France,
La parole : Sainte-Hélène.

The word goes round the ranks,
Resounds along the Seine ;
That word they give is—France,
The answer—Sainte-Hélène.

C'est là la grande revue
Qu'aux Champs-Élysées,
A l'heure de minuit
Tient César décédé.

'Tis there, at midnight hour,
The grand review, they say,
Is by dead Cæsar held,
In the Champs-Élysées.

H

VI

It is curious how, in spite of their manifold follies and shortcomings—which were sometimes almost criminal—the Bourbons managed to inspire certain of their adherents with an almost fanatical devotion. Many and many a brave man sacrificed life and property for the ancient Royal line of France. Of this stamp were the gallant Vicomte de Frotté, shot by Napoleon in 1811, and the Marquise de la Rouérie, the organiser and leader of the Chouan revolt. It is, indeed, almost impossible to conceive the intense loyalty displayed by those Frenchmen and Frenchwomen who cherished the traditions of the old régime.

In 1842 I knew at Florence a lady—Mademoiselle Félicie de Fauveau, a sculptress of some note—who belonged to a noble French family. At that time somewhat advanced in years, she had been much with the Duchesse de Berri, and still

remained a devoted supporter of the ancient monarchy.   To such an extent indeed was this the case
that, inspired by a feeling of the most ardent loyalty,
Mademoiselle de Fauveau had made a vow never
to let her hair grow till the Comte de Chambord
should as Henry V. ascend the throne of France,
and this resolution she carried out with an utter
disregard of the graces.   The Comte de Chambord
never reigned, and therefore to the end of her life
she kept her head closely cropped.   I very well
remember seeing him at Vicenza in the same
year as I met Mademoiselle de Fauveau.   He
was not at all a remarkable-looking man, and
walked with a slight limp, the consequence of
an accident which had occurred to him as a young
man, when his horse had fallen upon him.   As
a matter of fact the fracture which he had sus-
tained would have left no traces had the doctors
in attendance shown any great surgical capacity.
This, however, they did not do, allowing their
patient to travel in a carriage over bad roads
before the fracture had been thoroughly reduced.
Dr. Récamier, it may be added, had especially
warned them against allowing such a thing, but no
notice was taken of his letter.

The Comte de Chambord was far more high-
minded than most of his line, and it was always
said that had he chosen to abandon some of his
convictions he would certainly have been King of
France.   His attitude, however, was always
straightforward, and for this reason it is in all

probability that he lies, the last of the Bourbons, uncrowned in his tomb at Frohsdorf.

I still possess a sketch of Mademoiselle de Fauveau standing with her hand on a favourite dog, which was drawn by my dear governess, Miss Redgrave, from a full-length statuette which the sculptress herself had modelled. The dress, oddly enough, is almost exactly similar to a tailor-made costume of to-day; but in 1842 it was considered a very great eccentricity, and used, I recollect, to excite almost as much astonishment as the lady's cropped head. Nevertheless, Mademoiselle de Fauveau was a very dignified figure, her face, curiously enough, bearing a considerable resemblance both in feature and expression to the martyred Queen whose memory she adored.

Though it is now a hundred and fourteen years since Marie Antoinette mounted the scaffold and became the victim of a crime which, according even to Napoleon, was far worse than regicide, the very mention of her name evokes as great a feeling of sympathetic compassion as it did at the time of her brutal execution. No one who has studied the story of the terrible persecution and mental torture to which she was subjected can fail to be moved by the sufferings of this royal martyr, whose dignified bearing in some measure actually impressed the howling mob which shouted for her blood. The progress of the unfortunate Queen to the place of execution was an awful one, for the squalid cart in which she was placed was escorted by a band of furies, whose raucous howls and ignoble jests disgusted even the rough soldiery who guarded the august prisoner's road to death. As the tumbril, it is said, passed the church of Saint Roch a band of wretches seated on the steps actually clapped their hands as if at a circus; the only open expression of sympathy, indeed, came fitly enough from a little child, which, as the rueful procession wended its way past the Oratoire, rose to its feet and kissed its little hands to the poor Queen, a last message of love, as it were, from the true heart of France.

When one thinks of the respectful affection, amounting almost to adoration, which Marie Antoinette inspired in men like Fersen, the Chevalier de Rougeville, and others, it would seem that there hung about her graceful personality an atmosphere of mesmeric fascination, something of which still seems to linger in certain places closely connected with her romantic memory. Notably is this the case at the Petit Trianon, where she must always remain almost a living figure to the visitor of any imagination. Strolling through the beautiful grounds on a fine spring day, the graceful trees bathed in a golden light, one well imagines the beautiful Queen surrounded by her children and friends wending her way to her *hameau*, the toy village in which she took so much interest and delight.

To this lovely retreat, when the leaves were beginning to fall and the lilies of France to fade came the news of the arrival at Versailles of the crowd of Parisian rabble, who on the 5th of October 1789 invaded that stately palace. The same day Marie Antoinette decided to join the King, and flying to his side, abandoned for ever her beautiful Trianon, the enchanting spot in which some of the happiest days of her life had been passed, and which she was never to see again.

From that moment nothing but sorrow and misfortune were to be her lot. Versailles was in a turmoil, and on her arrival there she soon found that her life itself was in danger. On the following day (6th October), she spent some terrible hours at the windows of the room known as the bedroom of Louis XV., to which she had been forced to fly from her own private apartments, whilst the crowd without the palace savagely called for her blood. Only did its fury abate when both she and the King, appearing on the balcony of an adjoining apartment, promised to set out forthwith for Paris and to take up their residence at the Tuileries.

A mysterious legend has always declared that before taking their departure the Royal couple caused a considerable sum of money, together with many valuables, to be secretly buried in the park adjoining the palace, but though careful search has often been made nothing has hitherto come to light. At the present time, however (April 1907), there is a rumour that, owing to the discovery of an old manuscript indicating the place of conceal-

ment, the authorities in charge of the palace of
Versailles are on the point of discovering the exact
locality of this long-hidden treasure.   It is much
to be hoped that such a report should prove true,
for in all probability, in addition to the financial
and artistic value of such a discovery, some
documents of the highest historical interest are
almost certain once more to be brought to the
light of day.

There must, undoubtedly, be much treasure and
many jewels buried during the great Revolution
still lying hidden under the soil of France, for
before going into exile numbers of *emigrés* buried
their most valuable possessions in the earth, with
the intention of recovering them on that return
which in many cases was never to take place.   A
great portion of the splendid jewellery of Madame
du Barry has never been satisfactorily accounted
for, though it has often been declared that it still
remains intact and untouched in an unopened case
lying in the strong-room of Coutts' Bank.   Be this
as it may, I believe that it is an absolute fact that
this famous firm of bankers are still the guardians
of a large number of cases deposited there by
French *emigrés*, who having returned to France
in order to forward the Royalist cause, met their
death without having left any instructions as to
the disposal of their property lodged in England.
The rule, I believe, in such cases is for the bank
to allow the boxes literally to moulder to pieces,
carefully wrapping up in paper any objects which

may fall out, and replacing them in a heap on the top of what is left. It seems a pity that no Act of Parliament should ever have been passed to deal with such cases, for there are probably many priceless works of art slowly drifting to utter decay in these old brass-bound chests fast mouldering into dust.

Though, as has been said, a legend declares that some of the jewels of Madame du Barry still lie in the strong-room of Coutts' Bank, it is difficult to see how such can be the case unless she deposited her valuables with more than one London banker; for it is absolutely certain that the firm with whom she usually banked when in England was that of Messrs. Hammersley and Morland of Pall Mall, in whose keeping, according to her own estimate, she at one time had over 300,000 livres' worth of diamonds. The firm in question has long ceased to exist, and I do not know who took over their business. At the end of 1794, after the death of Madame du Barry, diamonds left by her in England were sold by order of the Court of Chancery, and realised 13,300 guineas.

As is well known, this poor woman was literally hounded to death by an Englishman, George Grieve by name; he was a native of Alnwick, in Northumberland, where he early in life distinguished himself by his Radical proclivities. Having squandered the patrimony bequeathed to him by his father, an attorney of some local

standing, he went to America in 1780, where, it
is said, he met Washington, Franklin, and other
lights of the young American Republic.   In 1783
he came to Paris, in which city he appears to have
posed, perhaps with authority, as an American
representative in the revolutionary demonstrations
which were already beginning to agitate the French.
Later on, grandiloquently styling himself, " Factieux
et anarchiste de premier ordre et désorganisateur du
despotisme dans les deux hémisphères depuis vingt
ans "—a title, by the way, which might be recommended to the consideration of some of our modern
socialists—Grieve took advantage of Madame du
Barry's absence in London in 1792 (to which city
she had gone to look after her stolen diamonds)
to take up his residence at Louveciennes, where
she possessed a splendid residence, and where
she was adored by the peasantry, to whom she ever
dispensed a truly regal charity.   By bribery and
persuasion this apostle of progress gained over two
of her servants, and then, managing to obtain an
order for seals to be placed on her papers and
valuables, installed himself in her house whilst pro-
curing its mistress's arrest on her return to France.
The villagers, however, mindful of the goodness of
their Lady Bountiful, petitioned for and obtained
her release.   Grieve, no doubt desiring that his
own very doubtful dealings with the contents of
her château should not be exposed, again managed
to get her arrested, but, as on the previous occasion,
a petition of the inhabitants of Louveciennes once

more set her free.   In November 1793, the wretch,
who was quite determined not to be balked of his
prey, finally ran his unfortunate quarry to ground,
and was successful in getting the favourite of
Louis XV. tried and led to the guillotine.   Her
persecutor, unlike many of his fellow-benefactors
of humanity, contrived to survive the Terror, and
died peacefully in Brussels in 1809, having in the
interval once more made a journey to America,
where he published a translation of Chastellux's
travels.

It is curious to learn that Grieve, who was
evidently full of Anglo-Saxon hypocrisy, had the
effrontery to make a personal appeal to the Conven-
tion, in which he demanded the head of the du Barry
"in the name of good morals."   The real truth
of course being, as has been said, that this scoundrel
(who had obtained permission to make an inventory
of her valuables, which he drew up absolutely
alone, entrance to her residence at Louveciennes
being closed to all but him) had made away with
much of her money and jewellery, and was in consequence determined to have their unfortunate
owner sent to another world in order that his own
defalcations might evade detection.   In all probability he buried a certain amount of treasure in
the grounds of Madame du Barry's house; at all
events local rumour has always declared that gold
and jewels lie hidden in the earth there.   Many
searches have been made, but no valuables discovered.   A skull, however,—in all probability that

of the Duc de Cossé-Brissac, the Royal favourite's last lover,—was dug up near the house. Brissac having been hacked to pieces at Versailles, some youths got hold of the head, and in high glee carried it on a dung-fork to Louveciennes, where they hurled it through the open windows of the du Barry's salon.

A principal agent of Grieve in his campaign against Madame du Barry was her black page, Zamor, who appears in many a picture, fantastically dressed, standing by the side of the beautiful mistress of Louis XV. The old King himself took the greatest interest in Zamor, and bored as he usually was with everything, would yet sometimes deign to smile at the pleasantries of the spoilt little negro, who was allowed to take pretty well any liberties he pleased. Zamor had been originally brought from Bengal as a child by an English sea-captain, and, having been made chief page to the favourite (who acquired him as a pleasing contrast to her white dog and her monkeys), received an excellent education after being baptized with the greatest pomp. Nevertheless, in spite of the favours with which his mistress had loaded him, Zamor turned against her at the time when one word from him could have saved her head. An ardent student of Rousseau and an enthusiastic democrat, this little negro attained a certain position in revolutionary circles, being given an official position in the district of Versailles. He was called as an important witness at the trial of his benefactress, and manifesting the greatest bitterness against her, coldly and brutally gave such testimony as directly contributed to her condemnation.

His ingratitude, however, did him no good, for, falling into disgrace with the revolutionary authorities, he soon sank into the most dire poverty, the property which he had amassed being got out of him by a designing milliner. In old age he supported life by giving elementary lessons to the children in the quarter of Paris which he inhabited, where the little wizened old man was well known as "the negro who had betrayed la du Barry."

Silent and taciturn, he retained the cult of the revolutionary doctrine to the end of his life, which seems to have occurred somewhere about 1820, his little room being decorated to the last with the portraits of Marat and Robespierre, whilst the works of Rousseau, his favourite author, occupied a prominent place upon his modest bookshelf.

Zamor was a traitor, it is true, but there is no doubt he was sincere in his devotion to the revolutionary ideal, whereas the arch-scoundrel Grieve was nothing but an egotistical hypocrite — a callous, canting rogue.

An ancient Norfolk family, which in old days had much to do with France, is that of Jerningham of Costessey Hall. Many of its members indeed, prevented from entering the English army owing to their unswerving adherence to the Roman Catholic faith, crossed the Channel and took

service under the banners of the French king,
attaining in several cases to high military command.   The last of these to do this was General
Jerningham, Colonel Commandant of several Irish
regiments under Louis XVI., who, returning to
England after the Revolution, died at Costessey in
1814.   At the present day the best known representatives of this old family are that distinguished
man, Sir Hubert Jerningham, and his brother, Mr.
Charles Edward Jerningham, a cultured collector
and authority upon prints of Old London.   A
peculiarity of the Jerninghams is that, though they
have steadfastly adhered to the Roman Catholic
Church, no one of them has ever been a priest, or,
on the other hand, become a Protestant; though
Mr. Edward Jerningham, the friend of Horace
Walpole, well known as a good scholar and elegant
poet, did, I believe, more or less abjure his faith
and declare himself an Agnostic.   Notwithstanding
the very strong anti-Catholic feeling which in old
days prevailed in Norfolk (the bells of the Norwich
churches were rung on the rejection of the Catholic
Emancipation Bill in 1825), the Jerninghams did
not, like so many of their co-religionists, abstain
from social intercourse with their Protestant neighbours, with whom, in spite of their faith, they were
always very popular.   One of the Dillons, a close
connection of the family of which I have been
speaking, took a leading part in the many attempts
made to rescue the unfortunate Dauphin who,
according to the most modern authorities, was

actually got out of the Temple, a substituted child being left in his stead. Another Norfolkian also made several strenuous efforts to the same end. This was a lady, Mrs. Atkyns of Ketteringham Hall, near Norwich, who expended practically her entire fortune in efforts to save the unfortunate Prince.

An energetic and adventurous woman, the story of her life has been given to the world in a French book published a short time ago. She was, before her marriage, Miss Charlotte Walpole, an actress of Drury Lane Theatre, and I like to believe that she was in some way connected with the Walpole family to which I belong; her father, Robert Walpole, was certainly a Norfolk man, but the exact degree of his relationship to us I have never been able to discover. Certain is it, however, that she used the Walpole crest with the addition of a lion, a circumstance which might possibly point to a descent from Colonel John Walpole, a Royalist who, for his services at Cropredy Bridge, was granted such an addition to his arms. Miss Walpole, who appears to have been exceedingly fascinating, before very long captured the heart of a Norfolk squire, and after their marriage the young people took up their abode at Ketteringham Hall, old Mrs. Walpole, the bride's mother, being installed in the Park close by in a house which has been long pulled down. Curiously enough, flowers still come up in the spring-time at this spot, which yet retains the name of Madame Walpole's garden. After a short time passed in Norfolk, Mr. and Mrs. Atkyns went to Versailles, where, introduced into the intimate entourage of Marie Antoinette by the Duchesse de Polignac, the lady conceived a respectful veneration for the unfortunate Queen, which, in after-years, caused her to penetrate, disguised as a member of the National Guard, into the prison of the Conciergerie. By means of a daring stratagem she actually contrived to obtain admission to the cell in which Marie Antoinette lay, her intention being to inform the Queen of a plan of escape. At the moment, however, of handing the royal captive a bouquet of flowers, the missive which was concealed amongst its leaves fell to the ground, when Mrs. Atkyns, seeing that a gaoler was about to read it, snatched the note from his hands and without a moment's hesitation swallowed it. Later on Mrs. Atkyns was the chief organiser of several attempts to save the Dauphin, and expended some very large sums of money in plots, actually hiring ships to lie off the French coast ready to receive the young Prince should one of the efforts made to rescue him prove successful.

Living to a great age, the poor woman eventually died almost penniless in Paris as late as the year 1836, for Louis XVIII. though admitting, on his restoration, that she had devoted her life and fortune to the service of his line, would never reimburse any serious portion of the sums which the mistress of Ketteringham Hall had, with the greatest difficulty, raised upon her estate.

He did once, however, under great pressure, send her some insignificant sum. Ketteringham Hall itself is now the property of Sir Francis and Lady Boileau, who, together with a few others, have, within the last year, erected a memorial tablet to the friend and would-be rescuer of Marie Antoinette. Owing to the comparative state of destitution in which the poor woman died her wish to be buried in Ketteringham church had not been respected. It is therefore pleasant to think that, owing to the kindly initiative of Lady Boileau, a memorial of her now exists close to those of her husband and son—the last members, it may be added, of a distinguished county family.

There exists a print of Mrs. Atkyns engraved by Watson and Dickinson after Bunbury. In this she is represented in the character of "Nancy," who, dressed as a young soldier, has followed her lover to the camp of Coxheath, a part which contemporary critics tell was enacted by the young actress with much dash and charm. In this character, indeed, she won the heart and hand of her Norfolk squire.

Retiring from the stage after the conclusion of the run of *The Camp*, her next appearance in a soldier's dress was to be in far different surroundings. Surely when assuming the costume of the National Guard in which she set out to attempt the rescue of the captive queen, her thoughts must have flown back to those careless days in which, miniature firelock in hand, she had gone through

the military exercise amidst the plaudits of the
audience at " Old Drury."

An inscription under the print runs :—

> My Nancy leaves the rural plain
> A camp's distress to prove,
> All other ills she can sustain
> But living from her love,

to which I have added on a small plaque attached
to the frame :—

> Elle poussa le dévouement jusqu'à l'héroisme
> et la courage jusqu'à la témérité,

a tribute paid to this brave Englishwoman by
that admirable writer, M. de la Sicotière, Sénateur
de l'Orne.

Mrs. Atkyns, whilst residing on her estate in
Norfolk, would seem to have taken a warm interest
in politics, her sympathies being, of course, strongly
anti-democratic.   The following letter was found
by my cousin, Sir Spencer Walpole, amongst the
papers of his grandfather, Mr. Perceval, the distinguished statesman who met with such a tragic
end :—

Sir—I flatter myself you will do me the honour to excuse
my intruding upon you at a time you must consequently be
extremely occupied. I most sincerely congratulate you on
your becoming one of His Majesty's ministers. I, with a
large majority of England, felicitate myself as a true and
faithful subject to my sovereign on seeing a gentleman of
your abilities and loyalty in the situation you now fill.   May
Heaven prosper your efforts to serve your King and country!
I take the liberty to suggest an idea, or rather, offer an
opinion. I have heard that the present Receiver-General
for the county of Norfolk, Sir Roger Kerrison of Norwich, is
likely to lose that place ; permit me, sir, to hint to you that

I

all the other bankers except Kett or Day are downright revolutionists. From the knowledge I have of the inhabitants of Norwich (my house being situated but five miles from that city), I have taken the liberty to recommend either the House of Kett or that of Day in case there should be a change. Mr. Day is an alderman of the City of Norwich, a man much respected. Kett was a Quaker, but was read out of the meeting for having subscribed to the volunteers. In case of a dissolution of Parliament either of these gentlemen will be useful and active agents. Do not think, sir, that I recommend them from my having any interest in their having such an advantageous place, or from having any particular acquaintance with either; on the contrary, I never spoke to Mr. Kett that I know of, and not twice in my life to Mr. Day, but they are loyal subjects to their King —that is enough for me—Day in particular. Norwich is famous for the number of its democrats. Excuse, sir, my troubling you, but it is for the public good; that, I think, with you will be sufficient apology. The present Receiver-General is not of what we call the Loyal Party. I shall not mention to mortal my having written this. Should there be a dissolution of Parliament, and that you think I can be of any service in this county or the city, having some interest in both, I request you will have the goodness to inform me. —I have, sir, the honour to be, your most obedient, very humble servant, CHARLOTTE ATKYNS.

KETTERINGHAM HALL,
WINDHAM, NORFOLK,
5th April 1807.

If, sir, at any time you think I can by any means be of the least use with regard to French affairs, having more knowledge of that country than, perhaps, sir, you are aware of, you may command me. There is a circumstance that most certainly may one day or other prove a severe check to the allied Powers should they attempt to enter France; it is a secret or artful menace that Buonaparte reserves for a last manoeuvre. When I come to town, which will be in less than a fortnight, I will, sir, if you please, explain my meaning. I need not request, sir, that any communication I give, or my *now* having taken the liberty to address you, may remain a profound secret.

The secret menace to which Mrs. Atkyns here alludes would seem to indicate that, in her opinion, Buonaparte was aware that Louis XVII.—the child supposed to have died in the Temple—was still alive, and was reserving this knowledge in order to make use of it should necessity arise.

It was another relative of Sir Spencer's, the Reverend Mr. Perceval, who took such a great interest in the pretender Naundorff, an individual claiming to be Louis XVII. Mr. Perceval it was who published a book called *The Misfortunes of the Dauphin*, in which the adventures of the Duc de Normandie, as Naundorff styled himself, are fully described. Much of this narrative, however, is very involved and unsatisfactory, whilst the account of the Dauphin's escape from the prison of the Temple, concealed in a coffin, carries but little conviction. The organiser of this rescue is stated to have been Josephine Beauharnais, afterwards Empress of the French.

It is not, in all probability, generally known that there were no less than thirty-six pretended Dauphins, including an American one — Eleazar Williams by name—about whose origin considerable mystery prevails. The story told about him was that he had been brought as a child to America by a French family in 1795, and placed in charge of an Iroquois half-breed, Thomas

Williams by name, being as a young man educated by a Mr. Nathaniel Ely, a deacon of the Congregational Church — Eleazar Williams himself afterwards entering the ministry. It was in 1851 that a Mr. Hanson began the investigations which brought Eleazar Williams before the world as the lost Dauphin.

The Duchesse d'Angoulême, sister of the child over whose fate such a mystery prevails, is declared, when on her deathbed, to have sent for General Larochejaquelein, a faithful adherent of the Bourbon cause. "General," she said, "I have a fact—a very important fact to reveal to you—the testament of a dying woman. My brother is not dead. This is the nightmare of my whole life. Promise me to use all possible means to find him. Travel by land and sea to discover some of the old servants or their descendants; for France can never be happy and tranquil until he is seated on the throne of his fathers."

Mr. Hanson was much struck with the words which the Duchess was supposed to have uttered, and applied them to Eleazar Williams. In 1853 he published an article embodying his researches and conclusions. It was entitled, "Have we a Bourbon among us?" and appeared in a number of *Putnam's Magazine*. But Eleazar Williams himself, who appears to have been a very quiet, dignified, and sincerely religious man, never made any particular effort to establish his claims as Dauphin, or rather as King of France, and passed most of his time in missionary work amongst the Indians. He carried on a large correspondence, however, with those interested in his history, and would sometimes discuss the question of his supposed birth. It was a constant practice of his to declare that there lingered in his memory vague recollections of a childhood passed amidst the greatest magnificence. In the freedom of private conversation he would also speak of a feeling of having passed through terrifying scenes as well as of noble edifices, beautiful gardens, troops on parade, and gorgeously furnished apartments— memories, indeed, such as might have been inspired by the splendid Court of Versailles.

Eleazar Williams died in 1858, and a grandson of his is, I believe, still living. The whole story of this American Dauphin—though, perhaps, of no serious historical importance—is a curious one, and the book in which it is set forth, *The Story of Louis XVII. of France*, merits some attention, especially as it deals at length with the pretender to whom allusion has already been made, the celebrated Naundorff, who is, in its pages, ruthlessly denounced as an impostor and cheat. Naundorff's grandson, it may be of interest to know, is, or was, engaged in commercial pursuits, and is styled Jean III. by the small band of adherents who believe in his claims to the throne of France, whilst the Dauphin, "Prince Henri Charles Louis," born in 1899, is the offspring of his marriage with the "Princesse Magdelaine," daughter of a worthy tradesman in the town of Lunel.

The whole story of the Dauphin seems destined to be wrapped in impenetrable mystery, but, as has been said, it is now believed by those most competent to judge, including M. Sardou (probably the greatest living authority on the French Revolution) that the Dauphin did not, as is generally supposed, die in the prison of the Temple. There is, indeed, good reason to assume that having been got out by some means or other (possibly in a package of dirty linen carried by the wife of Simon, his gaoler), he was conveyed without the walls which encircled his prison. Once liberated, however, his rescuers must have become dispersed, very likely being themselves executed or imprisoned for some reason other than their share in his escape, and the child, already enfeebled by his captivity, alone in the seething whirlpool of revolutionary Paris, entirely devoid of resources of any kind, would under such circumstances have been in a very hopeless position. So in all probability poor little Louis XVII., a forlorn and friendless wanderer, died a miserable death in some obscure part of that vast city over which his ancestors had held such absolute sway. As for the numerous pretenders, some of them, there is no doubt, must have heard the tale of the Dauphin's rescue from persons who had a hand in it, thus obtaining the material for the more or less plausible stories which made a considerable impression upon certain people who certainly should have known better. The Duchesse d'Angoulême, to the very end of her life, as has been said, was always declared to entertain grave doubts as to her brother having died in the Temple,—a fact which would account for her refusal to accept the heart of the boy buried as the Dauphin by the revolutionary authorities, a gruesome relic which was offered to her by Dr. Pelletan. There exists a story that she left Memoirs with a definite injunction that they were not to be published till one hundred years after her death—1951—and should there be any foundation for such a report it is therefore possible that those who live till that date may see some definite light thrown upon not the least fascinating of historical mysteries.

VII

TRAVELLING on the Continent in old days was attended with many discomforts, which to the present generation would appear almost inconceivably irksome. In the first place, there was the passport nuisance, whilst the Customs regulations were infinitely more complicated and tedious than is at present the case. I remember that, in 1844, I nearly involved an old lady we knew — Miss Astley—in very serious trouble through innocently begging her to take a sealed packet to my sister, then staying at Mayence. In my little parcel were, amongst other things, four pairs of Tyrolean gloves, then much in fashion, and these nearly caused the arrest of this poor lady on the Belgian frontier, where the officials threatened the most frightful penalties, amongst them a fine of £50, for attempting to smuggle a lesser number of pairs of gloves through the Customs than the Belgian law

120

allowed—the regulation being that nothing under
a dozen pairs could be carried by travellers without
liability to a very severe penalty. The postal
arrangements abroad in old days were also totally
inadequate.

As a child at Munich, in 1837, I recollect
that our opportunities of communicating with
friends in England were extremely limited, for
we were practically dependent, so far as sending letters was concerned, upon our Minister
or upon stray travellers passing through the city.
Unfortunately for our correspondence, the English
Minister had very little to communicate to the
Foreign Office at home, and only sent a bag of
dispatches about once a month, whilst the arrival
of an English visitor was, in those days, quite an
event in the old Bavarian city. Many of the
habits and customs of the people of Munich were
very strange and uncomfortable. The great
families, for instance, entertained a strong dislike to
having servants to board and sleep in their houses,
and the consequence of this was that ladies, on
returning from some grand party or other in a
gorgeous carriage with two footmen behind,
dressed in rich liveries and hats loaded with plumes
and feathers, used to descend from their chariots,
light their solitary night-lamps from the flam-
beaux of their departing footmen, and then sadly
creep up to bed amidst the dreary and dismal
solitude of a dark and deserted mansion.

At that time it was not at all an unusual thing

on a cloudy day to see Bavarian officers, in full
regimentals covered with enormous military cloaks,
walking about attended by their footmen carrying
umbrellas. Some of the young officers were very
pleasant ; we used to meet them at the *table
d'hôte*, where, when tired of our own company, we
used occasionally to dine. On one occasion I was
very much amused at a newly fledged subaltern—a
lieutenant, as he told us, of but six weeks' standing
—bashful and timid as a girl. That evening, for
the first time, there happened to be a band at
dinner, which surprised my mother, who inquired
of the young officer—" D'où vient cette musique ? "
Blushing up to the eyes, he answered, " Madame
la Comtesse, de la part du diable." We had been
talking of the opera, and the poor young man
thought that my mother was asking what was the
music which the band had been playing, which,
oddly enough, happened to be a selection from a
piece called " De la part du diable."

We were all convulsed with laughter at this
incident, which was rendered the more amusing on
account of the complete mystification of the lieutenant as to what indiscretion he could have committed ; however, when the matter was explained,
he himself laughed just as merrily as the rest
of us.

At that time an open fireplace was seldom seen
in Munich, whilst carpets were practically unknown. In the house which my father took there
was not even a drugget in any of the rooms,

though in other respects they were quite elegantly
furnished.   The whole life of the place was quaint
and old-fashioned—a certain amount of state and
magnificence being pervaded by a homely simplicity
which would arouse amusement in these more
luxurious days.   In the early morning or as late as
noon, for instance, all of us used to go with my
father to the market, where he himself would
choose and buy vegetables, fruit, and game, some
of which he would stuff into his pockets, whilst
the main portion was placed in an enormous
basket which two of us would carry, and so would
we perambulate the principal streets back to our
palace.   After a great " chasse" of the king's
a good deal of the spoils used to be put
up for public sale, and on these occasions my
father would add a man-servant to our marketing
party, in order to assist in carrying home, as if in
triumph, the roebuck which it was his usual
custom to purchase.

Well do I remember the extremely meagre provision which in those days was made on the Continent for the performance of the ordinary ablutions,
but even at home in England things were not very
much better.   Very few country houses had bath-
rooms, and even where they did exist the hot water
had generally to be brought up in cans.   Baths,
indeed, were considered more as luxuries than as
anything else, whilst children, owing to the water
being generally cold or at best lukewarm, regarded
their weekly tub with dread rather than affection.

That Saturday tubbing of my youth is now, I suppose, in these days of almost universal bath-rooms, quite a forgotten function. Modern mechanical arrangements provide a more or less constant supply of hot and cold water, and children are very rightly brought up to regard a daily bath as one of the necessities of life, which was, of course, not the case in the days when can after can of hot water had to be laboriously carried all over the house from the kitchen. Saturday night tub-bing was, indeed, a sort of regular English institu-tion, dating, I believe, from the reign of King Henry VIII., who is declared to have performed certain partial ablutions on occasional Saturday evenings, on which occasions His Majesty's barber, John Penne or Penn, was expected to be in attendance. This John Penn was an ancestor of the famous Quaker who bore the same name, and was a man of some importance in his day.

In the famous picture by Holbein of Henry VIII. delivering a charter to the barbers and surgeons on the occasion of their amalgamation into one body, John Penn stands out as a prom-inent figure. There is a story, indeed, which, I fancy, rests upon no solid foundation, that the first Sir Robert Peel always expressed the greatest admiration for this painting on account of the fine portrait of the royal barber, and once actually offered the Barbers' Corporation £2000 to allow him to have it cut out after a copy had been made to put in its place. An even more fantastic legend used to declare that Sir Robert had often expressed an intense desire to be allowed to have a bed made up upon the dining-table of the Barbers' Company, in order that on awakening in the morning his eyes might rest upon his favourite Penn. The table in question, as a matter of fact, is an ancient dissecting table on which, previous to 1745, the bodies of criminals and malefactors were laid — the executions at Tyburn furnishing the Barber Surgeons' Company with a constant supply of anatomical specimens.

Up to comparatively recent years the country houses, as I have said, which could boast a bathroom were very few in number, whilst in the 'forties and 'fifties, and even later, such conveniences were practically unknown. In some houses, indeed, there were no big baths at all, guests being expected to perform their ablutions in the so-called foot-baths, which were a sort of cross between a wine cooler and a soup tureen. At the same time it must be added that people were probably not so very much dirtier than they are to-day, for the modern practice of lying in hot water need not necessarily be any more cleansing than the vigorous rubbing of a soaped flannel which, in old days, children were taught to apply. I remember going to stay at a country house, shortly after my marriage, where there were no baths at all. However, I determined not to be beaten; I sent to the laundry for a large wooden wash-tub, which was brought up into my bed-

room, and answered its purpose uncommonly
well.

Some people there were who declared baths to
be dangerous, as inducing a tendency to catch constant chills. Untidiness in dress and the like were,
on the whole, I think, regarded with more toler-
ance than is the case to-day—to go even farther
back, the beautiful costumes of the eighteenth
century, there is reason to believe, in many cases
covered people none too careful about their personal toilet. The travelling of the past, when
comparatively little luggage could be taken, was
rather apt to promote careless habits of dress, and
several great travellers were quite notorious for
this sort of thing, their economy of linen being
regarded with considerable lenience.

I recall to mind a story which used to be told
of a celebrated traveller who, almost alone, had
made several wonderful journeys into the Far East,
and wandered over many strange and wild places
on the earth's surface, in the course of which
wanderings he was declared to have contracted a
supreme contempt for some of the ordinary ways
of civilised society. Careless to a degree, the
changing of his shirts appeared to him as nothing
but an irksome usage, and, consequently, it was by
no means often that a snowy expanse of shirt front
graced his breast. On one occasion, when about
to visit a country house at which he was to be the
lion of the party, his wife, who was not accompanying him, determined that this once at least he

should do her honour. The visit was to last three days, and so carefully packing three spotless shirts in his bag, she bade him at their adieu to take particular care to don one of these shirts regularly every evening. The three days passed and her husband returned. " I hope you did as I told you," said she. " Of course I did, my dear," was the reply. " I put on a clean shirt every evening, so with the one I started in, that makes four I am wearing at the present moment."

When travelling on the Continent in old days we drove most of the way in our own carriages, which, when we came across the few railways which then existed, were hoisted up on to trucks. This practice was not very agreeable, for one was exposed to many discomforts, and I had always supposed that it had long been totally extinct. This, however, appears not to be the case, for such a mode of railway travelling has been seen in England as recently as the summer of 1889, when, I am informed, the nieces of the late Archdeacon Hindes Groome (the friend of Edward FitzGerald, and a most delightful character, who remembered the rejoicings after Waterloo), saw at Bournemouth Station a large open barouche standing on an ordinary truck at the end of a train which had just arrived. In the carriage sat—quite at their ease with their sunshades up—two elderly ladies. A coachman and footman met the train ; the carriage was drawn on to the platform with the ladies still in it, and from thence it was hauled outside the

station, where, a pair of horses being quickly har-
nessed, the whole party, with the addition of a
maid who had travelled in a second-class compart-
ment, drove off.

Another curious survival was also witnessed by
Miss Hindes Groome, who, when staying at
Cheltenham in the early 'sixties, was told by her
mother one cold Sunday morning in the winter:
" I shall send for a Sedan-chair so that we can go
to church in comfort. Perhaps they still have
them at the place where in former days I remember
that they could be hired." The message was
sent, and to the surprise of the household the Sedan-
chair, borne by two men, duly arrived. The chair
was brought into the house, the front door being
shut, and Mrs. Hindes Groome and her little girl
got in, being carried to Trinity Church, into a sort
of inside lobby, in which, after the service, they
once more entered the chair, and were carried home
and deposited in the hall, being on both journeys
completely protected from the outside air and
quite immune from draughts. It may be assumed
that this was about the last time that a public
Sedan-chair was made use of for ordinary purposes,
though I believe that at certain health resorts
invalids still make occasional use of a somewhat
similar conveyance. Mrs. Hindes Groome, it
appears, was rather surprised, though very pleased,
when she saw the men bringing up the old chair,
which revived in her memory many recollections
of a past age. She always declared that no modern

vehicle could match a Sedan-chair for comfort in
wet or rough weather.   This lady's father, who
had been born in 1779, remembered the first stage-
coach which ran from Cheltenham to London,
at which time it was considered a wonderful improvement, for, previous to its introduction, everything came across the hills on pack-horses.

The early days of railway travelling were very
unpleasant in many ways, whilst journeys on the
Continent were regarded as positive adventures.
Such a thing as a train *de luxe* was, of course,
undreamt of, whilst feeble linguists were terribly
handicapped on account of there being no officials
well acquainted with foreign languages as is now
the case; only too often the instructions to
travellers purporting to be written in English were
quite unintelligible.   Even in comparatively recent
years mistakes in the phraseology and spelling of
English in foreign guide-books, time-tables, and
the like, have not been uncommon ; but I think the
following menu, which dates from the early days of
the station refreshment-room at Modane, is an
almost perfect example of " English as she is wrote."
It was sent to me by a friend, and I was so much
struck with it that it has been given a prominent
position in a scrap-book of mine filled with cards
and menus of every kind, interesting souvenirs, in
many cases, of political and other banquets.   One
side of this menu, I must add, is printed in French,
the following translation being appended on the
adjoining sheet.   It runs exactly as I give it here—

K

MODANE STATION

Travellers will find in the Refreshment Room (Buffet of the Station) which is in direct communication with the Custom Office, luncheon and dinner at the price of 3 frs., wine included.

———

Porridge.

———

Slender at the Saint Germain.
Pike forced meat ball sauce of the financial
        Beef to bake vegetables.
Poultry snow-drop of the Bresse at the
        Jelly.
Salad of the time.
Side dish, chees and desert.
        ($\frac{1}{2}$ bottle of wine.)

———

The prolonged stoppage of this train to Modane is long enough to allow travellers to lunch and look over their baggage at the Custom Office.

People when on a journey in old days were not very particular about their food; indeed, too often thoroughly tired and worn out, they were thankful to get anything to eat at all. Now pretty well every one who is able to afford it is luxurious, and Spartan habits are at a discount. Nevertheless there seem to be no noted gourmets to-day such as used to exist in the past. Foremost amongst those, of course, was Abraham Hayward, whose *Art of Dining* is, I suppose, but little read at the present time, when many of his gastronomic ideas would be considered quite out of date. His contention, for instance, that the comparative merits of pies and puddings present a problem difficult to decide, would seem somewhat ridiculous to *bons vivants* of the present day, when puddings, formerly so popular, are, except in the sick-room, rarely seen. Plum-pudding, of course, still maintains its ancient place. It may not be generally known that it originated from plum-porridge, a first course always served at Christmas in the seventeenth century. This was prepared by boiling beef or mutton with a broth thickened by brown bread, raisins, currants, cloves, nutmegs, ginger, and other condiments being inserted when it was half-cooked.

The English are very contemptuous of many excellent things which their country affords. Amongst these is the truffle, which, though perhaps not equal in flavour to that of Périgord—called by Brillat Savarin the diamond of the kitchen—is yet most delicious when properly cooked. Besides this, owing to the small esteem in which it is held, its price is exceedingly moderate, English truffles being purchasable in Covent Garden Market at about one-eighth the price of the French variety. Years ago, when staying at the Grange in Hampshire, I asked my host, the late Lord Ashburton, whether he had ever thought of hunting for truffles in his park, abounding as it did in beech trees, under which, in this country, these esculents are found. He told me that he believed there were plenty of truffles, but it was not worth the trouble of searching for them, as no one cared for English truffles. I assured him that he was wrong, for they were excellent; and, yielding to my entreaties, he sent out orders for search to be made, and the next evening we had English truffles for dinner, which were served merely as truffles, without any announcement as to their nationality. Every one ate them, and every one said they were delicious, and from that day to this the English truffle, when in season, has continually been included in the menu of the dinners served at the country house in question. Truffles exist also at Goodwood and in Highclere Park—in fact, pretty well everywhere where there are beech trees. The difficulty in obtaining them seems to lie in the paucity of truffle-hunting dogs, which, of course, have to be specially trained for their work. No doubt, were some easy means discovered of finding truffles, their excellences would become better known, and a home-grown delicacy, which is now almost overlooked, would take its proper place in public appreciation.

Crayfish are excellent eating, as I believe the Germans realised when they entered France in 1870. I was told that for years afterwards the supply of *écrevisses* was very limited indeed.

Many years ago, at a time when I was living in Sussex, I formed the idea of attempting to acclimatise the crayfish in a little stream which appeared suitable to their habits, and accordingly, after everything had been prepared under expert direction, a consignment of *écrevisses*, sent from France, were duly placed in a pool specially enclosed with gratings, and furnished with everything

that the most luxurious crayfish could possibly
desire. The experiment, however, proved totally
unsuccessful, for after a time not so much as even
a morsel of shell was to be found. Another consignment shared exactly the same fate, and Lord
Onslow, who made a similar experiment in acclim-
atisation, informed me that his efforts, like mine,
had also ended in disaster. For a long time I was
much puzzled as to what might have caused the
death and also the mysterious disappearance
of any remains of these *écrevisses*, but am now
convinced that it was the result of raids by
predatory water-rats, the possibility of which we
had left out of our calculations.

A rather curious thing in connection with
gastronomy is that for the last two hundred years
the dinner hour in England has been getting later
and later.

In Addison's time people dined at two o'clock,
but gradually dinner was put off and put off till
four or five became the popular hour for dining
amongst the well-to-do classes. With the beginning of the nineteenth century came a further
postponement, and the dinner hour soon came to
be fixed at some time about seven o'clock; since
which period further encroachments upon the
evening have taken place, and now half-past eight
is by no means an unusual hour.

The old English dinner which I remember in
my childhood was, of course, simplicity itself as
compared with the elaborate banquets of to-day.

Nevertheless, a well-cooked English dinner, now almost unobtainable, was not by any means a thing to be despised.

A small turbot, some well-roasted lamb or duckling, with green peas, followed by a good apple or apricot tart, are, when well cooked, as Lord Dudley used to say, a dinner for an emperor, and, in addition, far more healthy than many a more costly and ambitious repast.

I well remember, as a child, my father sitting at the head of the table and carving the joints himself, even when he gave a dinner-party. In consequence of this we were in terror of asking for a second helping, for even when only the family was present it was as much as he could do to find time to eat his own dinner. The modern system is without doubt much more convenient for everybody.

In the education of young ladies in England too little attention is as a rule, I think, devoted to the inculcation of the principles of sound housekeeping, and in consequence a good many mistresses of households are quite ignorant of the important details of domestic management. Many jokes, I remember, were current about one of this sort, a distinguished matron of society, whom I may mention as Lady Caroline, a dear, portly dame of high degree. Entering the married condition rather late in life (despite a good average weight of some sixteen stone) as second wife to a West-Country squire of limited estates, she undertook the management of his household with a firm determination to conduct it on unswerving principles of domestic economy. This truly admirable resolution was unfortunately unenlightened by even a glimmer of elementary knowledge of housekeeping, and her unsuccessful attempts at starting greatly entertained her numerous friends. Her prompt dismissal of her first cook in particular created much amusement. In vain had the poor woman, when taxed with dishonesty, tried to persuade her mistress that only two legs of mutton pertained to each sheep; for had not the lady, as she somewhat angrily declared, all through her life seen them grazing with four!

In these days, however, there are so many admirable books published which deal with household management and cookery in general, that little excuse can be found for those who wilfully remain ignorant of the essential amenities of existence.

I have a good collection of cookery books which I began to get together at the time when the famous Soyer, who had been cook to Lady Blessington, was creating quite a sensation in London. I remember being taken to see him, and I also recollect his wife, who was a woman of considerable artistic attainments, executing very pretty little sketches in water-colour.

Both Soyer and his wife are buried, I believe, in a sort of mausoleum in Kensal Green Cemetery, and on Soyer's tomb is the very appropriate inscription, " Soyer tranquil."

Gentlemen used formerly to sit long in the dining-room over their wine, of which they often drank a considerable quantity; but all this has now been changed, and to-day they soon join the ladies, whose society they very naturally prefer to the mineral waters in which so many of them indulge instead of wine. People certainly seem to me to drink much less nowadays, and of late years, I am informed, the consumption of wine at dinner-parties has sunk to a very small quantity indeed, many men drinking almost no wine at all. These would, I fancy, be bad days for people like Abraham Hayward, who, when a friend of his remarked, "Why, Hayward, I believe you could drink really any quantity of port, couldn't you?" is said to have replied, "Yes, my dear fellow, any *given* quantity." On the other hand, I believe that ladies who, up to comparatively recent years, nearly all drank water, take a good deal more wine, especially champagne, than was formerly the case.

The old custom of people asking one another to have a glass of wine at dinner has long since died out. No doubt its disappearance is a good thing, though there were occasions when it distinctly conduced to pleasant sociability. A shy man, for instance, at a dinner-party of strangers was soon put at his ease by kindly intimations that Mr. So-and-so would like to take a glass of wine with him. Not a few, however, carried the old custom too far, and, besides this, a set could be so easily made against any especial individual whom mischievous schemers might wish to exhilarate unduly.

Cigarette-smoking after dinner has undoubtedly been a great factor in the cause of temperance. In old days such a thing would have been regarded with horror; indeed, I think the greatest minor change in social habits which I have witnessed is that in the attitude assumed towards tobacco-smoking, which in my youth, and even later, was, except in certain well-defined circumstances, regarded as little less than a heinous crime.

Smoking-rooms in country houses were absolutely unknown, and such gentlemen as wished to smoke after the ladies had gone to bed used, as a matter of course, to go either to the servants' hall or to the harness-room in the stables, where at night some sort of rough preparation was generally made for their accommodation. To smoke in Hyde Park, even up to comparatively recent years, was looked upon as absolutely unpardonable, while smoking anywhere with a lady would have been classed as an almost disgraceful social crime.

The first gentleman of whom I heard as having been seen smoking a cigar in the Park was the late Duke of Sutherland, and the lady who told me spoke of it as if she had been present at an earthquake!

Well do I remember the immense care which devotees of tobacco used to take, when sallying forth in the country to enjoy it, not to allow the faintest whiff of smoke to penetrate into the hall as they lit their cigars at the door. The whole thing was really ridiculous, but I suppose it would have still been going on had it not been for our present King, who most sensibly took the lead in promoting the toleration of what is, after all, a great addition to the pleasures of life.

Besides this, there can be no doubt that the cigarette-smoking now practically universally prevalent after lunch and dinner has been a considerable factor in the direction of temperance, and has ended the practice of consuming large quantities of wine, which in old days was more or less universal. On the whole, I believe that smoking does more good than harm, in spite of the attacks sometimes levelled against it. Cigarettes, of course, are a modern invention, but I believe they already existed in a slightly different form at the beginning of the nineteenth century, when old Peninsular officers used to smoke tobacco rolled up tight in a piece of paper. They called this a *papelito*, and I fancy it was much the same thing as a cigarette. The exact time when cigars were introduced into England seems very uncertain. In *Westward Ho!* Charles Kingsley pictures Amyas Leigh smoking a cigar, and it is to be presumed that he had authority for this. At the same time it is quite clear that cigars were hardly known in England at all as late as 1730, for the writer of a book published about that time, when describing the adventures of certain English sailors taken prisoners by a Spanish pirate in South America, notes with

special astonishment that the captives were presented with "segars," of which he gives a detailed
description.

The greatest traditionary smoker is, of course,
Dr. Parr, whose motto is said to have been, "No
pipe—no Parr." He is also declared to have once
very wittily told a lady, who had triumphantly
prevented him from indulging in his beloved
tobacco, that "she was the greatest tobacco stopper
in England."

VIII

SINCE the days when as a child I first knew London the outward aspect of most of the streets may be said to have completely changed. Up to within the last twenty years the alteration was not very marked, being for the most part gradual, but now a veritable architectural revolution seems to be taking place. Everywhere the boxlike Georgian house is passing away, and on all sides towering mansions with elaborate frontages in every possible style (some indeed being little but collections of decorative samples jumbled up together) are making their appearance. Amongst other eccentricities modern architects seem to have an especial love for small windows, which, considering the not over-abundant supply of sunshine and light available in London, seem somewhat out of place. On one estate (I believe that belonging to the Duke of

140

Westminster), a clause in every lease forbids the building of a house with any but windows of very moderate dimensions. In modern street architecture uniformity seems to have little place; it is, I fancy, considered inartistic by English architects, who, careless of the example of Mansard (the designer of the Place de la Concorde) and other men of the past, who were capable of really great architectural conceptions, imagine that decoration, no matter how exotic or inappropriate, produces a more striking effect than that well-proportioned, dignified, and graceful uniformity of construction to which, I fear, they are quite unable to attain. The best modern street in the West End, I think, is Mount Street, which, notwithstanding the diversity of style exhibited in the façades of the houses, is a really fine street, and one, moreover, not entirely unpicturesque. Most of the old streets in the West End are too narrow for the lofty houses now so frequently being erected. How the occupants of these mansions— overshadowed as they must be by other giant constructions facing them, and for the most part only furnished with ridiculous little windows— ever obtain any light, is a mystery which I think their builders would be considerably puzzled to explain. The old Georgian houses were quite devoid of any pretension to especial decorative merit, but some of them were not lacking in a certain dignity of proportion, whilst ample provision for the admission of light was always to be found.

ment, but there was something rather picturesque about the lamplighter who, at the dusk of a winter's evening, kindled the old gas-lamps which are now things of the past. When the electric light first came in most people viewed it with the greatest suspicion, which for some time seemed rather justified, for, owing to an absolutely safe method of installation not being perfectly understood, there were a good many slight outbreaks of fire, for the most part happily extinguished before much damage had been done. About the first people to make use of the new illuminant in their house were Lord and Lady Randolph Churchill.

A certain architectural symmetry was always observed by the architects who built the houses around the old squares of London, but to-day there is no uniformity at all—buildings of every sort of style and size jostling each other like toys in a shop window. In our streets and squares, indeed, we may see attempts at every kind of style, from the Byzantine to a sort of spurious Queen Anne, whilst terra-cotta decorations (peculiarly unsuited, I fancy, to our atmosphere) ramble in meaningless riot over many a sham Renaissance façade. Proportion, the real foundation of true artistic effect, is totally neglected in favour of laboured originality of design, whilst hardly ever do any of our modern buildings convey that idea of dignified stability which should be the thoughtful architect's chief aim. It is true we have what might well be termed "the prison style," in which enormous arches of ponderous design support minute pillars, which in turn are crowned with some eccentric terminal, the whole being liberally topped by a series of domes, pepper-boxes, or miniature steeples embellished with ornamentation of a more or less insignificant kind.

Old London, from an architectural point of view, was a very unpretentious city, as may be seen from many an old print; but there was a certain air of solid comfort about it as well as a good deal of old-fashioned dignity.

Few streets in the West End have escaped being modernised, and façades of every period and style may now be seen side by side with such old Georgian mansions as still remain. On the whole, however, Berkeley Square has survived pretty well, and still retains a good deal of its old appearance.

The streets leading out of it, though in many cases some of the houses have been altered, also keep that air of quiet repose which makes this part of London so pleasant to live in.

I have lived in Charles Street now for some thirty-eight years, and have naturally become much attached to it and to Berkeley Square, where I was born, and where nearly every house possesses memories which to me recall the past. Charles Street boasts one of the most curious old tavern signs in London—"The Running Footman"— though I fear that the sign itself is but a modern reproduction of the original one. Be this as it may, no similar signboard exists; it recalls the days

L

when noblemen were preceded by runners, whose especial duty lay in clearing the way. The legend beneath the footman, clad in green coat and knee-breeches, states, "I am the only running footman," and such as a matter of fact is the case, for there exists no other sign of this kind. Long may this interesting survival of other days maintain its position!

The Duke of Queensberry,—"Old Q.," the star of Piccadilly,—is believed to have been the last nobleman to retain running footmen. These he himself was in the habit of engaging after having made them give an exhibition of such fleetness of foot as they might possess. A well-known story used to be told of the trick which one of these gentlemen played his Grace. A man desirous of serving "Old Q." in the capacity of running footman had to run a sort of trial up Piccadilly, whilst his future master sat on the balcony of his house carefully watching the performance. On one occasion, a particularly likely-looking candidate having presented himself, orders were given that he should exhibit his running powers in the Duke's livery, in which accordingly he was equipped. The man ran well, and "Old Q.," who was delighted, shouted out to him from his balcony: "You will do very well for me." "And your livery will do very well for me," replied the man, after which reply he made off at top speed, and could never be caught nor found again.

Running footmen were wont to sustain their

energies by drinking a mixture composed of white wine and eggs—a small supply of the wine being frequently carried in the large silver ball which topped their tall canes. About seven miles an hour was by no means an unusual speed for them to attain, but when put upon their mettle they would do even better.

In the eighteenth century these men were frequently matched to run against horses and carriages, and one of the last recorded contests of this sort was between a celebrated running foot- man and the Duke of Marlborough, some time before 1770. The wager was that the footman would run to Windsor from London quicker than the Duke could drive there in his phaeton and four, both to start at the same time. The result was that his Grace just (but only just) won, whilst the poor footman, worn out by his tremendous exertions, and very much chagrined at his defeat, died from the effects, it was said, of over-fatigue.

Some of these men wore no breeches at all, but a sort of short silk petticoat kept down by a deep gold fringe.

In the north of England the calling of running footmen was not totally extinct till well into the middle of the last century, for as late as 1851 the Sheriff and Judges were announced, on the opening of a North of England Assize Court, as being pre- ceded by two running footmen, whilst about the same date the carriage of the High Sheriff of Northumberland, on its way to meet the Judges of Assize, was attended by two pages on foot, holding on to the door handles of the carriage and running beside it. These running footmen were dressed in a short livery jacket and white trousers, and wore a jockey cap.

In the old days, when communication between towns and villages was by no means easy, swift runners were often of the greatest service to their employers, especially in cases of illness when a doctor lived far away. The story of the Scotch running footman is a very old one; still I hope I may be excused for repeating it here. This man was on his way from Glasgow to Edinburgh in order to requisition the services of two noted physicians for his sick master, when he was stopped by an inquirer who wished to know how the invalid was.

"He's no dead yet," was the reply, "but he soon will be dead, for I'm fast on the way to fetch twa Edinbro' doctors to come and visit him."

In a small street at the foot of Hay Hill, leading towards Burton Mews, used to be another quaint old sign—"The Three Chairmen"—a relic of the days when Sedan-chairs were in fashion. I do not know whether this public-house still exists, but rather think it has disappeared.

In 1774 a party of people driving in a coach were attacked and robbed on Hay Hill; the reputation of this locality, indeed, was very bad, as George IV. and the Duke of York, when very young men, discovered to their cost, for they also were made to stand and deliver by highwaymen who stopped their hackney carriage at this place. George IV. always used to declare that the man who robbed him was none other than Champneys the singer. The reason, as a matter of fact, why no great stir was made about this affair, was that the Prince Regent would have had to account for his whereabouts the evening before the robbery took place, and this he was for certain reasons unwilling to do.

The whole neighbourhood, indeed, is full of memories of old days when life in London was totally different from that of the present time—witness the stout iron bar which stands in the doorway of Lansdowne Passage in Berkeley Street. This was put up to hamper highwaymen, one of these gentry having effected his escape after a robbery in Piccadilly by galloping through the passage from Curzon Street, his horse successfully negotiating the steps. This happened in comparatively recent times—at the end of the eighteenth century.

It might be thought that in these more peaceful times highwaymen had long been extinct in the West End of London, but such is not the case, for within the last twenty years they reappeared in modern guise in the very centre of Mayfair. One winter's night in 1889, the French naval *attaché*, who was going home from his club, was set upon in Curzon Street by four men who, after violently assaulting and robbing him, left

him senseless upon the ground, where he was
discovered by the police a short time afterwards.
The assailants in this case were never, I believe,
arrested, though the whole affair created a great
sensation, occurring as it did in the very centre
of a quarter generally considered to be about the
safest in London.

Peaceful as Berkeley Square is to-day, it came
near being a scene of carnage at the time of Lord
Liverpool's ministry, when artillerymen stood there,
lighted match in hand, by the side of loaded field-
pieces which they were quite prepared to fire.
Mount Street also has had a military day, owing
its very existence indeed to rumours of battle, for
on its site stood a bastion or mount—part of the
line of fortifications hastily thrown up to defend
the western suburbs of London in 1643, when the
Parliament was expecting an attack from the
forces of King Charles I.   In the centre of
Berkeley Square stood, up to comparatively recent
times, an equestrian statue of George III. as
Marcus Aurelius. This had been erected by the
Princess Amelia ; it had no particular artistic merit,
and was perched upon a very clumsy pedestal.

Berkeley Chapel, at the other end of Charles
Street, has been but recently demolished ; it may
not be generally known that at one time the
celebrated Sydney Smith was its minister.   In
after-years this celebrated divine took up his abode
in Charles Street, at No. 33.   At No. 42 in this
old street lived the celebrated and unfortunate

dandy " Beau Brummell "—this was about the year
1792 ; whilst a more intellectual occupant of one of
its houses was Bulwer Lytton, in whose house was
a room fitted up in exact facsimile of an apartment
at Pompeii—everything being in keeping. Charles
Street, in all probability, did not derive its name
from the Merry Monarch, but from Charles, Earl
of Falmouth, brother of the first Lord Berkeley
of Stratton. Berkeley Square, though begun
about 1698, was not finished till the time when
Sir Robert Walpole was Prime Minister; he,
indeed, made a note of the last houses being built
there. Many distinguished people have lived in
this old square—Lord Clive amongst others. It
was at a house in Berkeley Square that a butler
murdered a certain nobleman, his master—a crime
which called forth from George Selwyn the remark : " Good God ! What an idea that butler
will give the convicts of us when he is sent to
Newgate ! "

In these days houses change owners very
quickly, and people, I think, rather like the amusement of taking new houses and redecorating them ;
but in the past this was not at all the case. There
is yet one house in Charles Street, " No. 41,"
which has been in the possession of the same
family for over one hundred and fifty years. Lord
Powis's house in Berkeley Square is another instance of a long continuity of tenure.

Another old-world square is St. James's. Passing
through it the other day my thoughts strayed back

to the memory of a great lady of old days, Lady
Cowper, who used to live there. She was the
mother of the late earl, and has long been dead.
Well do I remember the ballroom, and especially
some magnificent silver chandeliers, which made a
great impression upon my girlish mind.

Lady Cowper was an amusing woman, and used
to say shrewd things at times. She once told me,
"To make a ball successful, three men should be
always asked to every lady—one to dance, one
to eat, and one to stare—that makes everything go
off well"—and her entertainments certainly did.

The beautiful drawing-room in this house is, I
believe, reproduced at No. 9 Grosvenor Square,
the residence of Lord and Lady Haversham, who
are endowed with a quite unusual share of artistic
taste, as is exemplified in their delightful country
residence, South Hill Park, in Berkshire.

There still remain in Charles Street, as well as
in Berkeley Square, several specimens of the old
iron extinguishers which were formerly used by
the linkboys in the days when torches served to
light people home and no regular system of street
lighting existed. For this reason the neighbourhood of Mayfair was at one time none too pleasant
at night, abounding, as it did, in riotous characters.

It was said that it was Lord Coventry, the
husband of the famous beauty, who finally caused
an end to be put to the "May fair" which used
to be held upon the ground now covered by Hertford Street, Curzon Street, Shepherd's Market,

and some other streets. Lord Coventry lived at the house at the corner of Engine Street (now Brick Street) which, in the middle of the eighteenth century, had been erected on the site of the large and ancient Greyhound Inn. The perpetual noise and uproar which went on by night as well as by day during the whole month of May, owing to the fair, so irritated and annoyed him that he determined to make an effort to have it totally suppressed. As early as 1709 it had been prohibited. but within a few years was once more revived, though the Grand Jury of the City of Westminster had characterised it as a vile and riotous assembly. Lord Coventry, however, by some means or other, was completely successful in his efforts to abolish finally what he considered to be an intolerable nuisance, and no "May fair" seems to have been held much after 1764, the date at which Lord Coventry entered into possession of his new house. Most of the ground on which the fair was held belonged to a Mr. Shepherd, whence has originated the present name of Shepherd's Market, which is sometimes wrongly called "Shepherd Market," as if it had been a meeting-place for shepherds in the past. This was never the case. Another gentleman of the same sounding name also lived in Mayfair for a time in 1723. This was the celebrated Jack Sheppard of notorious memory.

In an attic in Curzon Street Sir Francis Chantrey, when quite an undistinguished young man, modelled his Head of Satan and the bust of Lord

St. Vincent; and in this street also lived Madame Vestris; the Miss Berrys, one of whom I knew, lived at No. 8, whilst Lord Beaconsfield went to reside in this street at No. 19 at the beginning of 1881, in which house he died some three months later.

Many have sought to trace the origin of the name Piccadilly, but I believe that no entirely satisfactory explanation has ever been given. The first mention of what is now a world - famous thoroughfare occurs (as is well known) in Gerard's *Herbal*, which has originated an erroneous idea that Piccadilly existed in 1596 when the work in question was published. As a matter of fact, it is not in the original edition of Gerard's *Herbal* that such a mention occurs, but in a much later one published in 1636, and edited by Thomas Johnson. It runs as follows:—"The little wild bugloss grows upon the dry ditch bank about Pickadella." It is pretty well authenticated that about 1630 a retired tailor, named Higgins, whose fortune had been in a great measure made by the sale of "pickadelles"—piccadillies or turnover collars— built himself a snug house in this locality which he called Pickadilla Hall; and Mr. Higgins, there- fore, it was who, in all probability, originated the name.

Up to about 1851, the year of the great Exhi- bition, Piccadilly was more a fashionable lounge than anything else, but since that time it has com- pletely changed, and from having been a purely

West End street has become an ordinary London
thoroughfare.

No. 22 Arlington Street, now Wimborne
House, has had a good many different names as
well as occupants. Once it was called Beaufort
House, then Hamilton House, then Walsingham
House, and now finally, as has been said, Wimborne House. Amongst other remarkable people
who have lived there was Lord Houghton, who
once took it for a year. It was the interior of this
house, it is said, that Hogarth utilised as the scene
of the wonderful series illustrating the marriage
à la mode of his day. In 1870 Mr. Pender (afterwards Sir John) gave a great party in this mansion
to inaugurate the opening of a telegraph cable to
India, in those days considered a great feat.
Messages, I remember, were sent to the Viceroy
during the evening, and congratulatory replies duly
received, whilst most of the intellect and rank of
London were amongst the guests. The present
King and Queen were there, and Mr. and Mrs.
Disraeli, and altogether the whole entertainment
was a most brilliant one. Just about this time
society was beginning to widen out, and the stamp
which once used so ruthlessly to hall-mark people
as belonging to the *crême de la crême* or as being outside the pale, to make a more feeble impression.
Nevertheless, the great millionaires had not yet
made their appearance, and if any one died and left
a hundred thousand it was still thought enormous.

The ways and things of the 'sixties seem very

strange to-day.   Oysters were a shilling a dozen, and people used to be made ill by arsenic green wall-paper.   The hideous crinoline was universally worn by ladies, and entailed untold inconvenience and discomfort.   Old Dr. Fuller of Piccadilly (the last of the apothecaries) was once summoned to dislodge a fish-bone from the throat of Frances Anne, Lady Londonderry, and when imperiously told to begin, was obliged to say that he was quite unable to get within many yards of her ladyship's throat in consequence of her crinoline being so enormous and so solid !

People were much more ignorant about health than is the case nowadays, when they discuss the un-romantic ailments of their interiors with the greatest freedom.   Formerly great reticence was observed about such subjects, which no one would have even dreamt of mentioning.   Doctors, and the medicine they gave, were still viewed with something of a mysterious awe.   In the days when the old Coliseum in Regent's Park was still in existence, a gentleman came out of his doctor's in Harley Street, looking very solemn, and met a friend on the doorstep, who said, " What on earth is the matter ?   You look like the man who lost a sovereign and found six-pence."   " Well," said the other, "my doctor tells me that I'm not at all the thing.   By the way, where is the ' Perineum ' ? "   " Oh," replied his friend, " that's easily answered ; straight down Portland Place, and turn to the right, and then you'll see it in front of you ! "

At a great party which was given at the India
Office during the Sultan's visit to England in 1867,
the wife of the Turkish Ambassador (who was,
of course, like most of the Turkish envoys sent
to England, a Christian), a lady weighing some
twenty-five stone, completely succumbed, being
overpowered by the heat. A doctor was present
in the room, being in close attendance upon the
Sultan, and every one thought that he would at
once be sent to revive the enormous and prostrate
Ambassadress. Her imperial master, however,
instead of thus despatching his medical adviser,
whom he kept in close attendance by his side, did
not show the slightest desire to dispense even for
a moment with his services, but on the contrary,
fearing that the excitement consequent upon this
unfortunate occurrence would heighten the august
temperature, bade the physician keep his hand
closely upon the imperial pulse till such time as all
inflammatory symptoms should have subsided.

Formerly, practically the whole of the West
End was more or less given up to the fashionable
world, and the great majority of people in Piccadilly or St. James's Street knew one another. The
men then thought a good deal more of their dress
than is to-day the case; indeed, having as a rule
no occupation, it was for many one of the principal
ends of their existence. The young man of that
day lived principally in Mount Street, where, before
it was rebuilt, comfortable furnished chambers
could be procured for about a hundred a year—

rather a difference this from the present Mount
Street, in which an unfurnished flat of the simplest
description costs about four or five hundred pounds
per annum. In spite of their greater attention
to dress, the dandies of another age were not so
luxurious as the men of to-day—at least theirs was
a different kind of luxury. They had no City
avocations to attend to during the day, or restaurants to dine at in the evening, and consequently
clubs played a much greater part in their lives than
is now the case. A sort of mysterious solemnity
used to attach to clubs in my youth, and we used
to regard them with the greatest awe. To-day
ladies frequently call for male relatives at their
clubs; years ago such a thing was absolutely unheard of, and would have been regarded with the
utmost consternation and horror.

In the 'forties, I remember, it was hardly considered proper for a young lady to walk past the
big bow-window at White's, at that time filled
with the dandies of the day; and I well remember
my father telling our governess to take care that
my sister and myself, when going down St. James's
Street, should walk on the other side of the road.
The peculiar charm of this old street has been best
expressed, I think, by my delightful friend of other
days, the late Mr. Frederick Locker :—

> Why, that's where Sacharissa sigh'd
>   When Waller read his ditty;
> Where Byron lived and Gibbon died,
>   And Alvanley was witty.

. . . . .

At dusk when I am strolling there
  Dim forms will rise around me,
Lepel flits past me in her chair,
  And Congreve's airs astound me.

And once Nell Gwynne, a frail young sprite,
  Look'd kindly when I met her;
I shook my head, perhaps,—but quite
  Forgot to quite forget her.

IX

THE history of the London parks is a very interesting one, tinged, as it is, with a certain amount of romance.

Of late a good deal of attention has been directed to prints of the parks by reason of Mr. Charles Edward Jerningham, the clever "Marmaduke" of *Truth*, having presented a collection of old prints, as well as of park keys, passes, and the like, to the nation—an interesting gift which, very appropriately, has now been permanently placed on view in a room specially set apart at Kensington Palace. As may be observed from those prints, the parks formerly had a much more rural air than is now the case, when they have become little more than regulated pleasure grounds for the people.

In the summer of 1739 an otter hunt took place in St. James's Park. A large dog otter, having taken up his abode there, played great havoc with the fish in the ponds and canal, and eventually, as he would take no notice of the traps set for his destruction, a regular otter hunt was organised by the ranger, then Lord Essex. At nine o'clock in the morning of a summer day, Sir Robert Walpole's pack of otter hounds, which had been borrowed for the occasion, appeared upon the scene, and after a hunt which lasted two hours the otter, having left the water and tried to run to the great canal, was speared by a Mr. Smith who hunted the hounds.

At one time, of course, deer were regularly hunted in Hyde Park, and in the seventeenth century several serious affrays took place between poachers and the park gamekeepers, one at least of which led to executions at Hyde Park Gate.

When I was a child there were still deer in Hyde Park, for they were only finally removed in 1831. One of the chief reasons for their removal was, it is said, that a great number of complaints were made concerning the keeper, who was in the habit of shooting pet dogs which then, as now, were taken to the park for exercise.

At the present time a vixen fox is said to have taken up her abode in Richmond Park. Indeed, once again wild life is making its way into the town, and of late years the advantages of the London parks as a haven of refuge have gradually become recognised by many different kinds of birds, which find in them a secure retreat. A kingfisher has, I believe, been seen in St. James's

M

Park, whilst at the moment of writing these lines a pair of magpies are busily engaged in building a nest in one of the trees of the Green Park, quite close to the railings which skirt Piccadilly. A curious fact in natural history is that pigeons which are wild in the country are quite tame in London, apparently recognising that once within the metropolis they have nothing to fear. So tame, indeed, are they that their practice of building nests in all sorts of places has of late begun to cause considerable inconvenience.

It was King Charles I. who threw open Hyde Park to the people, and this he did, not owing to the force of circumstances, but quite of his own free will. To-day the fact that this park was once the absolute property of the Crown, and only thrown open by a royal concession, is more or less forgotten, and, in common with other parks, it has long been regarded as the property of the people, and is generally spoken of as such. Some years ago a rather purse - proud millionaire was complaining at a dinner-party of the worry that the two parks attached to his country houses caused him, whereupon some one sitting at the other end of the table said in a loud voice which every one could hear, " My parks don't worry me, though I have many more than that." Somewhat humbled, the millionaire, much taken aback at meeting some one, as he supposed, more richly dowered than himself, immediately inquired where these properties might be, and was completely silenced by the prompt reply : "Hyde Park, St. James's Park, the Green Park, and all the other parks."

My eccentric ancestor, George Lord Orford, who once drove a four-in-hand of stags, held the rangership of the parks from 1762 to 1791, it having been offered to him through Horace Walpole by Henry Fox, first Lord Holland, in the hope, as he said, that it would at least delay his ruin. Previous to his receiving this sinecure, for it was little else, Lord Orford had created some sensation in London when marching at the head of the Norfolk Militia, 1100 strong, at a review in Hyde Park, his martial appearance having much pleased the King. Pitt, in a letter to Lady Hester Stanhope, wrote : " Nothing could have made a better appearance than the two Norfolk battalions. Lord Orford, with the port of Mars himself, and really the genteelest figure under arms I ever saw, was the theme of every tongue."

The old Ranger's Lodge in the Green Park was removed in the spring of 1842 by Lord Duncannon (afterwards Earl of Bessborough), at which time the gardens attached to the building were also thrown into the park. Sir Robert Peel, who was then Prime Minister, wished other alterations to be made in the shape of a terrace, adorned with fountains, statues, and flower vases, from the gate at Hyde Park Corner to the houses at the eastern end. These, however, were never begun. It may be mentioned that the stags which formerly adorned the entrance to the Ranger's Lodge were removed to Albert Gate, where they still remain.

It is a curious fact that the principal gate of Hyde Park, which is close to Apsley House, possesses no name whatever, being simply known as Hyde Park Corner. The north-east entrance of the park, the Marble Arch, was removed to its present position in 1851; before that date it stood in front of Buckingham Palace. Near the gate, facing Great Cumberland Place, was the place of execution known as Tyburn, and when a wall used to enclose this corner military executions were carried out within it. In this spot were erected the only gallows ever set up in Hyde Park; this was for the purpose of hanging a Sergeant Smith who, two years previously, in 1745, had deserted to the Scotch rebels.

In the Green Park the ancient course of the Tyburn has not entirely disappeared, and may even be traced by the winding depression which remains where it formerly flowed. There was formerly a pond in the middle of this park, but this was filled up in 1842, at the same time that the Ranger's Lodge was razed to the ground. The design for Spencer House, which looks into the Green Park, though known as having been the work of Vardy, is also said to have in reality been taken from a drawing by Inigo Jones, the pediment alone being purely original.

Probably few people have any idea that a serious

proposal was once actually made to erect a railway station in Hyde Park. This was to be inside the park, on the left-hand side, not very far from the entrance at Hyde Park Corner, and was to serve as terminus to a projected London and Richmond railway.

At the upper end of the road skirting the garden wall of Buckingham Palace, now called Constitution Hill, the great Sir Robert Peel met his death on a June afternoon in 1850, when his horse, having shied at something, threw its rider over his head, an accident which led to a fatal termination a day or two later.

On Constitution Hill, by a somewhat strange coincidence, two attempts were made upon the late Queen Victoria by individuals who were more or less of deranged mind—Edward Oxford, on June 10, 1840, and John Francis, on May 30, 1842. A little more than a month later a hunchbacked youth also levelled a pistol at Her Majesty not very far away from the same locality. His name was Bean, and the outrage occurred whilst the Queen was proceeding from Buckingham Palace to the Chapel Royal. A madman who entertained similar murderous designs also attempted to enter Buckingham Palace in 1839, but was fortunately seized by a sentry before he could do any harm. In former days lunatics were not kept under such strict observation and control as is at present the case. In the early 'forties, for instance, a regular panic was produced in Kensington Gardens by the appearance of a half-clad lunatic on horseback, who created a great deal of confusion amongst the people listening to a band.

The quaint old name of Constitution Hill was the "King's coach-way" to Kensington, whilst the Green Park was at one time known as Upper St. James's Park.

In old days there were occasional riots in Hyde Park, notably in 1855, when a Bill to prevent Sunday trading aroused much irritation. Frequenters of the park were a good deal molested by these disturbances, which occurred several Sundays in succession. In 1862 there was also a riot in the same park, which arose from a difference of opinion as to the French occupation of Rome. A free fight took place, indeed, between a number of working men and a body of Irish Catholics, in the course of which a good many people were seriously injured. The breaking down of the park railings during the Reform agitation was, however, a much more serious affair, quiet being only restored by the arrival of the Life Guards.

For the last forty years or so, with the exception of the Trafalgar Square riots, the great demonstrations which are a regular feature of London Sundays have passed off quite peaceably, those taking part in the processions being drawn from a more orderly class than was formerly the case. Even the demonstrations organised by the unemployed have been of a law-abiding character. In connection with these I remember rather an amusing little incident. A certain lady had been invited to view a procession of the unemployed from the windows of a house belonging to a hostess much interested in philanthropic endeavour. On that particular occasion the unemployed had made but a sorry muster, and the lady in question, with every desire to say the right thing, remarked on leaving, "A most delightful afternoon, and I feel sure you are doing a great deal of good ; but it was disappointing, wasn't it, that after all your trouble there should have been so few unemployed ? "

Whilst speaking of Hyde Park I am reminded of the various legends prevailing as to the origin of the name Rotten Row, which some people maintain is nothing else than a corruption of *Route du Roi*. I do not believe there is any real authority for this derivation, which seems to me somewhat speculative and fanciful, and rests upon no serious foundation of historical evidence. There were formerly many streets in England, and especially in Scotland, which were called Ratton Row, either from alliteration, or allusion to the locality being infested with rats. There was, for instance, a Ratones Lane or Rat Lane in the parish of St. Michael, Greenhithe, as early as the 14th century, whilst coming down to later times a portion of Old Street, just where it joined with Goswell Street, was called Rotten Row in 1720, the houses being appropriately enough in a bad state of decay ; the name of this street was afterwards changed to Russel Row. The most fanciful derivation of Rotten Row is the one which declares it to have originated from *Rattanreigh*, a Celtic term for a good mountain path or road as contrasted with a bad one. Rotten Row in Hyde Park can, by no stretch of imagination, be termed mountainous, and the name of this pleasant ride, which is not an ancient one, in all probability actually arose from the loose state of the mixture of sand and gravel of which its surface is composed.

It was Sheridan who, in a debate in the House of Commons in 1808 on the question of building houses on a part of Hyde Park, jokingly suggested that both sides of Rotten Row might be built on, in order that gentlemen taking their rides there might have the advantage of being gazed at by ladies in the balcony.

Thanks to his efforts, and those of Sir Francis Burdett, Mr. Windham, and Mr Creevy, the scheme was abandoned and the park saved.

As has been said, the name of Rotten Row is not of any great antiquity, the first printed mention of it being only found as recently as 1781, though it is believed that the ride in question was known by that name for some years anterior to that date. Though it is still much frequented at certain hours, Rotten Row does not now evoke the idea of fashion and pleasure, combined with a certain air of luxurious dissipation, which it formerly did. People nowadays, I fancy, go there more to take a ride for the benefit of their health than anything else, and the joking letter written by a friend of mine in the early 'sixties would to-day be quite meaningless. The writer was under the impression that I was out of town, but, chancing to be taking a stroll in Hyde Park, caught sight of me riding there, which prompted the following missive :—

DEAR LADY DOROTHY—I thought you were in innocence with your flowers, but, instead, find you caracoling in the paradise of the lost—in Rotten Row.

In old days no one would have dreamt of riding in the Row in country costume ; but now, I fancy, no rule whatever prevails about this, and people ride in anything they like, whilst the brilliant and eccentric figures which at times used to make their appearance have now totally disappeared, having given way to a dull and monotonous uniformity of costume.

During the season white duck trousers used to be much worn by gentlemen in the park, and the extreme tightness which fashion at one time prescribed for these occasionally led to some ludicrous incidents. A former Duchess of Beaufort, I remember, used to relate a story of such a mishap having happened to one of her admirers. Years ago there was a good deal more romance surrounding the love-making and engagements of young people than prevails to-day, and young men would often send a little present to the lady of their choice with the message that its acceptance would signify that their suit had proved successful, and its return the opposite.   At the time before the Duchess's marriage, when she was Lady Georgiana Curzon, a certain peer who was very much in love with her at last determined to learn his fate, and so sent her a beautiful little riding-whip, together with an impassioned note, in which he said that he should be in the park the next morning, when he would expect to discover her decision.   This would be indicated by her riding-whip ; that is to say, the presence of one he had sent her would mean accept-ance, and its absence refusal.

The next morning the young lady duly rode in the park, but, to his extreme disgust, her expectant swain saw that the riding-whip she carried was not the previous day's gift, whereupon, overcome with rage and mortification, he at once put his horse into a gallop, with the result (at the recol-lection of which the Duchess could never help laughing) that his tight white trousers burst right up the side.

In Rotten Row Lady Diana Beauclerk was once wont to ride in a green velvet riding habit, whilst the Prince of Orange caracoled by her side. Here also used to canter the dashing Baron de Géramb, whose plumed kalpack and furred pelisse made such an impression upon the British military authorities as to cause the creation of certain cavalry regiments dressed as hussars, which are still part of the English army.   This Baron, who ended his days as the chief of a Trappist monastery,

was an extraordinary and somewhat mysterious
character, who, after having offered to raise 24,000
Croatian troops to assist in the overthrow of Buonaparte, was denounced as an impostor and ordered
out of England.   Upon this he barricaded himself
in his house, hanging out a board on which was
written, "My house is my castle," and announced
that he would sustain a long siege whilst awaiting
the arrival of his Croatians, and at the last extremity
would blow up his house and all Bayswater
rather than yield.   His resistance, however, did
not last long, for that very evening he was captured,
taken to Harwich, and sent out of the country.   In
later life Géramb, becoming a monk, rose, as has
been said, to a very high position in the Trappist
community.   Indeed, when he went to Rome in
1837 he created such a sensation that Pope
Gregory XVI. said, "There are two popes now—
Pope Géramb and myself."   The favourite motto
of Géramb, in his later years, when he had become
a pattern of simple devotion and zeal, was "*se taire,
souffrir et mourir,*" words which he caused to be
inscribed on the walls of his modest cell.   This
Procureur-Général of the Trappist Order, who
was the creator of the English hussar, died at Rome
on the 15th of March 1848.

The era of the dandies has long since passed
away, and were he to return to the scene of his
sartorial triumphs, D'Orsay,

> Prince of unblemished boots and short napped hat,

would find that his well - thought - out costume,

far from evoking admiration, would be regarded only with ridicule and contempt.   The days of the gorgeous equipages which at one time formed one of the principal sights in Hyde Park during the season are also over; there seems a strong probability, indeed, that in the not very distant future horsed carriages in London will become something very like curiosities, being supplanted by motors, which, notwithstanding certain inconveniences, are essentially suited to a modern city.

Probably the only person now living who used a *vis-à-vis*, a form of carriage once very fashionable but now totally obsolete, is the present Lady Cardigan, who now, I believe, seldom leaves Deene Park, her lovely place in Northamptonshire.   I remember my brother once being very much amused, after having been on a visit there, at a little incident of which he was the hero.   Met at the station by a dogcart, he observed that the driver treated his attempts at conversation with a somewhat tolerant familiarity.   On coming up to the house and finding that no stop was made at the front door, he proceeded to inquire the reason, when he was told that the servants' entrance was elsewhere.   He then found that he had been taken for a French cook, whose arrival had been eagerly looked for—a discovery which caused him the greatest amusement and delight, for there was nothing that he liked more than telling a joke against himself.

At the east end of Hyde Park once stood a fine avenue of walnut trees, but these were destroyed in the early part of the nineteenth century, when the wood was sold to be made into gunstocks.

Duelling, though practically obsolete in England after the first quarter of the nineteenth century, lingered on up to about the middle of the 'forties, when an encounter between Lieutenant-Colonel Fawcett and Lieutenant Munro, in which the former was shot dead, led to a debate in the House of Commons owing to the wife of the former being refused a pension. On this occasion Sir Charles Napier declared that but one way existed of effectually putting an end to duelling. No duel should be allowed which was not fought across a table. Of the two pistols used only one should be loaded with ball, lots being drawn to see who should have the loaded one. If this produced no result, then both pistols should be loaded with ball, and the survivor, should there be one, hanged. The last duel actually fought in Hyde Park is believed to have taken place in April 1817, when two gentlemen exchanged shots, both of them being wounded. As late, however, as 1822 a duel was fought in Kensington Gardens between the Dukes of Buckingham and Bedford.

At one time a perfect mania prevailed for fighting duels, and this was by no means confined to the well-to-do classes. In 1780 two negro servants fought a duel in Hyde Park, neither of the combatants, however, being seriously hurt; but an encounter which occurred some three years later between two footmen in the same place was of a much more serious character, both being severely wounded.   Towards the beginning of the nineteenth century, however, duels began to be much fewer in number.

At my old home in Norfolk—Wolterton Hall—my nephew, the present Lord Orford, recently came upon a number of curious old documents, amongst them a copy of the codicil to the will of the eccentric Lord Camelford, drawn up by him two days before his fatal duel with Mr. Best.   The reasons for this codicil being at Wolterton was no doubt that Lord Camelford's mother had been a Miss Wilkinson, a family connected with Burnham, a property which for generations has belonged to the Walpoles.

Lord Camelford, it will be remembered, was called out by Mr. Best under great provocation, of which an officious person was the cause.   This individual had represented to Lord Camelford that Mr. Best had spoken slightingly of him to a Mrs. Simmons, a lady with whom Lord Camelford was on terms of considerable intimacy, whilst Mr. Best had formerly been her lover.   The latter, who was noted as a deadly shot, did everything he could to avoid a conflict, and others also attempted to use their influence, but their efforts were all in vain, Lord Camelford declaring that the thing must go on.   Accordingly a duel was fought in the fields behind Holland House, with the result that Lord

Camelford was mortally wounded, expiring some four days after the fatal meeting.

The codicil, drawn up in the very face of impending death and containing, as it does, a manly reference to Lord Camelford's adversary, is a dignified and interesting document, the full contents of which, I believe, have never before been made public. For this reason I now venture to give a copy of it here:—

I Thomas Lord Camelford of the Parish of Boconnoc in the County of Cornwall deliver this paper as an explanatory note and Codicil to my Will; There are certain Sums of money of mine in the Hands of Mr. Colin de la Brunerie, who lives at No. 396, Rue de L'Université at Paris, with this money he has purchased two Estates the one in Picardy, the other near Lausanne, the whole of these Lands, with whatever Money of mine may be in his Hands I bequeath to the Grenvilles in the same manner as the rest of my property described in my Will, after a settlement shall have been upon him and his Wife (that is upon their joint lives) of a salary equal to what he at present enjoys from me which I believe is somewhere about 240£ a Year   I likewise bequeath him 500£ as a proof of my esteem and respect for his talents and integrity   I have likewise certain Sums of money in the Hands of Mr. Nicholson School Master of Soho Sqr. greatest part of which is vested in two Ships destined for the South Sea fishing, these I likewise bequeath to the Grenvilles in the same way as the other that is in the manner described in my Will, *fifteen Hundred* Pounds of this Money *is a loan* to Mr. Nicholson made on former occasion for the extending his establishment, this Money (namely 1500£) I bequeath to him as a reward for his private confidential Labours in my affairs, but the file patent Machine will go to the Grenvilles. I likewise bequeath to my good Friend and old Shipmate Captn. Burrie a full discharge of all his debts to be paid by my Heirs as soon as may be together with the redemption of his half pay, which I have reason to fear he has sold, and I furthermore bequeath to him a yearly Annuity of 200£ whenever he is not employed in Service, on Condition that he does not reside in town or within one hundred miles of it. To my friend Devereux I bequeath my little Brown Hunter together with my Guns, Dogs and other sporting apparatus which I think will amuse him, and tend to drive away the recollection of the tedious Hours I have made him spend. He will understand what that means, and I beg that the whole of that business in every way may be forgot with me that is not mentioned by him.   Having now mentioned all those to whom I am bound by sentiment of regard and esteem I will say a Word of perhaps one of the worst men that ever disgraced humanity — I mean my former Steward Berlingdon, he has got the command of a Ship of mine called the Weldon, the particulars of which are in the Hands of Mr. Nicholson part of her is his own as I allowed him to vest somewhere about 500£ in her, the precise Sum is mentioned in the paper at Mr. Nicholson's, as there will be no doubt, but that he will use every artifice in his power to defraud my heirs.   I hereby declare that except that share in the vessel I do not owe him to my knowledge a single farthing and I advise them to take the earliest opportunity of recovering their own.   There are many other matters at any other Time I might be inclined to mention but I will say nothing more at present than that in the present contest I am fully and entirely the Aggressor as well in the spirit as in the letter of the Word, should I therefore lose my life in a contest of my own seeking I most solemnly forbid any of my friends or relations let them be of whatsoever description they may be from instituting any vexatious proceedings against my Antagonist, and should notwithstanding the above declaration on my part the Law of the Land be put in force against him I desire that this part of my Will be made known to the King in order that his Royal breast may be moved to extend his mercy towards him.   With respect to myself I have ever entertained an anxious desire that my remains may be deposited in some *region of the Earth* distant from the place of my Nativity and where the surrounding scenery will smile upon me, others adorn their abode while living and it is my fancy to adorn mine when dead for this purpose I beseech most earnestly that whenever the times will permit my body may be removed in the cheapest manner to the Island of St. Pierre in the Lake of Berne in Switzerland there to be deposited in the Centre between the 3 trees that stand on the right of the Tavillon a bush or some such thing may be planted over me but without any Stone or Masonry in any shape or form whatever   and for the permission to have this my last wish carried into execution I bequeath one thousand pounds to be paid to the Hospital at Berne to whom the Island belongs   I appoint Devereux my Executor for all these things relating to my burial on which I attach more importance than a sensible man perhaps ought to do   With respect to all my other friends and relations I beg that they will not wear mourning on my account or shew any outward mark of regret for my loss (signed) CAMELFORD (L. S.) Richard Wilson for *Lord Camelford* by his express direction and authority. Signed by Richard Wilson in the presence of and by the express directions of the within named Thomas Lord Camelford and sealed published and declared this eight day of March one thousand Eight hundred and four as an explanatory Note and Codicil to his Will referred to by him herein (he having written and signed the Contents hereof on the sixth of this instant March on two Sheets and a half of paper and being unable to resign the same of this present Date) in the presence of us whose names are hereunder written who in his presence and in the presence of each other have subscribed our Names as Witnesses attesting the same—P. E. OTTEY—H. U. THOMSON—S. NICHOLSON.

After Lord Camelford's death an inquest was duly held and a verdict of wilful murder returned against some person or persons unknown. A bill of indictment was then prepared against Mr. Best and his friend, which was ignored by the Grand

N

Jury, who thus carried out the desire expressed in the codicil.   Lord Camelford's other wish was also respected, and his body was duly removed to Switzerland, where in a secluded spot near the Lake of St. Lampierre this eccentric but dignified nobleman of another age sleeps his last sleep. According to his instructions, no monument or stone marks his resting-place.

This Lord Camelford was the second and last of the name, his father, Thomas Pitt, a nephew of the great Lord Chatham, having received the Barony. The first Lord Camelford was a cultivated man and something of a poet, for when Lord Hervey stayed with him at Boconnoc in 1775 he wrote the following pretty lines (which are not, I think, generally known) in memory of his visitor's mother, Lady Hervey, who had been the beautiful Molly Lepell :—

> Of manners gentle with strong sense combin'd,
> All grace her form, all elegance her mind ;
> Thro' every stage acquiring powers to please,
> Wit without malice, dignity with ease ;
> Learn'd, tho' no pedant, by reflection sage,
> Smiling thro' pain and beautiful in age.
> Such Hervey was, but is, alas ! no more—
> All we once loved and all we now deplore.

X

Family pictures—Nelson and the Walpoles—A group by Devis—A fine old French picture saved by Mr. Cobden—Eccentricity of Lord Hertford—Dr. Schliemann's bequest—Some beautiful books in Lord Carnarvon's collection—Fashion in art—Sir Patrick Grant and the red cloak—Mr. Graves—Lord Leighton—Mr. Aidé —A genial artist—Sir David Wilkie—Scene-painting and art— Stewart relics—Silhouettes—Anecdotes of William IV.—Lady Georgiana Curzon and "Ugly Mugs"—Watch-papers—The origin of Christmas cards.

POSSESSING a certain number of family pictures, the majority of which are portraits of Walpoles, I have for many years past seized every opportunity of adding to their number.

Many years ago I was fortunate enough to secure at a sale a fine miniature of Horace Walpole as a child, dressed in a fanciful costume —the work of Nathaniel Hone. Owing to people being out of town and to its being a wet day, the bidding was very feeble, and this little gem, which I have several times lent for exhibitions, became my property for the insignificant sum of two pounds. Besides this I have also a small portrait of Horace Walpole which had become the property of Lady Blessington, at whose sale I bought it.

Amongst other family pictures I have also four pastels by Rosalba, representing different members of the Walpole family.   One of them is an excellent portrait of the owner of Strawberry Hill, whilst another represents Sir Robert's brother, the Admiral Galfridus, whose sword was one of Nelson's most valued possessions.   Galfridus Walpole himself had a not undistinguished naval career, losing his right arm in a sea fight in the Mediterranean, on which occasion he was in command of the *Lion*, a ship of eighty guns which, single-handed, fought four French ships mounting sixty guns apiece.   When the Rev. Maurice Suckling married the grand-daughter of Sir Robert Walpole's sister, Captain Suckling presented him with this sword, the recipient in course of time bequeathing it to his grandson, Horatio Nelson, who always wore it, and was grasping it in his hand when so severely wounded at the battle of Teneriffe.

Always particularly interested in memorials of Nelson, I have managed to collect a few things connected with the great admiral, amongst others some curious pieces of a dessert service owned by him.

It is, I believe, a well-authenticated fact that Wellington and Nelson only met once.   On this occasion Wellington was going upstairs at Downing Street and met a man coming down.   He afterwards found, on making inquiries, that this man was Nelson, who, on his side, told some one that he had met a most remarkable-looking young man on the stairs at Downing Street. There exists, I have been told, a print depicting what is nothing but a purely imaginary interview between these two great men, for there is no record that any regular meeting ever took place between them.

Another interesting picture which I possess is one representing the Vanneck family grouped on the lawn of their house at Fulham, with old Putney Bridge (destroyed only a few years ago) standing out in the background. This picture was the work of Arthur Devis, an eighteenth - century painter of portraits and also of what are known as "conversation pieces." The work of Devis is not very much known to-day, but during his lifetime the painter in question attracted a good deal of attention owing to his very remarkable likeness to the Pretender ; indeed, during a period of political excitement he was actually obliged to leave Preston in disguise. Appropriately enough he painted a picture of the " Pretender and his Friends."

Two prominent figures in my picture are two ladies, daughters of Sir Joshua Vanneck, who both married Walpoles. One became the grandmother of my husband (I have also a miniature of her by Smart), and the other the great grandmother of my cousin, the late Sir Spencer Walpole. Her husband was the Hon. Thomas Walpole, Horace Walpole's cousin, who lost his fortune owing to the capture of the West Indian Islands by the French, having had the bad luck to accept bills

drawn by the Scotch firm of Alexander upon
his real property in that quarter of the world.
The French Government after this capture at once
declared all debts due to English creditors to be
annulled; but Mr. Walpole, betaking himself to
Paris, after a protracted struggle in the French
Courts, eventually obtained a judgment in his
favour, and then very honourably handed over his
recovered estates to the Bank of England in discharge of his obligations.

After the death of his first wife Mr. Walpole
married in Paris Madame de Villegagnon, the
widow of the Comte de Villegagnon, and Sir
Spencer Walpole possessed the permission signed
by the French King—the unfortunate Louis XVI.
—which, under such circumstances, it was in those
days necessary to obtain.

In addition to pictures I have also a certain
number of Walpole relics, amongst them a fine
marqueterie clock which formerly belonged to
Horace Walpole at Strawberry Hill.

In former years, before the rage for collecting
had reached its present pitch, and the extravagant
prices of to-day were as yet undreamt of, French
art occupied a very different position in the estima-
tion of collectors from that which it does to-day,
and occasionally fine old French pictures were to
be found in very queer places.

In one of my scrap-books I have a photograph
of an old French picture with some notes written
at the side which recall to my mind a very kindly

action which was performed by Mr. Cobden, and by which he greatly assisted a poor labourer and his family.

Mr. Cobden chanced to be one day walking in a Sussex village with his friend Mr. Robinson (afterwards Sir Charles), of the South Kensington Museum, and came across a child trailing what appeared to be a piece of old board by a string run through two roughly made holes. For some reason or other this board attracted his attention, and examining it, he discovered it to be an old picture evidently of considerable artistic merit.

Conducted by the child to its home, Mr. Cobden interviewed the father—a poor labourer with a large family—to whom he suggested that as the picture might possibly be of some value he should allow it to be restored, and afterwards privately raffled amongst some friends; in this way a nice little sum would be brought in to the poor household. The labourer willingly gave his consent, and, after careful restoration, the picture turned out to be a graceful and elegant portrait of Madame la Duchesse de Bourgogne, a Princess of the House of Savoy and the mother of Louis XV. From the style and brilliant colouring of the painting it was declared to be the work of Largillière, and in all probability had once hung at Cowdray, the ancient home of the Brownes, the ruins of which stood not very far away.

The raffle was duly organised by Mr. Cobden,

twenty-five tickets at a guinea apiece being disposed of amongst friends.   Of course I took one, but, alas, I did not win the picture.

Since those days works of art of all kinds have largely increased in value, and realise sums which would have fairly staggered the collectors of the past.

It is said that the Bernal Collection, which in 1855 realised £69,000, would to-day fetch close on half a million.   Many things, indeed, which were then sold have since changed hands at a profit of a thousand per cent, and even more. A Dutch picture, for instance, which was sold at the Bernal sale for eighty guineas, was bought by Mr. Wertheimer, when Mr. Adrian Hope's pictures were sold, for no less a sum than £3200.

It is not, I think, generally known that before Mr. Bernal began his great collection he had already formed a small collection of pictures. These he sold on the death of his first wife, who met with such a tragic end, being burnt to death while dressing for a party.   She was Mr. Bernal Osborne's mother.

Many collectors are very careless of their treasures, and, once a coveted *objet d'art* is obtained, · forget all about it.   The Marquis of Hertford, who did so much to make the Wallace Collection what it now is, had a good deal of this tendency, and would keep some of his finest and most valuable pictures piled up in heaps against

the wall, not troubling to have them hung, or indeed paying any attention to them at all.

Lord Hertford was in the habit of employing certain agents to buy for him, and on one occasion, it is said, sending for one of the most able of these men, bade him spare no expense or trouble in the effort to secure a certain picture, the details of which he minutely described. The collector accordingly set out, telling his lordship that his wishes should certainly be fulfilled; but in spite of the most strenuous exertions the much-sought-for picture could not be discovered, and Lord Hertford eventually received a letter from the man saying that, much to his regret, he was abandoning the search, feeling convinced that it was useless.

A year or two later, however, this very collector, whilst travelling on the Continent, chanced to come across a shrewd dealer whom he had not yet questioned about this picture. He accordingly asked the man whether he knew anything about it, to which the latter replied: "Know anything about it? Of course I do; but you need not trouble any further about it, for it has gone into a collection from which no money will cause it to emerge. Lord Hertford bought it of me three or four years ago, and, as you know, he never parts with anything." The collector at once informed Lord Hertford of what he had been told, and on a search being made the picture was duly discovered, propped up behind several others with its face to the wall.

The splendid Wallace Collection, as is well known, was lost to France by the scant consideration which the French Government showed to Lady Wallace ; but it is said that England, on the other hand, failed to secure another very interesting and valuable bequest entirely through a misunderstanding.

Dr. Schliemann, the famous excavator of Troy, had, it is said, quite made up his mind to leave his collection, which included many objects of great antiquarian value, to this country, but oddly enough his election as an honorary member of a very learned club caused him to alter his decision. On receiving the notification of this election the distinguished antiquarian (who did not understand that honorary members paid no subscription) sent £10 to the secretary of the club, thinking that he would at once acquit himself of his obligations as a new member.

The secretary, however, on receipt of this sum, interpreted it as being either an insult or a bribe, and a great fuss was made, which so disgusted Dr. Schliemann that he determined to reconsider his bequest, and did so, with the consequence that the whole of his collection went elsewhere at his death.

Lord Hertford, though a great connoisseur of French art, did not, I believe, make any great collection of French eighteenth-century books, such as the little almanacks, illustrated by good artists, which were produced in such abundance during the reign of Louis XV.

Lord Carnarvon has a fine collection of these, amongst them being an *Almanach des Muses* bearing the arms of Marie Antoinette.   Another of his treasures is *Les bienfaits du sommeil,* an exceptionally scarce and practically unknown almanack, embellished with four plates engraved by Delaunay after Moreau.   He also possesses a perfect copy of the very rare *Suite d'estampes pour servir à la mode*—a reduction of the *Monument de costume* of Moreau le jeune.   This, by great good fortune, he found whilst looking through a vast assortment of rubbish at a shop in Constantinople, one Turkish pound only being asked for two perfect copies. Other rarities in this most careful collection of scarce and beautiful books are the tallest known copy of that rarest of Elzevirs, *Le pastissier François,* and a first edition of the *Art of Cookery,* with H. Glasse, the autograph of Mrs. Glasse, written upon the title-page.   The well-known remark, "First catch your hare," does not occur in the first edition.

Lord Carnarvon also has many splendid bindings, as well as an ancient morocco box, covered with gold tooling and made to hold prayer-books, which once belonged to Gabrielle d'Estrées.

A collection of books of this kind, many of them containing sketches by great artists such as Fragonard and Moreau, is exceedingly difficult to get together—taste and knowledge being indispensable requisites as well as the possession of a well-filled purse.

At one time massive folio volumes were the delight of the bibliophile, but that day has long since passed : small and beautifully bound and illustrated volumes are now the collector's especial delight.   Fashion, indeed, exercises her sway here as in other forms of art.   I remember, for instance, a regular craze which was originated by Sir Francis Grant, a fashionable painter of other days, who was a great favourite in society.   A portrait painted by him of his daughter (a singularly good-looking girl), wearing a red cloak, created a great sensation, and in consequence of the happy effect produced by the brilliant colouring of this picture, every one, old or young, ugly or beautiful, rushed to have their portrait painted in a similar costume. The result in most cases, however, was far from being as successful as in the case of Miss Grant. She afterwards became Lady Annesley.

Sir Francis painted a picture of my sister and myself which now hangs at Methley.   This, in my opinion, was a great failure, for my sister looks like a murderess, whilst I am represented as apparently suffering from the effects of a narcotic which she has just administered.   Nevertheless, many people said it was not at all a bad picture, but I never liked it.   Sir Francis was an agreeable man, and we often used to go to his house in Regent's Park to sit to him in the evenings.   He was the only painter I ever heard of who painted by gas-light, a feat which has always lingered in my memory as a somewhat remarkable thing.

Lady Dorothy Nevill

from a portrait by the Hon. Henry Graves

Emery Walker Ph. Sc.

The Hon. Henry Graves was another popular portrait-painter of the past. I think that in all probability the best thing he ever did was a miniature portrait of myself, which, on account of its beautiful execution, is quite a little gem. For some years Mr. Graves had no success at all, but a portrait of the late Lady Alexandra Lennox being very much admired, he leapt into popularity, and afterwards, I believe, regularly made several thousands every year. Thorburn also painted what I suppose would be called a miniature of me. His particular bent lay in painting portraits rather like miniatures, but covering a very much larger surface. Another fashionable painter was Buckner, who painted my portrait in what may be called the keepsake style (as a matter of fact, an engraving of it actually appeared in a number of the *Keepsake*). Though somewhat artificial in pose, this picture was not at all unpleasing, being far more graceful than any modern effort of the same sort. At the present time, alas, the art of portrait-painting, except in one or two cases, cannot be said to stand at anything but a very moderate level.

Buckner, it was said, invariably made his portraits more beautiful than the sitters really were, in order to please people and thus cause their friends to flock to his studio.

Lithographs after Count D'Orsay's drawings of well-known people of his day, which were once so popular, are now seldom to be seen. I well remember Lord Beaconsfield telling me how

anxious he was to secure a picture of Napoleon
the Third done by D'Orsay ; it was coming up for
sale at Christie's, and he feared that it would fetch
at least two hundred pounds, a sum which he
declared himself ill able to afford. However, when
the day came, the bidding was very feeble, and he
secured the picture for twenty pounds. I suppose
it still hangs at Hughenden.

Sir John Millais I used to meet every year at
the shooting parties given by that most delightful
of hosts, Sir Henry (now Lord) James. I remember
that, by a curious fatality, the weather during
these shooting parties was always execrable, but
the clever and pleasant guests, together with
the most excellent of hosts, used to make us all
forget the torrents of rain which fell most of the
time.

Lord Leighton also for many years I regularly
saw, for he always formed one of a party which
came to us every Easter. Nevertheless I cannot
say that I ever really knew Lord Leighton well,
for there always seemed to be something mysterious about him—a sort of curious reticence, as it
were, which prevented one becoming intimate with
him. Perhaps this was but fancy ; in any case we
always remained the best of friends.

A newspaper once mentioned Lord Leighton's
picture of Cimabue finding Giotto at work on his
sketches as the "Discovery of Grotto."

Another criticism of the same sort which
appeared in 1884 was the one which described

Walker's " Harbour of Refuge "—a representation
of an almshouse, in the swarded quadrangle of
which a mower plies his scythe—as a good sea-
piece.

Mr. Hamilton Aidé—one of the last survivors
of the little group of which I have just spoken—
passed away only a few months ago.   A man of
singularly refined taste and literary culture, Mr.
Aidé was also a very talented painter in water-
colours.   The most charitable of men, he would
occasionally have little exhibitions of his works,
and as they secured a ready sale, many poor
people benefited by his artistic gifts.   His works,
principally landscapes in Italy and Sicily, always
sold well ; at the last exhibition of them in
Bond Street, only a few months before his death,
they were purchased with great rapidity, and the
poor, I believe, benefited to the extent of four or
five hundred pounds.

I used at one time to hear a good deal about
various artists and their work from my dear
governess, Miss Redgrave, whose family (one of
which, Mr. Samuel Redgrave, wrote the invaluable
Dictionary of Artists of the English School) was
well known in artistic circles.

A great friend of the Redgraves was Webster,
whose pictures were at one time very popular on
account of their genial humour and gaiety.   Many,
indeed, were engraved.   Among his best-known
works were " The Smile and the Frown," illustrating the two different moods of the schoolmaster

in Goldsmith's *Deserted Village*—"The Boy with many Friends"—"The Village Choir"—"The Dame School"—"Coming out of School," and others depicting subjects of a similar kind. Mr. Webster was very lively and full of fun, and devoted to children, like many people who have none of their own. He would describe how, as a boy, he had once, by mistake, been locked into the village stocks by his brother, and kept there for some time, owing to the key having been mislaid. He would laugh very much over the recollection of the gibes levelled at him by the village boys whilst he was awaiting his release, adding, however, that the actual experience was anything but pleasant. Another great joke of his was that when he wanted to join the Civil Service Stores, at the time when they were first started, he was informed that only persons connected with the Civil Service could be admitted as members, but triumphantly obtained his ticket as the orphan of a Civil Servant, being then over seventy years of age. Up to about the year 1856 Mr. Webster resided in Kensington, but the rest of his life was spent at a charming old house at Cranbrook, in Kent. During a severe attack of gout, he went one winter's day, wrapped up in blankets in a bath-chair, to the Round Pond in Kensington Gardens, in order to note some ice and snow effects for his picture of "Boys at a Slide," his reason being that he feared a thaw might set in and lose him the opportunity for observation. In his later years he suffered terribly from the same affection, and would constantly declare that it was only with the greatest difficulty he could put an eye to a small figure or a curl of hair in its proper place, as his poor fingers and trembling hands caused him to paint details, and even features, in quite wrong positions.

The Redgrave family had also known Sir David Wilkie, whose picture "Rent Day" created such a sensation. By a veritable *tour de force* the painter contrived in this work to represent a man coughing. The figure in question is in the very centre of this picture. As a rule, attempts to depict people coughing, yawning, or the like, are far from successful.

There was, for instance, a picture I remember which was called "A Pinch of Snuff," in which the artist had made an effort to represent a sneeze, and the result was not very satisfactory. Morland, however, in his "Connoisseur and Tired Boy," has shown the latter gaping in a very realistic manner.

"The Long Sermon" (a picture by Hunt) also contained a study of gaping—a young man being depicted as being quite unable to repress this somewhat curious natural effect of being bored.

William Hunt, who died in 1864, was a fine painter of still life, and a sturdy and genial humorist in art as well as one of the greatest (if not the greatest) English flower painters in water-colours who ever lived. A loving painter of rustic life, he cared little for professional models, preferring to paint the real villagers whom he knew and understood. "The Blessing," a country-man returning thanks for his humble meal, is probably Hunt's masterpiece. Of this Ruskin said, "It is more than a sermon; it is a poem."

Hunt being a cripple, he was, as his family said, "good for nothing," so they made him an artist. In early life he assisted in the redecoration of the rebuilt Drury Lane Theatre, and painted part of a drop-scene. Curiously enough, a great many artists who have achieved success originally began their careers as scene-painters. Amongst them may be mentioned De Loutherbourg, the con-temporary of Rowlandson, who was a scene-painter at Drury Lane Theatre; Stanfield and Roberts, as well as David Cox, who, in the early part of the nineteenth century, was assistant painter at the Birmingham Theatre. The late Mr. Thomas Sidney Cooper also, I believe, once did a little in this line. George Chambers, marine painter to William IV., was scene-painter at the Pavilion Theatre.

Amongst architects, Inigo Jones must not be forgotten as having practically been a scene-painter, for his genius largely contributed to the success of the masques which were so popular in his day.

A relative of Inigo Jones, who was also his pupil, attained some celebrity as a designer of the scenery and accessories used in these entertain-ments. This was John Webb, some of whose

sketches and designs are still, I believe, in the
Duke of Devonshire's library.

The first piece of regular scenery used on the
English stage is said to have figured in a play at
the Duke's Theatre, Lincoln's Inn Fields, in 1662.
Evelyn, of course, mentions "sceanery" in his
diary some three years before that date, but this
in all probability merely consisted of hangings of
figured tapestry.

My eldest brother, the late Lord Orford, was
an ardent collector of everything connected with
the Stewarts and possessed a good many interesting portraits. Amongst these was a painting of
Prince Charlie executed by Blanchet in 1730 for
the Grand Duke of Tuscany; this formerly belonged
to the Duchesse de Berri when she lived at Venice,
and is now, together with a picture of Cardinal
York, in the possession of Colonel Walpole of
Heckfield Place, Hants, who has a considerable
number of valuable Stewart relics, amongst them
a gold snuff-box with a secret spring revealing a
miniature of Prince Charlie, whilst outside are inscribed the names of those killed in 1745. Though
there are many collectors of memorials of the
Stewarts, portraits of members of that family are
occasionally unrecognised at auctions. Such a case
occurred quite recently when an excellent portrait
of the old Pretender was labelled at the Duke of
Fife's sale as "the Comte d'Artois by Danloux"!
This was the more extraordinary as the Pretender
is shown wearing the Order of the Garter, a decora-

tion which the Comte d'Artois never received.
The portrait in question, being purchased by a
friend of mine for a very moderate figure, was discovered by him to have been the work of Batoni,
an Italian artist, who executed an almost precisely
similar portrait of Prince Charlie, but of smaller
size, which may be seen hanging in the National
Portrait Gallery.

A younger brother of mine was also much
interested in the Stewarts, and possessed some
curious letters from the Pretender, certain of
which are dealt with in the Appendix to this book.

I possess a number of the old silhouette portraits
very skilfully cut out of black paper, amongst them
one of George III. Silhouettes, in the days before
photography, were given to relatives and friends
just as photographs are to-day. At Eridge Castle
there are several very good ones of unusual size.
Everybody knows the small silhouette in a black
frame so often seen in curiosity shops, but big
ones are, I think, much less frequently to be
met with. Elaborate coats of arms used also
formerly to be cut out of white paper; these,
when pasted upon a black background, produced
a very good effect. Some little time ago I was
fortunate enough to come across some Walpole
arms done in this fashion, which I at once secured,
as a specimen of really good work of this kind is
by no means easy to procure. Silhouette cutting
of every sort is now more or less a lost art; it
belonged, indeed, to a period when people had

plenty of time, and women were content to stay at home, beguiling the long winter evenings with simple work of one kind or another, which would be not at all to the taste of their more luxurious descendants.

Princess Elizabeth, daughter of King George III., was an adept at cutting silhouettes and figures out of paper. I possess a little volume which is entirely filled with her work. Some of the designs, instead of being black, are white, and with each of these is a slip of green paper to serve as a background. This little portfolio was formerly in the possession of Lady Banks, to whom it was given by the Princess.

The best silhouette I have is one representing Mrs. Jordan—I think in the character of " Sir Harry Wildair "—the pretty features (immortalised by Chantrey in the monument at Père la Chaise) crowned by a profusely plumed cocked hat. Of her royal lover, William IV., in whose reign I lived, many stories used to be told illustrating his kindly nature and great devotion to children, in whose society he absolutely revelled. Lady Georgiana Curzon, for instance, well remembered how this kindly monarch kept a whole cupboard full of dolls to give to little girls.

This cupboard was under the care of a favourite Hanoverian servant, whose peculiar personal appearance had caused the King to nickname him " Ugly Mugs." Lady Georgiana used to tell how, when she was taken to the palace, King William

would say, " Now, little girl, you can go and ask
Ugly Mugs for a doll," upon which, running off
to the individual in question, she made her request,
" Please, Mr. Ugly Mugs, may I have a doll ? "
The Hanoverian invariably met this by pretending
to be very angry, and by saying, " My name is
not Ugly Mugs," in a tone of simulated rage, but
the doll was always produced, whilst the kindly
King never failed to laugh at the description of
Ugly Mugs's rage.

As a child Lady Georgiana Curzon was present
at the wedding of Lord de Ros's sister to Lord
Cowley, which, by the wish of King William, took
place at St. George's Chapel, Windsor—I rather
think she was one of the bridesmaids. Anyhow,
I know that she used to describe her great excitement on the occasion in question, and how much
she looked forward to the ceremony, and especially
to the wedding breakfast and other festivities
which would come after its celebration.

Lord de Ros, however, who was fond of a joke,
took her aside the day before the wedding, and
addressed her very gravely. " My dear child,"
said he, " I know you are looking forward very
much to the breakfast and amusements which you
imagine are going to follow this wedding, but
don't count too much upon them, for I may tell
you in confidence that everything depends upon
whether my sister can make up her mind or not,
and I warn you that she is extremely unreliable.
When you hear the Dean ask, ' Will you have

this man for your wedded husband?' prick up
your ears, for everything depends upon her answer.
As a matter of fact I half believe she will say 'No,'
in which case you may say good-bye to breakfast
and everything else."

Little Lady Georgiana was so upset at this
that that night she hardly slept at all, and words
could not describe her excitement in the chapel
next day. The fateful moment, however, at
last arrived, and when the bride repeated in a
clear voice the words "I will," Lady Georgiana,
who could contain herself no longer, immediately
shouted out, "You all heard her! You all heard
her!" So great was her excitement that only the
assurance that everything was all right could restore
order.

One occasionally comes across queer little
paper circles elaborately ornamented and engraved. These are old watch-papers, which it was
formerly the custom for watchmakers to put in
the outside cases of old-fashioned watches which
came to them to be repaired. These watch-papers
generally bore the repairer's name and address,
surrounded with an appropriate design, and sometimes also contained a motto. William Teanby,
a Lincolnshire schoolmaster, achieved a certain
celebrity on account of his great skill in writing
manuscript watch-papers with a crow-quill pen.
There are still in existence some very pretty
old watch-paper designs printed on white satin.
One of the best of these shows a mass of coloured

garlands enclosing a miniature silhouette of King George III.

These watch-papers, like engravings, are sometimes found in different states. I have the first state of a very quaint one issued by J. Woolett, watchmaker, Maidstone. On it is shown the figure of Time pointing to a dial, whilst his scythe is seen lying at his feet. Around the rim of this watch-paper are simple directions for regulating the watch.

I possess a good many engraved concert and ball tickets, the work of Bartolozzi, Smirke, Ibbetson, Legoux, and others. Legoux, in particular, executed a number of benefit tickets closely following the style of his master, Bartolozzi, whose own productions in this line, unlike most of his stippled work, were invariably engraved by his own hand. These tickets, generally designed in a spirit of fanciful allegory by his friend Cipriani, were, as a rule, intended for benefits and charitable entertainments, in which case Bartolozzi would engrave them for nothing. There is a splendid collection of them in the British Museum, presented in 1818 by Lady Banks.

Amongst other odds and ends which I have collected are a number of old bill-heads, several of which are prettily engraved in quite an elaborate fashion. The best of these dates from about the middle of the eighteenth century, and on it, within an elaborate border, is a representation of a merchant showing some elaborate wall-papers to a lady in a huge hooped skirt, who is accompanied by a richly dressed gallant. The whole composition is quite a work of art, and contrasts most favourably with the bill forms in use at the present day. Many bill-heads continued to have little engravings upon them till about the middle of the last century, when this pretty custom practically died out.

Up to quite recent years an enormous number of valentines used to be sent on the 14th of February, St. Valentine's day. Most of these, it must be confessed, were of a very inartistic and tawdry character, whilst in some cases ridiculous and even insulting pictures were sent to unpopular people. This custom, however, for some reason or other has now completely died out, though it is not so very many years ago that thousands of valentines must have passed through the post. On the other hand, many more Christmas cards are sent than was formerly the case. Sending Christmas cards, it may be added, is a custom of comparatively recent introduction, the first of these cards having been printed in England about the year 1846. This, I believe, was drawn by Mr. J. C. Horsley, R.A., at the suggestion of Mr. (afterwards Sir Henry) Cole, well known in his day as " King Cole." The card in question was divided into three parts by a trellis-work design, and in the two side panels were designs representing " Feeding the hungry," and " Clothing the naked," whilst the centre panel contained a merry family group drinking the toast which was printed beneath—" A merry Christmas and a happy New Year to you." About a thousand only of these cards were produced, and it was not until 1862 that Messrs. Goodall and Sons issued the first series of Christmas cards which came into general use. These had border designs of holly, mistletoe, and robins. Messrs. Goodall did not, however, continue to produce Christmas cards, but after a few years relinquished this portion of their business to Messrs. Marcus Ward and Co., under whose auspices the Christmas card attained the great vogue which shows no signs of abating.

XI

In these days the number of collectors has
become enormous. Besides those who collect
pictures, old furniture, and china, many people
make a special hobby of prints, old glass, old
watches, and even old watchstands, not to mention
many other trifling relics of the past to which time
has imparted some share of interest and value.
Some of the old wooden watchstands just mentioned are exceedingly pretty, being formed of
cleverly carved wood in most cases covered with a
coating of gilt, whilst many specimens would appear
to be of French origin, some of the finest recalling
the graceful timepieces of the eighteenth century.
Watchstands may still occasionally be picked up
for a very moderate price, though when of exceptional quality they may cost something between

fifteen and twenty pounds. Such watchstands, it must be clearly understood, have nothing in common with the hideous Victorian wire arrangement which the grandfathers of the present generation were wont to place on their dressing-tables or by their bedside. In the old wooden watchstand the dial alone of the watch is shown within a circular space so contrived that the watchstand, as has before been said, presents the appearance of an old clock.

Samplers, which not so very many years ago were only to be found in old nurseries and forgotten attics, are now eagerly sought for, as are old needle-work pictures, which in many instances are highly ornamental. A similar kind of picture is that in which the dress of the figures is formed of coloured pieces of silk, cleverly worked on to an eighteenth century print. A very interesting specimen of this work which I possess represents an officer engaged in conversation with an elaborately dressed lady, every detail of the costumes being carefully reproduced in appropriate colours, whilst the figures themselves are cut out of two prints published by Carington Bowles. The whole composition of these pictures is most cleverly carried out, the wall-hangings and carpets being accurately represented by stuffs of suitable pattern. Signed and dated 1784, this composition, as was usually the case with needlework pictures, was the work of an amateur. In past days many of the common sort of prints were utilised in this manner, many hours being whiled away by ladies whose sphere of activity would to-day be thought somewhat limited.

Print-collecting, in which so many people are now interested, has of late years become a very expensive hobby, but there are still some minor forms of it which are accessible to those of moderate purses. Military prints, that is, representations of old uniforms, are as yet not particularly costly, and their brilliant colouring produces an exceedingly decorative effect. Such prints are very fascinating to lovers of past fashions, besides according very well with the hunting and coaching prints which have now for many years been in considerable request. A very pretty set of military prints is one drawn by Dayes and engraved by Kirk in 1792. These prints, six in number, representing the uniform of the Guards of that day, were published by Captain Hewgill of the Coldstream regiment, and sold by Boydell at the Shakespeare gallery.

Of late, French engravings have come into great favour with many English collectors. They are, as a rule, exceedingly pretty, expressing as it were the very spirit of that pleasure-loving France which disappeared in the blood-stained days of the Terror.

About the most valuable French line engraving, as well as one of the prettiest, is "Les Hasards heureux de l'Escarpolette," engraved by Nicolas de Launay, after the picture by Fragonard, a replica of which hangs in the Wallace Collection, where it is known as "The Swing." The little lady in the Wallace Collection, it may be observed, has no plumes upon her hat, whilst these exist in the engraving, which is taken from another similar picture now in the possession of a French collector, Baron Edmond de Rothschild.

Other beautiful French prints are " Le Coucher de la Mariée," by Moreau le jeune ; " La Soirée des Thuileries," by Simonet ; " La Toilette," by Ponce ; and " Le Prélude de Nina," by Chaponier. The coloured French prints by Debucourt and Janinet are also exceedingly beautiful, but their high price places them above the reach of any but a wealthy collector.

Within the last twenty years French eighteenth-century art has become highly appreciated in England, and the fine furniture of that epoch has in consequence greatly increased in price. Nevertheless, there were connoisseurs even in old days who estimated the beautiful work of the French *ébénistes* at its proper worth. A conspicuous example was the late Mr. Jones, who cheerfully paid sums which were considered wildly extravagant at the time for some of the choice specimens which now form the Jones Collection at South Kensington.

Rooms fitted up entirely in the French style have recently been increasingly popular in England, and in several cases old houses have been purchased outright, in order that the fine *boiseries* decorating their walls might be removed to this country. This quite recently occurred in the case of the Hôtel de Ménars, a splendid old house standing not far from the Bourse, which once belonged to the celebrated Fermier-Général of that name. Its fine panelling, enriched with carving in the best style of the reign of Louis XV., has been most artistically re-erected by the purchaser, a gentleman of very cultivated taste, who has thus embellished three rooms of his mansion in Belgrave Square. Here, once more restored to its original condition, this superb *boiserie* stands forth as a splendid example of French eighteenth-century art. It may be added that during the repair and cleaning of the panelling in question no less than forty coats of paint had to be carefully scraped off. One of these was bright red, a thick coating of which would seem to have been applied at the time of the Revolution. It may be added that in the same house there is now an almost exact reproduction of the dining-room which formerly existed in the Hôtel de Ménars, the two original marble alcoves with scooped-out basins for cooling wine having been retained, together with a massive marble sideboard once more restored to its original use.

Amongst living collectors of fine French furniture, china, and pictures, in England, Mr. Alfred Rothschild undoubtedly takes the first place. Others there may be who also have fine collections ; it is easy to purchase rare and beautiful things if money is no consideration, but taste and know-

ledge cannot be bought, and he is one of the very
few who is endowed with these very valuable
attributes, too seldom possessed by those of very
large fortune.   The best things, I think, in his
possession amongst the French pictures are a
" Pater," bought from the late Lord Lonsdale ; the
"Baiser Envoyé," by Greuze ; and the "Toilette
de Venus," by Boucher ; whilst two unrivalled
pieces of French furniture are a *bureau cylindre*
in mother-of-pearl, once the property of Marie
Antoinette, and two Sèvres *coffres de mariage.*
He also possesses two very fine Sèvres tables, as well
as two superb sets of Rose du Barry vases, five in
each set.   At Waddesdon, the home of Miss Alice
Rothschild, are also many beautiful specimens of
French art, a splendid example of which is the
superb timepiece known as "the Fitzwilliam
clock."   Here also is the beautiful "Fortune-
teller," by Sir Joshua Reynolds, which once hung
at Knole.   The whole house, however, is so full
of fine things that it is difficult to particularise.

An interesting example of fine French furniture
is the table, now in the Wallace Collection, on
which the Treaty of Tilsit was signed in 1807.   Of
pale green lacquer and gilt bronze, it is said to have
been made by Dubois for the Empress Catherine
of Russia in the last years of the reign of Louis
XV.   This table was purchased by Lord Hertford,
about the year 1867, from the late Mr. Frederick
Davis, into whose possession it came in a somewhat
curious way.   Mr. Davis and his son, Mr. Charles

Davis, happened to be staying at an hotel in St. Petersburg towards the end of the year 1866, when an individual brought to them, for sale, a snuff-box with paintings by Von Blarenberghe, refusing, however, to divulge the name of the owner. His curious attitude in the matter excited a good deal of suspicion, and Mr. Davis, at length deciding that the box had been stolen, was on the point of calling the police when the vendor admitted that it was the property of Prince Kourakin. In order to verify this statement, Mr. Davis and his son proceeded to call upon the magnate in question, at whose house they were shown the famous "Tilsit table," which, after some negotiation, they succeeded in purchasing, Prince Kourakin certifying that the Treaty of Tilsit had been signed upon it, and adding that on the night of the signature there had been a fire, from which the table had very luckily been saved.

A few months later the table was sold to Lord Hertford, who was, of course, told its history. At the time Lord Hertford laughed at the story, declaring that he purchased the table more on account of its being a fine work of art than for any other reason ; but, nevertheless, he would appear to have made some investigations into its history, for he subsequently told Mr. Davis that he had found his statement to be perfectly correct, and had identified the table as being the identical one upon which the Treaty had been signed. Lord Hertford added that he had been present at

P

Tilsit at the time, and now perfectly recalled to mind this particular piece of furniture having been rescued from the fire.

Another exceptionally fine relic of the best days of art, which passed through Mr Davis's hands, was the famous Sèvres commode with mounts by Gouthière, which he purchased from the late Lord Conyngham for £20,000. This commode had once been in Windsor Castle, and was said to have been purchased for George IV., at the time of the Treaty of Amiens, for the sum of £200. When Mr. Davis had finished his negotiations (he just managed to outbid the late Lord Dudley, who was especially anxious to secure such a splendid example of French art) he sent his son in a van to fetch it—a special precaution, to prevent the precious commode from being damaged. To the horror of Mr. Charles Davis, on the return journey his unwonted convey-ance, suddenly coming to a dead stop, began to rock about in a most disquieting manner, and in a few seconds he realised from the sounds which reached him that the horse had been seized with a fit of the staggers, and that the van was fast nearing a perilous position close to the curb-stone, where it must almost inevitably be upset. Rising to the situation, however, he shouted out, "A fiver to any man who holds up the van," and in con-sequence of this presence of mind the van was somehow saved from overturning and the precious commode rescued from what would have been certain destruction. Mr. Charles Davis possesses

a perfectly unique knowledge of French art, and
having had many varied experiences in European
capitals, has naturally some very interesting stories
to tell—there are few things, indeed, which I enjoy
more than a chat with him about the great
connoisseurs of the past.

The late Mr. Hawkins, whose snuff-boxes
created such a sensation at Christie's not so very
long ago, was a particularly eccentric collector.
Buying very largely, he would often not trouble to
unpack his purchases once they were made.   A
Sèvres tea-service, for instance, was found in its
packing-case in Mr. Hawkins's hall in exactly the
same place where it had been deposited after its
purchase, some twenty-five years before, whilst
valuable snuff-boxes were discovered put away in
all sorts of odd corners.

The late Lord Revelstoke probably possessed
the finest set of green Sèvres vases in existence ;
these, seven in number, were sold to the late Baron
Nathaniel Rothschild of Vienna.

Whilst in the Wallace Collection England
possesses a superlatively excellent collection of
French furniture, the finest English furniture of
the eighteenth-century period is only to be found
in the hands of private collectors.   It is much to
be deplored that the Victoria and Albert Museum
contains no thoroughly representative collection of
old English furniture.   True is it that a certain
number of good examples are to be seen there, but
these are more or less scattered about, no special

section existing to show the evolution of style from Elizabethan times to the end of the eighteenth century. This is the more to be regretted, as an assemblage of the best work of English cabinet-makers such as Chippendale, Sheraton, Hepple-white, and others, could not fail to have an admirable educational effect upon public taste, especially were it displayed in rooms decorated in the style of their epoch. Mr. James Orrock, so well known as a fine judge of old English furniture, once attacked Mr. Gladstone upon this subject. He had long been anxious to place before that great statesman a scheme to erect a National Gallery of British Art on a site behind the great collection in Trafalgar Square, in a position quite secure from all danger of fire, his idea being that such a building should contain selected pictures from the National Gallery, from the Victoria and Albert Museum, the British Museum—in fact, from each of the National Collections. In addition to this, adequate space was to be allotted to a per-manent exhibition of Elizabethan, Jacobean, and Queen Anne furniture, and rooms set aside to contain the best work of Chippendale, Sheraton, and other great English cabinetmakers. Intro-duced to Mr. Gladstone by Sir William Agnew, Mr Orrock at once commenced his attack, pointing out the extreme desirability, and even the necessity, of the creation of what would be a temple of British art. He added that the encouragement to collectors to give and bequeath valuable works to such an institution could not fail to have its effect, whilst the historical and educational value of the collection must obviously be enormous.

Mr. Gladstone listened to all this in the most earnest manner, and cordially agreed that the idea was in every way most admirable. His opportunity appearing to have now really come, Mr. Orrock went on to point out that the cost of a building such as he proposed would most certainly be not more than half the sum expended upon the construction of a battleship. In reply to which Mr. Gladstone, after a remark as to the deplorable necessity of expending money upon such dreadful engines of destruction, said, "But, Mr. Orrock, you forget I am not now in power"; to which the latter very cleverly replied, "Mr. Gladstone, you are always in power."

Though the veteran leader of the Liberal Party promised at the end of this interview that he would see what he could do to help forward the suggested scheme, political strife must have obliterated it from his recollection, for in spite of his assurance he never made any move in the matter at all; and so it comes about that there is still no National Collection of fine old English furniture. Most of the best pieces are in private hands; for to-day the work of Chippendale and Sheraton is eagerly sought for, and never fails to command huge prices when put up to auction. Furniture after the designs of Hepplewhite has also many admirers, but Dutch pieces are often passed off as being his work ; these, however, may be known on account of their being of a somewhat heavier style of construction.

Sheraton and Hepplewhite chairs are of very much the same design—the Prince of Wales's feather ornament, so often found in the work of both, was, it may be added, no mere piece of fancy decoration, but the badge of the young Court party which was led by George IV. when Prince of Wales.

Sheraton himself appears to have held Chippendale in but very small esteem as a cabinetmaker, for in one of his books he speaks of the designs of the latter as being " wholly antiquated and laid aside." Possibly Chippendale's somewhat ornate designs may have appeared frivolous to the austere Sheraton, who was an ardent Baptist and wrote a good deal in furtherance of his religious views.

A great deal of wood was used in genuine Chippendale chairs, and an infallible sign of a copy is when the carving seems cramped and flat owing to the shallowness of the frame out of which it has been scooped. Much so-called Chippendale furniture has not even a semblance of being the work of that cabinetmaker.

One of the most ridiculous things possible, from an artistic point of view, for instance, is a Chippendale overmantel—that is to say, an overmantel constructed in the modern Chippendale style. Nothing of this sort was even made in the eighteenth century, though of course mirrors to go over mantelpieces were, and occasionally the decorative woodwork surrounding them was very elaborate and graceful. Really old work, however, is generally much more simple and dignified in style than the so-called reproductions. A great quantity of good old furniture, especially bureaus and book-cases, has been completely spoilt by additional inlay and superfluous carving, in order to render it more attractive to the unskilled buyer. As a rule, the sole ornamentation originally lavished on such things was a more or less elaborate moulding. It should always be borne in mind that in all really good pieces ornamentation is strictly subordinate to use. Chairs and settees were not made to exhibit eccentricity and flamboyant design, but to be sat upon, though, of course, in many specimen pieces the carving, whilst in no way flimsy or weak, is flowing and elaborate. Chippendale and other great cabinetmakers invariably started with plenty of material to work upon, and a sure sign of a spurious piece is a shallow frame, upon which the carving is cramped and flat.

Modern cabinetmakers delight in producing *marqueterie* furniture embellished with elaborate vases, trophies, scrolls, and bouquets. Sheraton and his contemporaries, on the other hand, produced their effects by relying upon the nice, graduated, and artistic tones of their veneers, rigorously excluding all over-elaboration of design. As for modern painting on furniture, it is as a rule so feeble in execution as hardly to deceive the most unskilled amateur—most of it, indeed, is nothing but a bad caricature compared with beautiful old work.

As a matter of fact, it is extremely difficult to come across good old English-painted furniture in first-class condition ; as a rule, it has been scratched or otherwise damaged in the course of moving, and the restorations which this has necessitated are generally only too apparent.

I suppose that taste, as regards furniture, was absolutely at its lowest point some seventy years ago, during which period much beautiful Queen Anne, Sheraton, and Chippendale was relegated to the attics and the servants' hall, its place being taken by the hideous and heavy early Victorian furniture, which the upholsterers managed to foist upon a somewhat inartistic generation.

In the 'forties, it is true, some slight signs of a reaction began to be visible, one of the first of those to lead it being the late Mr. John Burgess, a fine architectural draughtsman and painter, whose talents are now hardly appreciated at their proper worth. He was a member of the old Society of Painters in Water-Colour, to which he was elected through the influence of George Cattermole. The latter, it is said, was so indignant at Mr. Burgess being rejected on the first occasion of his seeking election, that he threatened to resign if his candidate were not admitted, with the result that at the next election everything turned out as he desired.

At Leamington Mr. Burgess lived in a house filled from top to bottom with English furniture, pictures, and drawings, all of the finest quality, and here it was that Mr. Orrock, the well-known connoisseur and collector, to whom allusion has before been made, first laid the foundation of his knowledge of English eighteenth-century art. He was a boy at the time, and accompanying his host in rambles over the surrounding country, very naturally imbibed a taste for collecting the beautiful old furniture at that time plentiful in country houses and cottages.

In the days when Mr. Orrock first became an enthusiastic searcher after fine old pieces of Sheraton and Chippendale, he brought down upon himself, as he has often been heard to say, much laughter and ridicule. His passion for "wormy" chairs in particular was a constant source of amusement to some of his friends, who wondered what on earth he could want with such rubbish. "You may laugh," he used to say, "but I shall laugh louder than you some day when my wormy chairs shall be appreciated at their proper worth— the worm-holes can be stopped—every one to his taste—some people like high game, I like high chairs." In the course of time his judgment was completely vindicated, and as an instance of the enormous rise in the value of really fine old furniture the story of two Elizabethan chairs which he bought in a cottage for ten shillings apiece may be given. One of these chairs was an especially fine one, having evidently drifted down into humble surroundings after having occupied an honourable place in an old country house near by. This particular chair Mr. Orrock soon sold for several pounds, a good price at that time. Some years later, however, when taste had begun to improve, he repurchased it for fifty pounds, almost immediately selling it again for one hundred and fifty. To-day it would be worth at least two hundred to two hundred and fifty pounds— not a bad increase on an expenditure of ten shillings.

The foundation of Mr. Orrock's collection began in rather a curious way. Chancing many years ago to be at Coventry with a friend, his attention was arrested by a sale of old furniture which was proceeding at an old coaching inn, "The King's Head" by name. A large quantity of chairs, tables, sideboards, and mirrors had overflowed into the street, and a quite superficial examination convinced him that here was a unique chance of acquiring some exceedingly rare and valuable specimens of Queen Anne, Chippendale, Sheraton, and Hepplewhite, for the old inn had been filled with the very finest work in several different styles, a great feature being the extraordinary sideboards. Entering the sale, Mr. Orrock, in concert with his friend, arranged to purchase the entire contents of the house from the dealers who were engaged in bidding for it, and the next day found himself in consequence possessed of a most splendid and

valuable collection.   Long before this time he
had christened himself "the voice crying in the
wilderness of British art," on account of his love of
vaunting the artistic merits of old English furniture ;
but after this purchase many fine judges of art,
observing the furniture in his house, began to
declare that they were coming round to his view.
Before long, requests poured in upon him from
every side for information as to where old
Chippendale and Sheraton could be procured, some
people, indeed, going so far as to beg him to furnish
their houses at no matter what expense.   So it
came about that this purchase of old furniture
at " The King's Head " played a considerable part
in accelerating the renaissance of artistic taste,
of which Mr. Orrock was undoubtedly one
of the chief originators.

Why old English furniture should have ever
been discarded in favour of the heavy horsehair
abominations once almost universal seems in these
more enlightened days something like a profound
mystery.   Some of the old designs, indeed, are
quite equal to the finest Gothic, whilst many
examples of the time of Queen Anne—the finest
period perhaps of all for English furniture—are
superb in their delicacy and exquisite finish.   Next
to this in beauty must be placed the early
Chippendale, certain specimens of which display
artistic qualities of the very highest kind.

With the death of King George III. fine old
English furniture ceased to be produced ; it may,

indeed, be said to have died with the monarch in question.

Within the last thirty years fine pieces have commanded prices which seem almost ludicrous in comparison with those of other days.   A gentleman, for instance, possessing two satinwood cabinets mounted in silver, which had belonged to Nelson's Lady Hamilton, actually obtained two thousand pounds for them—rather, let it be added, against his will.   He had originally given a hundred pounds for the two—sixty for one, and forty for the other —and had no intention of parting with them again. A rich American, however, somehow heard of the cabinets in question, and after obtaining a glimpse of them in the owner's absence, at once determined to become their possessor.   With this purpose in view he despatched an emissary to the gentleman, who was then away at the seaside.   The emissary, however, sought him out, went down by the newspaper train, and confronting him early one morning, said, "I have come to buy your cabinets." "You have come to do nothing of the sort," was the reply.   "I don't want to sell them ; tell your principal that when he offers a thousand apiece I will think about it."   The man sat down at a table, pulled out his cheque-book and wrote a cheque for two thousand pounds.   "There, will you take that?" he said.   The offer was too tempting, and the gentleman did.   In the end the American was so delighted with the cabinets that he insisted upon purchasing all the other old furniture in the house, for which he paid some seven thousand pounds. The wife of the original owner was much incensed on her return to town to find an empty house, but an explanation as well as a timely and handsome gift soon allayed her irritation.

Occasionally one comes across curious and interesting pieces in the most unexpected places, but in these days when every one is more or less on the alert to pick up antiquities, and dealers scour the country from end to end, anything of value is almost immediately snapped up, whilst as a rule larger prices are asked out of London than in it.

A friend of mine who is a great and discriminating collector of all sorts of antiquities, the Hon. Gerald Ponsonby, some years ago discovered, in Dublin, a set of what are known as "furniture supports," which are extremely rarely to be met with. They were never general all over the kingdom, and, to the best of my belief, were confined to the South of England. There are four of these supports, which are formed of Staffordshire pottery. The face of one of them is believed to be intended to represent Sir Robert Peel. The coat is scarlet with a black stock; the hair and whiskers are brown; the eyes black, and the eyebrows black also; the cheeks are a vivid red; whilst the stand itself is of a deep mottled pink. The base is $2\frac{7}{8}$ inches in length by 2 inches in width, and it is $2\frac{1}{4}$ inches in height. The height from where the head begins, taken over the nose to the base, is 4½ inches, the circumference immediately under the chin being 8 inches. These supports were used to stand chests of drawers upon, so that when cottage floors were washed the bright woodwork of the legs should not be spoilt. The legs of the chest of drawers were placed upon the stand at the back of the head, the face of the support being outwards.

The old four-posters which were once absolutely discarded and considered fit for nothing but the lumber-room or the wood-heap have now once more come into fashion, being eagerly sought for by collectors in old-world villages and country towns. When thoroughly cleaned and put into good order, with the addition of a modern spring mattress, they make by no means an unattractive couch. As a rule those four-posters are low, for people had low bedrooms in old days. In many of them the woodwork above the shelf at the head of the bed is a good deal charred—this is the result of burning by the candles placed there by their former occupants, who would seem to have been very careless as to fire. A great many oak bedsteads have very thick pillars at the foot, the bases of which in some cases resemble the legs of the old dining-tables, which were in most cases relegated to outhouses and attics about the time of the downfall of the Stuarts. These tables were in many cases adorned with some slight degree of inlaid work, and could be lengthened by pulling out flaps at each end. At the particular period when these tables were in use, furniture was not very abundant in English houses, but what there was of it was very useful and solid, elaborate ornamentation being principally confined to the chairs, specimens of which may still sometimes be found in out-of-the-way villages.   Authentic pieces of Jacobean furniture of oak of English growth and of somewhat severe design may generally be recognised by its colour, which is something quite different from the dull black surface of modern imitations.   Its patina, indeed, if such a word can be applied to furniture, is one which time alone can give, and this not even the most skilled manipulator can copy.   In the time of the Charleses there was also a certain quantity of richly upholstered furniture in which velvet and tapestry had their place.   At Knole, Lord Sackville's beautiful treasure-house, are many fine examples of this sort of work, amongst them a bed and a complete set of bedroom furniture given by King James I., the coverings being of red silk ornamented with gold thread and silver spangles.

A curious feature of Knole is the attic which for generations has been known as the Dumb-bell Gallery, on account of its containing a quaint wooden machine something like a windlass without handles.   Around the middle of the roller is wound a rope, and at each end are four iron arms terminating in a ball of lead.   The rope formerly passed through a hole in the floor into a gallery below, and any one pulling it would cause the roller to revolve and rewind the rope again, giving the person pulling it the same exercise as is obtained by ringing a church bell. In the seventeenth century, bell-ringing was a very popular pastime, and probably it was about this time that the machine was set up in order to afford opportunities for silent practice.

In all likelihood the modern wooden dumb-bell was developed from the handles of the windlass dumb-bell by some athlete who understood its possibilities. An illustration of this windlass and its handles is given in an excellent privately printed account of Knole which Colonel Sackville West has written.

A dumb-bell machine of the same kind, or rather the remains of it, was also in existence up to some few years ago at New College, Oxford —indeed, it may be still there to-day.

The leaden waterspouts at Knole are other very curious features, most of them being some two hundred years old and bearing the initials and arms of Thomas Sackville. There is also some chintz in the house which is over a hundred years old. Made of a material known as *Toile de Jouy*, it still retains its colour in spite of the countless cleanings which it must have undergone. The old English furniture at Knole with its original coverings is one of the marvels of the place—the rare old stuffs being in a most unusual state of preservation.

Some time ago, when one of the sofas from a set covered with old red velvet belonging to the

Great Gallery was under repair, a yet older covering, dating from the reign of Elizabeth, came to light. The woodwork of the set in question, it may be added, is elaborately carved, the work in all probability of Italian workmen who were imported into England in Jacobean days. Few old mansions are in such a wonderful state of preservation as Knole, which in its present condition may be called a monument of judicious taste. This happy effect, I may add, has been in a great measure produced by the reverent restorations and judicious care exercised by Mrs. Sackville West, a lady whose knowledge of art and whose artistic discrimination are of the highest possible character. Of these gifts Knole itself as it is to-day forms a sufficiently convincing demonstration.

XII

IN some of my old scrap and photograph books I have many memorials of long dead and gone animal favourites, such as horses and dogs, besides one or two pictures of the Siamese cats which at one time were great favourites of mine. It was the late Mr. Harrison Weir, a true lover of animals if ever there was one, who first brought these beautiful creatures to my notice, and by a fortunate chance I became possessed of several of them, which had been imported from Siam and were presented to me by Sir R. Herbert of the Colonial Office. Exceedingly docile and domesticated, as well as ornamental in the highest degree, these cats were unfortunately very delicate in their constitution, and I never managed to keep any one of them alive longer than two years. At that time the only pure breed was kept by

226

the King of Siam, and specimens were very difficult to procure, for they could only be obtained by those having high influence in the palace. Of a beautiful dun colour, the nose, face, ears, feet, and tail of a dark chocolate brown, and with a tail shorter and finer than that of our own English species, the " royal cat of Siam " (as the animal is properly called) is exceptionally loving and affectionate in its nature, following its owner from room to room more after the manner of a dog than that of an ordinary puss. Curiously enough these cats as a rule are quite friendly with the dogs of the house they inhabit, frequently occupying the same baskets. The best I ever had was a lady cat which I called Mrs. Poodles, and exhibited at the Crystal Palace Show, where it was awarded the gold medal. It had three kittens by an English cat, but oddly enough none of them exhibited the slightest trace of their Siamese descent, all being pure tabbies. Since those days—I am speaking of the 'seventies—I fancy the mania for Siamese cats has died away, for I have never come across any in recent years. I myself gave up keeping them on account of their extreme delicacy of constitution, to which I have already alluded, and also on account of the sad end of another Poodles to which I was much attached. She also, like my prize cat, contented herself with an ordinary plebeian cat as a husband, for I was unable to obtain any suitor of her own royal line, though many people did their best to help me to do so. Amongst these was that delightful man the late Sir William Gregory, who before setting out for the East wrote me an amusing letter, in which he said :—

> I shall enter into relations with mercenary and desperate men to steal a tom cat from the palace of the King of Siam, and when stolen he shall be conveyed as a comfort to your Siamese tabby.

However, as no royal lover could be procured, this poor Poodles became visibly more and more depressed, and as time went on developed a mania for strolling off into the woods, where I fancy she dallied with certain humble admirers who began to hang around the grounds. This partiality for wandering did not cause me much alarm, as she always came safely back, remaining away, as a rule, for but a short time ; but, alas, there came the fatal day when my poor Poodles did not appear for twenty-four hours. She had been caught in a trap, and we should never have known her fate had it not been for the devotion of a humble cat, evidently her lover, who hung around the house uttering such piercing wails that he at last induced some one to follow him into a little wood just out-side the garden, where we found his suffering love —a touching instance of feline devotion. Though we did everything we could for her, the accident ended in poor puss's premature death, and after her demise I ceased, as I have said, to keep any more Siamese cats. I still have a memento of this Poodles in the shape of a muff made of her coat, very much resembling beautiful sealskin, which it is usually taken to be.

Of dogs I have always been very fond, and have had many in my possession of all sorts, breeds, and sizes. Looking over one of my old scrap-books the other day, I came upon a little sketch of a pet of long ago to which I was particularly devoted. This was a little dog called Shuck, after the phantom dog which is supposed to haunt the Norfolk lanes round Cromer and the country-side in that part of Norfolk in which was my old home. Poor little Shuck lived far longer than most of his race, for when he died he had reached the age of seventeen years—a sort of canine Methuselah. His end was pathetic in the extreme. He always slept at the foot of my bed, and I was one night awakened by feeling him creep up and gently lick my hand, after which he somewhat laboriously returned to his usual place, once more to relapse, as I thought, into peaceful slumber. From this sleep, however, he was not to awake, for in the morning I found him dead. It has always seemed to me that the caress which he gave me that night was a last farewell, bestowed whilst dimly conscious of his impending end.

For some years I always had one or two of the dogs known as the "lion dogs of China," most beautiful little animals with a luxuriant coat of a light brown colour, and having particularly fine tails. These were given me by the late Duchess of Richmond; indeed the breed was then only to be obtained from Goodwood, the late Duke of Richmond having been sent some of them from China. I believe, however, that now there are other families of these Chinese dogs in England, for of late I have occasionally observed them in the streets. Every dog of this kind which I possessed was called Goodie, from Goodwood, the home of its family. These Goodies were dogs of very curious characters and marked individuality. One especially I recall to mind, an extremely fine dog, who was a canine misogynist of the most pronounced kind. On one occasion it was arranged that he should accompany me on a visit to Goodwood, there to form a matrimonial alliance with a distant cousin—a charming little lady Goodie. Her attractions, however, did not appeal to him, and the moment that he set eyes upon his *fiancée* he became moody and ill-tempered, immediately attempting to run away. The extreme disgust he manifested was only too visibly shown in a photograph taken of the couple (the *fiancée*, by the way, looking somewhat ashamed and embarrassed), side by side, sitting up on their hind legs. Nothing would induce him to stay with her, and when he eventually escaped he at once demonstrated his extreme joy by racing all over the house, barking in the most obstreperous manner. All ideas of the contemplated alliance had to be dropped, and when my Goodie returned with me to London he was still a bachelor, in which celibate condition he ever afterwards remained.

A breed of dogs somewhat resembling the " lion dogs " are the little Pekinese, some beautiful specimens of which are owned by Lady Algernon Gordon-Lennox. I believe that there is only one other possessor of the true breed of these very valuable little dogs in England.

Amongst other dogs which I have possessed, I very well remember a Kurdish sheep-dog which was sent me by my brother from Turkey. It had an extraordinary name, Bedar Khan Beg, I think it was, and this, together with the £40 which its journey to England cost me, causes it to linger in my recollection. It was not a particularly attractive animal, and I never got to care for it very much. I hardly had time to do so, indeed, for it only lived a month after it arrived, never recovering from the fatigue of its very costly voyage.

In the letter which my brother wrote announcing the despatch of this canine gift, he told me that an interview he had had with a certain Pasha had much amused him—amongst other humorous incidents, his dragoman translated a remark made in Turkish by the Pasha, "The dog lies," as "Le Pasha dit que monsieur se trompe!"

Sir Edwin Landseer once gave me a collie, and a very beautiful animal it was, with one rather annoying fault, however, that of barking on every possible opportunity—a habit, I believe, which is very often found amongst collies.

Looking back upon the many canine pets which have lived out their little lives by my side, it is a

pleasure for me to think that their existence was
in every case about as happy as a dog's life can be,
for their faithfulness and affection I delighted to
repay in the best manner I could; and when, in
the natural course of events, they sank into their
eternal slumber, I felt that I had nothing wherewith to reproach myself on the score of neglect or
inhumanity.   Many of my dogs lie peacefully
buried in an animals' cemetery which I had laid out
at our house in Hampshire, and over the graves of
some of them I even put up short epitaphs, one
of the best of which was written by Mr. W. H.
Mallock, who at that time had just created a
considerable sensation with his very clever book,
The New Republic :—

ON TOPSY

Where art thou now, little wandering
Life, that so faithfully dwelt with us,
Played with us, felt with us, fed with us,
Years we grew fonder and fonder in?
You who but yesterday sprang to us,
Are we for ever bereft of thee,
And is this all that is left of thee,
One little grave and a pang to us?

I do not know whether the lines written by
Louis XVIII., to be inscribed on the collar of a
dog belonging to Madame de Caylus, are generally
known :—

On n'offre point de largesse à celui qui me trouvera,
Qui me rapporte à ma maîtresse pour récompense il la verra.

The dogs most to be envied in England are
certainly those at Sandringham, King Edward's

Norfolk home.   Here Queen Alexandra, kindest
and most feminine of queens, whose love of animals
is quite unbounded, has always several beautiful
indoor pets who are looked after with the most
loving care; whilst the splendid condition of a
number of more robust dogs, who live out of doors
under the most perfect conditions possible, attests
the great attention devoted to their welfare.

Besides dogs, I have had many horses which
were more or less pets.   Such a one was a mare,
Black Bess by name, who was so gentle that I
could ride her up close to a street door and ring
the bell from her back.   I rode more or less for
the greater portion of my life, but I cannot say
that I was ever very devoted to riding—perhaps
I had too much of it when I was a child, when
a very great deal of my time was spent in the
saddle.

The first horse which I recollect being allowed
to have for my very own was a beautiful grey
mare, Testina, so called on account of her little
head.   She was the daughter of my father's racehorse, Clearwell, the winner of the Two Thousand
Guineas, and on her, as a little girl, I rode with him
from Antwerp to Munich in the 'thirties, when railways were scarcely in existence.   After this I had
many other horses, but I eventually gave up riding
with but little regret; my early experiences with
Testina, who was seventeen hands high, and extremely difficult to manage, having rather set me
against that form of exercise.

Driving appealed to me much more in the 'sixties and early 'seventies. I had two ponies which I really loved. These I used to drive in the low pony-chaise so fashionable at that date, controlling them with the whip combined with a parasol, which the present generation only knows from Leech's drawings in *Punch*. At the slightest touch they would (though in reality perfectly manageable) perform the most astounding antics, rearing up in the air and shaking their heads in a manner which startled every one except myself, who knew the real gentleness of their disposition. These ponies lived to a great age, and when they were past work I took care that they should spend their last years in well-earned peace and happiness in a pleasant paddock.

Birds of all sorts I have owned in numbers, amongst them a parrot which never talked at all for a year, till one day when we had a luncheon-party it burst out into a torrent of bad language which much disconcerted everybody.

Mr. Bernal Osborne, I remember, used to have an amusing story about a parrot, which he used to tell when desirous of administering a sly dig at any one who had contrived to obtain a reputation for cleverness by merely saying nothing at all. A great ornithologist, he declared, once advertised for sale the cleverest parrot in the world. The price was large—£500—but would-be purchasers were asked to realise that the bird was absolutely the cleverest in the world. This announcement created a considerable sensation amongst lovers of parrots, and eventually a rich old lady, having somewhat reluctantly paid the required price, secured the treasure. She kept it for some months, during which it said not a single word; but thinking the bird still felt strange amidst its new surroundings she determined to wait a year, and if she had waited a hundred the result would have been the same—never a word did the parrot utter. At the end of this time, being very naturally annoyed, she went to the ornithologist and expressed her surprise and disappointment. "The parrot you sold me," said she,—"the cleverest bird in the world, you called it,—never speaks at all." "No," was the reply, "but remember, it's a very devil to think."

At the time of the Crimean War General Sir John Mitchell sent me a live demoiselle crane—whether the bird was a demoiselle or a monsieur we never discovered, but she or he lived with us at our home in Hampshire in the greatest amity and peace. There were, indeed, occasional insinuations that fresh eggs disappeared in a mysterious manner, but we did our best not to believe these base accusations against our dear friend. At one time, I remember, she insisted on taking care of a little family of chickens, leaving the inconsolable mother to go crying about in a despondent manner. In addition to the crane we usually used to have two storks striding about the grounds, but I do not believe they were ever really happy; possibly they did not easily resign themselves to the want of water to bathe and splash about in. I fear also that there must have been something wanting in the food we gave them, for after a short sojourn with us pair after pair went to a better land. In consequence of this continued mortality we eventually had recourse to a post-mortem examination, in order to discover the exact cause of their death. It was then found that the responsibility lay with their diet, which was shown to have been somewhat Spartan in character, and to have consisted for the most part of small pieces of slate, bricks, and what was still more singular, brass buttons of various sizes. The digestion of these poor birds, strong as it was, had not been able to cope with this extraordinary collection of hardware, which they had probably been forced to adopt as a menu owing to the lack of some substance which the soil did not supply.

For many years I delighted in the possession of two choughs,—delightful birds, with red feet and beaks, as tame as magpies. A pair of them, to our great astonishment and delight, made a nest in a tower of our house, laid a couple of eggs, and gave every appearance of preparing for the advent of a family. We were all much excited about it, for it is, I believe, an unheard-of thing for choughs to breed in captivity. In the expectation of an event which seemed likely to cause a considerable stir in natural history circles, we forbore from disturbing the enterprising couple in any way; but at last it became clear from careful observation that the blessed day of hatching would never arrive.

Sir William (then Mr.) Flower was immensely interested in our choughs, so when all hope of offspring was at an end I wrote informing him of the sad downfall of our anticipations, and received the following letter in return :—

ST. JOHN'S LODGE, nr. AYLESBURY,
Sept. 5, 1882.

MY DEAR LADY DOROTHY—I am sorry to hear that the choughs did not hatch, but hope that they will do better next year; it is something that you have saved two of the eggs, and I shall be very pleased to add one of them to the collection under my care, if you will kindly send it addressed to me at the College of Surgeons, any time after the 16th of this month, when I return to town.

It will be safer than sending it here, where we are all spending a pleasant autumn holiday.

We were for a week, last month, at Norfolk, at Lord Walsingham's, whose beautiful entomological collections you are probably acquainted with. He is a very enthusiastic naturalist.

We have not been to Combe Lodge or Dangstein since the spring, though Lady Thompson has kindly asked us to go again; but as we have several other visits to pay, I am not sure whether we shall be able to accomplish it before the autumn has gone.

I trust that when you are in London again you will not forget to come to see my museum; just now we are full of painters, and I am afraid it will be two months at least before it is restored to its normal condition of order.

With kind regards, in which Mrs. Flower joins,—I remain, yours very truly,   W. H. FLOWER.

The following year our choughs were once again observed building a nest in the same tower, and in due course our eyes were gladdened by the sight

of eggs lying peacefully in the nest, at which we
used to peer through a trap-door which could be
opened without arousing the choughs' alarm. At
last came the happy day when one little fledgling
actually made its appearance; at last we seemed
certain of being able to announce that we had
achieved an ornithological record. From time to
time, however, further peeps at the new arrival
began to disconcert and puzzle us, for its plumage
of the most unchoughlike character did not at all
accord with that of its parents; and one fine day,
alas, the dreadful truth was at last forced upon us
—the choughs had hatched out a little starling!

In the end everything was explained, for, on
investigation, it was discovered that our pair of
choughs were both of them hens—the reason that
the two eggs had never produced offspring! The
two poor birds, evidently realising that their only
hope of a family lay in adoption, had the next
year annexed the eggs of some unfortunate starling, and then hatched out the little alien, whose
arrival in the world was the cause of our disappointment and disgust.

At our place in Sussex, just on the borders of
Hampshire, I had a very large garden, and here,
besides greenhouses, was an aviary in which were
kept many different kinds of birds. I do not
know, however, that aviaries are ever a great
success; it is far more pleasant, indeed, to see
birds at liberty like my choughs, who used to stalk
about the grounds as if the whole place belonged

to them, as did also the poor storks ; these latter, however, always looked melancholy, owing, I suppose, to the permanent state of indigestion produced by their partiality for dining off broken crockery. I was very proud of my garden, in which most of the distinguished botanists and biologists of that day, including Sir Joseph Hooker and Charles Darwin, took a great interest.

In my greenhouses I had at one time a large collection of insectivorous plants, specimens of which I used occasionally to send to Mr. Darwin, who carried on a correspondence with me about these curious things, in which he was very much interested. I went once to pay him a visit at his house at Down, in Kent, but unluckily found him suffering from one of those attacks from which he perpetually suffered, he having never perfectly recovered from the terrible sea-sickness which tortured him during his voyage on the *Beagle*. In consequence of his indisposition I was only able to talk to him for a short while, but, nevertheless, he told me a great deal about the digestive powers of the secretion of the *drosera* or sun-dew, which, as he had actually proved by experiment, acted upon albuminous compounds in exactly the same manner as does the gastric juice of mammals.

One or two of our greenhouses were entirely devoted to rare plants and orchids, which were sent to me by my friends from every part of the world. The late Lord Sherbrooke, then Mr. Lowe, and Mr. Bernal Osborne, I remember, used rather to laugh at my partiality for horticulture—the latter especially used to declare that ladies liked taking in scientific men by pretending an interest in the subjects which were their especial study. Mr. Cobden, however, took the warmest interest in my gardening experiments, and wrote to me often on the subject. In 1861, when in Algiers, which in those days was, of course, not nearly so well known as at present, he sent me the following letter :—

ALGIERS,
19th January 1861.

MY DEAR LADY DOROTHY—It was, indeed, very kind of you to think of me when in another quarter of the globe. I will not lose a post in replying to your kind inquiries. The weather here is delightful. It is an English summer. I suspect from the admission of the natives that we have an exceptional fine season. However, I have derived great benefit from the change. There is really no excuse for coughs or asthmas here, for we have generally a blue sky, and never any fogs or white frosts. I have been annoyed for many months with a sort of stiff neck. It is precisely the same as if I had sat in a draught and caught cold yesterday. I have a difficulty in turning my head without turning my body. You know I have been (all my life) rather stiff-necked in a moral sense, but this permanent muscular affection is rather novel and puzzling. However, I hope it will yield to the warm weather and other remedies. You would be delighted to see the fields and the gardens covered with roses and flowers. In walking in the country the other day I plucked a little wild flower like a larkspur, with leaves somewhat resembling parsley, and I remarked to my wife, "If we had found this in Lady Dorothy's conservatory, how we should have admired it !" The hedges are generally made of cactus and aloes, and they would puzzle the fox-hunters to go through them. The country is generally very uncultivated, and is covered with dwarf palms. The date-palm does not bear fruit here, though the trees grow very tall. You must penetrate some hundreds of miles into the interior to find the best dates. The city of Algiers, which stands on the steep slope of a hill, presents a strange aspect to the European visitor. There is a greater variety of costume than even at Cairo. You see Arabs, Turks, Jews, and Greeks mixed up with every variety of military French uniforms. There are a great many soldiers here, and I confess I should not feel quite so safe among the Arabs (who in their heart have no love for the infidel) if we had not a strong garrison of the *pantalons rouges.* The Moorish women walk about with their figures enveloped in white muslin, leaving only holes for the eyes. If one of these were seen walking near Dangstein the country people would be frightened, and would think that a newly buried corpse had escaped from the churchyard. There is a Jardin d'Essai, or experimental nursery garden, near Algiers, kept up by Government, which affords pleasant walks. A great number of the shrubs which you have under glass are flourishing here. The custard-apple flourishes. What surprises one is the rapidity with which the trees grow. There are some which in fifteen years have grown as large as they would have grown in forty or fifty in England. They have very little idle time, for there is no winter, and, if they get plenty of water, they grow rapidly in the summer. The orange tree is very fine in Algeria, but they are cultivated more extensively at Blidah, thirty miles in the interior, than here. They require a great deal of water at their roots. In fact, all the fruit, whether dates or other things, depends on irrigation. "Their feet in water and their heads in the fire" is the phrase used by the natives to show the treatment that agrees with them. If the climate did not make people idle, what an immense production there might be where there is no winter and the land of waters requires no rest ! The vegetable market in Algiers at eight in the morning is a sight to see, such piles of cauliflowers, beans, peas, and new potatoes. I cannot say a word about politics ; I am

R

busy with *Adam Bede*, *The Woman in White*, and other equally amusing volumes. I spend as much time as possible out of doors. There are forty or fifty English visitors here for their health, besides a few residents, and there is a staff of engineers and navvies employed by Peto and Co. on a railway and a boulevard, for which they have a contract. The hotels are good, but not cheap. Many people find lodgings a little way in the country. There—I am afraid I have exhausted nearly all my Algerian news. Pray give my kind regards to Mr. Nevill. I hope the severe weather has not interfered with his farming operations. I hear a good account of my lambs. I shall remain here till I get quite strong, and my return home will depend on the weather in England. I shall not attempt to be in the House at the opening of Parliament. I was working in Paris the whole of last summer and autumn, and can therefore take a little holiday with a clear conscience. My wife joins me in kind regards to you and family.—Very truly yours,

R. C.

It was through Mr. Cobden that I obtained a special sort of silkworm which at one time I kept in my garden. Before this I had from time to time experimented with the ordinary silkworm which feeds upon mulberry leaves; but my experiences had not been very satisfactory, for, in addition to other inconveniences, my silkworms, which were kept in the house, used occasionally to stray about and get up people's trousers, much to their inconvenience and horror. So I determined to make an altogether new departure, and had a sort of regular silkworm farm laid out in a part of the garden where it could be under constant observation. A certain portion of this ground was entirely devoted to the *Ailanthus glandulosa*, or "Tree of

Heaven," which is quite hardy. On its leaves lives
the Ailanthus silkworm, which I then set about
to procure, and wrote to several of my friends
asking them to assist me. Eventually it was
through the kindly efforts of Mr. Cobden that my
ambition was achieved, as the following letter will
show :—

ALGIERS, *23rd February* 1861.

MY DEAR LADY DOROTHY—My wife will have the pleasure
of writing to you with the beads, and I merely wish to add
that I am also sending some amber beads they procured for
me. Having called at the Jardin d'Essai here, and spoken
with the intelligent director, he tells me that he has only
about one hundred cocoons of the kind of silkworm you allude
to, and that he obtained them from Paris, where he advises me
to apply for some. He wrote me the following :—" Pour
avoir des œufs ou des cocons de ver à soie de l'Ailante,
s'addresser à M. G. Ménéirlle, secrétaire de la société
Impériale d'acclimatation à Paris." I give you this address
so minutely that you may be enabled, if you are impatient
to possess these little animals, to send for them before I
return through Paris, otherwise, if you will be so good as to
express the wish, I shall be delighted to execute the commission for you on my way home. The weather is delightful
here. Last week I placed a thermometer on a table in the
sun in front of the house, and it stood up to 95°. We find
it too warm. With kind remembrances to Mr. Nevill,—
I remain, very truly yours,   R. C.

These silkworms did very well indeed, and I
actually obtained enough silk to have a dress made
out of it ; but in the end I was compelled to give
up keeping the Ailanthus moth on account of
the small birds—tits in particular—which were
so taken with what they came to regard as an

irresistible gastronomic treat, that all precautions, such as nets, scarecrows, and the like, proved powerless to save the poor silkworms from destruction.

At that time the cult of gardens was not, as now, universally popular; it was before the day of garden books, though some very good works on horticulture of a more serious type were occasionally published. Such a one was a very interesting book called *My Garden*, written by a Mr. Smee, who had a beautiful garden near Carshalton. This was embellished with cuts of nearly every plant, bird, or insect which the owner had observed upon his domain—a most excellent idea which was admirably carried out. Of course, amongst modern garden books there is none to compare with the delightful *Potpourri from a Surrey Garden*, a work which, in addition to containing much valuable horticultural information, is also permeated with the personal charm and originality of its gifted writer.

Though people did not, as a rule, formerly devote so much care and attention to their gardens as is now the case, many country houses had attached to them " a garden of friendship." One of these, at Cortachy, in Scotland, I particularly recall to mind, on account of the many happy days I have spent with its mistress, Lady Airlie, a very dear and old friend of mine. Mr. Lowe (afterwards Lord Sherbrooke) once wrote on this garden some very pretty verses, a tribute to a hostess for whom he entertained the very highest admiration. It was, alas, but seldom that Mr. Lowe exercised his gift of graceful versification, but the lines in question show that his talents in this direction were of no mean order :—

THE GARDEN OF FRIENDSHIP AT CORTACHY

Is life a good ? then if a good it be,
Mine be a life like thine, thou steadfast tree ;
The selfsame earth that gave the sapling place
Receives the mouldering trunk in soft embrace,
The selfsame comrades ever at thy side,
Who knows not Envy, Wilfulness, or Pride.
The Winter's waste repaired by lavish Spring,
The rustling breezes that about thee sing,
The intertwining shadows at thy feet,
Make up thy life, and such a life is sweet.
What though beneath this artificial shade
No Fauns have gambolled and no Dryads strayed !
Though the coy nurslings of serener skies
Shudder when Caledonian tempests rise,
Yet sways a cheering influence o'er the grove
More soft than nature, more sedate than love.
And not unhonoured shall thy grove ascend
For every stem was planted by a friend,
And she, at whose command its shades arise,
Is good and gracious, true and fair and wise.

XIII

A Diorama at Florence—Vauxhall Gardens—Causes of their end in 1855—*Fête* at Cremorne—The Coliseum—Rinks and roller-skating —Aquariums—Zazel and Mr. Watts—Nelly Farren—The rise of the Music Hall—A visit to Evans'—Paddy Green as a collector— The Opera in old days—Taglioni and Cerito—Paul Bedford—Mr. Toole—His joke upon Sir Henry Irving—The Exhibition of 1851 —Houdin, the Prince of Conjurers—Theatre at Rome—Old days at Töplitz—A libel upon the Queen.

ABOUT the first public entertainment which I remember was a diorama of the Church of Santa Croce at Florence which I was taken to see when quite a child. It made a great impression upon my mind, and the recollection of the delight it gave me still lingers in my memory. The effect was beautiful and greatly enhanced by some extremely fine music which exactly simulated the swelling strains of an organ.

I suppose there are not many people alive who remember Vauxhall Gardens, an historic place of amusement to which I went several times—and very delightful I thought it. This, of course, was almost in the last days of prosperity which this once fashionable resort enjoyed, for towards the end it had become but a feeble and, I fear, none too reputable shadow of its former self.

246

Well do I recollect the ham sandwiches for which Vauxhall, or rather its expert carver, was famed. Rumour indeed declared that so great was this official's talent for cutting transparent slices of ham that, if put upon his mettle, he could cut from one single ham sufficient slices to cover the whole gardens, which were by no means inextensive in area. It was a pleasant place with its music and coloured lights, and, above all, the many memories of the eighteenth century which clung about the old gardens. Some of the decorative paintings were by Hogarth, and the artistic taste of another age could clearly be discerned, though time and the weather had done their work in the way of spoiling a good deal which would otherwise have been artistic and interesting. To such an extent was this the case, that when the pictures came to be sold (there were, I think, two sales, the last in 1859) ridiculously small prices were realised, though many were the work of well-known and highly gifted painters.

Vauxhall Gardens were finally closed about 1855. I fancy that a succession of unfavourable and rainy seasons greatly contributed to their end, for in spite of the added interest of balloon ascents and other sensational performances the public declined to be attracted. So bad was the weather one season that the management, with considerable sense of humour, sent out men bearing huge umbrellas upon which the attractions of Vauxhall as an open-air pleasure resort were vividly set forth.

At Cremorne, which lasted well into the 'seventies

(when its reputation became such as to call forth loud Puritanical protests which eventually caused its closure), fashionable *fêtes* used sometimes to be held, when the gardens presented much the same appearance as Vauxhall in its palmy days.   I went to some of these *fêtes*, but not to the last, on which occasion, I believe, considerable disorder prevailed on account of a number of the usual frequenters of Cremorne obtaining admission and squirting ink at the ladies' dresses as a sign of their displeasure at the intrusion of another society than their own.   In consequence of this no more of these *fêtes* were held, the gardens being entirely abandoned to the class which eventually caused their end.

As a girl I used often to go with my sister to the Coliseum, a pseudo-classical building erected in 1824 from the designs of Decimus Burton.   The buildings and grounds covered about an acre, and in addition to the main attraction, which was always a panorama, there were various other sights to be seen, such as to-day would be termed "side shows," the chief of these being, I remember, a stalactite cavern.   In 1844 the directorate made the first attempt to introduce roller-skating (or rather "wheel-skating," as it was then called) upon a floor of boards; this, however, proved an unsuitable surface, and the new amusement did not at all take the public fancy and had a very short vogue.   Some thirty years later, however, it was revived, under more favourable and more modern conditions with extraordinary and, for a time, almost frenzied

success.   In the middle 'seventies, indeed, the
mania for roller-skating suddenly caught hold of
every class, and rinks, some improvised and some
specially built, sprang up in almost every town
of any importance; whilst London, and more
especially fashionable London, went mad about
the new amusement.   The craze, however, did not
last as long as many speculators had confidently
anticipated, and a great deal of money was
eventually lost by those who, convinced of the
permanency of the roller-skating rage, had invested or rather risked their money in the construction of rinks.   The mania indeed died out as
suddenly as it had originated, though some years
ago skating on artificial ice secured a certain
amount of popular support.

Roller-skating whilst it lasted called forth many
witticisms and jokes, some of them, it must be
added, of none too refined a taste.   Certain ladies,
for instance, were said to stand on a very unsteady
footing, whilst others of irreproachable conduct
and stern demeanour were spoken of as constantly
falling.   One could not help smiling to hear that
people regarded as models of decorum had recently
had many a slip.   The whole craze, indeed, with
the comical accidents it entailed, produced general
and widespread hilarity.

Another craze of a somewhat more lasting
nature was that for aquariums, which were greatly
patronised when they were first started with the
object, according to the promoters, of providing

the public with palaces where amusement was to be unobtrusively blended with instruction.

The best known and, for a time, the most successful of these was the Westminster Aquarium, quite recently demolished, the opening of which created quite a sensation. For a time all London flocked to this resort, where, in addition to the denizens of the deep, there was generally some extraordinarily daring acrobatic feat to be seen. The most sensational of these performers was Zazel, a graceful female acrobat who was fired out of a cannon and caught a trapeze, if I remember rightly, at the end of her flight. In reality the mode of propulsion was a strong spring, though the illusion of a real cannon being fired was produced by the volumes of smoke which surged from the cannon's mouth as the performer flew through the air. Zazel was presented to the public by Mr. Farini, an unrivalled purveyor of wonders. I was much struck by the grace and daring which this young lady exhibited, and being acquainted with some of the directors managed to get a quiet talk with her. I went one morning, I remember, and she explained to me exactly how the feat was performed, giving, indeed, a special and private performance of it for my benefit, in her working dress.

Zazel—a model, I may add, of the domestic virtues—was a singularly graceful athlete, and, in addition to the sensational cannon act, used to perform upon a trapeze slung high up near the aquarium roof. Her grace of movement, indeed, was such that many artistic people were attracted to the performance ; amongst others, I remember, the late Mr. Watts, whom, on more than one occasion, I met observing this artiste with the greatest interest and delight. He told me that he had seldom seen a more perfect example of graceful human motion, and had come there as much for the purpose of study as for the sake of amusement. When Zazel's cannon feat was first performed a considerable outcry was raised on account of the supposed danger to the human missile, and a high Government functionary was said to have been about to interfere, whereupon Mr. Farini (so ran the story) completely set the public mind at rest by proposing to demonstrate the safety of the performance by shooting the august official himself out of the cannon, not once only but as many times as he might like, undertaking that on each occasion he should be returned to his office perfectly unharmed and intact.

Seldom, I should say, has any acrobatic performance caused so much excitement in London as Zazel's, and those who went to the Gaiety at that time will remember the amusing burlesque of the feat (given in, I think, " Little Doctor Faust ") by Edward Terry and that never-to-be-forgotten incarnation of clever vitality, Nelly Farren, in which the latter, having climbed into a burlesque cannon, was asked, " Are you in ? Are you far in ? Are you Nearly Far-in ? "—sallies which were greeted with thunders of applause.

The music halls, to which to-day every one goes, were formerly not considered at all correct places for ladies. About the first time that society began seriously to realise their existence was, I think, at the time of the Russo-Turkish war, when Plevna, a sort of spectacular ballet, was being given at the Canterbury. A great benefit was organised in aid of the Turkish wounded, and a good many people crossed the river and took boxes. This incursion into what was to them an unknown world produced a certain taste for this kind of amusement, and led to music halls being gradually patronised by a very different sort of audience from the one which was formerly enraptured by the singing of the *lions comiques*. As years went on music hall after music hall abandoned its chairman, —a man, as a rule, of stentorian voice who in old days was a principal feature of these places. The entertainments given then gradually changed their character, and to-day every one goes to the music hall, where, for the most part, the performance is quite as innocent as a village penny-reading presided over by the vicar.

Before the days when the music hall had attained the popularity which it now enjoys, vague rumours, of course, used to reach society as to its chief stars, and occasionally some of us used to be unobtrusively taken to see them. One of the chief was George Leybourne, whose song "Champagne Charlie," with its sparkling music and catchy refrain, combined with the fact that he used to drive about in a carriage drawn by four horses, created quite a sensation in London.   Another was the great Macdermott, whose song " We don't want to fight, but by Jingo if we do," originated the expression a "jingo," so often used in political controversy.   The *lion comique* is now but a memory of the past, his very direct and somewhat robust methods being unsuited to the taste of the generation which takes its pleasures in a very different way from that popular in less squeamish times.

I well remember once going with a party— amongst others Lady Molesworth, Lord Torrington and Mr. Bernal Osborne—to Evans' Supper Rooms. It was not a place, I fancy, to which ladies went as a rule, but both Lady Molesworth and I had wished to see it, and so it was arranged that we should go.   The evening was not as successful as it might have been, as some of the party were in a bad temper ; but we tasted the potatoes, for which the place was famous, and, during the course of the visit, I was introduced to the celebrated Paddy Green.   He was brought up into the sort of box in which we sat by Mr. Bernal Osborne, who presented him to me with a long sort of speech in which he informed the old man that he was meeting a connection of the well-known Horace Walpole.   Paddy Green, contrary to my expectation, was immensely interested at this, and, telling me he would go and get something which I ought to see, disappeared for a

moment, only to return bearing with him the
"Opera Pass" which had belonged to my literary
kinsman, and which the old man was quite delighted
to show me. He kept declaring, I recollect, that
some day I should have it, and I always had a sort
of idea that he would leave it to me. He did not
do so, however, and at his death it was sold by
auction, when it was purchased by Mr. Hambro
of Milton Abbey.

Forty or fifty years ago theatres were few in
number, and a visit to the play was considered a
serious adventure and not a mere casual distraction
as it is to-day, when places of entertainment are
almost too plentiful in number. As girls, we used,
I remember, to be sent to bed for two or three
hours in the afternoon in order to rest before the
excitement of witnessing a dramatic performance.
The opera then, as now, was the most fashionable
resort during the season ; not, I think, that the opera
itself excited any very keen interest—the ballet
was the main thing ; but as these were the days of
Cerito and Taglioni there is little cause for wonder
at such having been the case. Taglioni, of course,
was not generally received, but, nevertheless, I once
met her at a party, though I cannot remember
where, or how she got there. Cerito, however, I
perfectly well recollect seeing at a Mr. Long's, at
whose house in Grafton Street one used to meet
all sorts of clever and interesting people, for he had
the especial gift of collecting together notabilities
of every sort. I was introduced to this famous

dancer, who looked very pretty and demure and made an excellent impression upon every one.

Taglioni was the very perfection of grace, and her name is still remembered as a queen amongst dancers. Poor woman, her latter years were clouded by poverty and misfortune, and she was obliged to give dancing lessons in order to support her children. Her opinion of the modern school of dancing was extremely low, and she did not scruple to declare that it appeared to her both ugly and improper. "Dieu, qu'elles sont laides avec leurs indécences," was the criticism she passed upon some ballerinas who claimed to be her successors at a time when the acrobatic distortion known as the cake-walk had not yet been invented. What indeed would she have thought of that? So-called dancing in these days is more often than not largely composed of wild gymnastic exercises, whilst skirt-dancing is too often but a series of feeble kicks executed by angular performers whose lack of grace is concealed by a number of voluminous swathings and petticoats.

When my sister and I went to the opera neither the performance nor the ballet attracted either of us as much as what was called "the crush-room," which was our principal delight. This social institution is now totally extinct. In those days, however, directly the opera was over the fashionable portion of the audience at once adjourned to a hall arranged for people to wait in whilst their carriages were being fetched, and here the gay world would linger generally for at least an hour. The crush-room, indeed, was like a sort of informal evening party; but such an institution would have no success in these days of bustle and rush when every one is only too anxious to be first away, and so many are eager to betake themselves to the fashionable restaurants, the possible existence of which was undreamt of up to comparatively recent years.

I have seen nearly all the actors and actresses whose names to-day are but dim recollections of the past. Paul Bedford I well remember in a burlesque of Norma singing an excruciatingly funny song with a wreath of carrots and turnips on his head. He was the funniest comedian I ever saw, though his methods would perhaps be thought too broad at the present time when the stage almost ranks with the Church, and not a few theatrical people are as proud as if they possessed three eyes and a tail. Paul Bedford, besides being a comedian of extraordinary though very rollicking talent, was an excellent vocalist as well. He had, indeed, originally made his reputation in Lablache's great part of Don Pasquale.

The late Mr. Toole, who often used to come and lunch with me, was the last of the comedians of the old school whose original personality was a principal cause of their success. Theatres to-day are, of course, far more luxurious than was formerly the case, everything being changed, from the lighting (in old days a very primitive affair) to the programmes, which used to be merely roughly printed slips of coarse paper.

Unfortunately I have no large collection of old theatrical programmes, and I always feel sorry that as a girl I did not keep the playbills of the day, which would now be of very considerable interest. One programme, however, I did carefully retain, treasuring it as a souvenir of two clever friends of mine—Sir Squire and Lady Bancroft, who retired from management in 1885, their last performance taking place on July 20 of that year. This farewell programme, as it was called, is decorated with a nice little photograph of the clever manager and manageress, whose retirement from the stage may be said at that time to have eclipsed the gaiety of the Metropolis.

The late Sir Henry Irving used constantly to send me any trifles which he thought likely to be of interest. I have a certain number of bookplates mostly sent me by friends, and having seen a new one designed for Sir Henry by Mr. Bernard Partridge, I told him how much I should like a specimen. Accordingly he sent me this bookplate, together with a rather amusing letter describing an adventure with Mr. Toole at Canterbury Cathedral, where the latter seized the opportunity of exercising his well-known love of joking—

15A GRAFTON STREET,
BOND STREET, W.

MY DEAR LADY DOROTHY—The 15th will soon be here, and I hope that you will soon afterwards come to " Becket."

S

Pray let me know when you can, on which night I may have pleasure of making you welcome.

On Saturday nights we play some other play, to be afterwards included in our American repertoire.

I was at Canterbury lately with our mutual friend, Toole, and greatly enjoyed the visit—until he began insisting to the attendants that I was a descendant of the great archbishop, and that my visit to the Cathedral would do much to make it popular.

So it seemed, for a little crowd soon collected, from which we were rescued by a most considerate canon, who insisted on conveying us safely to the crypt.

I am glad you like the bookplate which was designed by Bernard Partridge.—Believe me, dear Lady Dorothy, sincerely yours,   H. IRVING.

13th April 1893.

The public nowadays may be said to be satiated with amusements, but formerly it was quite otherwise, and anything new in this line was considered as a positive wonder. I well remember the sensation caused by the Exhibition of 1851, which in some mysterious manner was supposed to be the inauguration of an era of perpetual peace. I went there once alone with Charles Greville—"the gruncher" as he used to be called (a nickname which, I suppose, originated from the French word *grincheux*, for there were times when he could be anything but pleasant)—and we had to make our way through most tremendous crowds. I shall also never forget being nearly crushed to death on the last day of the same Exhibition, when I had gone quite alone. I got caught in the crowd, and being very small would have certainly been at least very seriously injured by the terrible crush, had not a friendly official thrust me into a place of safety in the shape of his little pay-box.

In old days conjuring (now almost entirely a children's amusement) was far more popular than is at present the case. The prince of conjurers was, of course, Robert Houdin, who carried sleight-of-hand and legerdemain pretty well to perfection; in addition to this he was also a very clever man, whose mind was constantly on the alert, as the following little incident will show. Houdin was very popular with the Sultan and performed before him on many occasions. Being one day asked to the palace to dine, he said to his imperial host, "Your Majesty has several times been pleased to express some very flattering opinions as to my magical powers, and it is true that I have performed some rather difficult tricks. They, however, are nothing to the feat I shall now perform, provided your Majesty accords me full permission to do what I like with the watch which lies on that table." At the same time he pointed to a wonderful specimen of the watchmaker's art which, beautifully enamelled and embellished in the Louis XV. style (a present indeed from that King himself to a former Sultan), lay in a glass case close at hand. The required permission was given, whereupon Houdin rose from the table, and to the horror of all present, and to the visible annoyance of the Sultan, took up the watch and in full sight of every one threw it out of the window into the sea.

An awkward pause now ensued, and one which seemed ominous for the conjurer; but the fish just then making its appearance, Houdin, with the greatest self-possession, bade one of the servants take a particular dish to the Sultan and beg him to cut right across the fine turbot which it contained. This the Sultan did, and to his stupefaction discovered the Louis quinze watch beneath his knife. From that day Houdin's prestige was greatly increased, whilst presents were heaped upon him by the Sultan, who thought it best to keep on good terms with such a wonderful magician. The explanation, however, of this feat — extraordinary as it appeared—is quite simple. Houdin had chanced to see the watch during a previous visit to the palace about a year before, and being a man of very alert intelligence, photographed, as it were, every detail upon his brain, having a vague idea that something might be made of it. Surely enough, he discovered the watch's exact double in a curiosity shop in London— another gift from Louis XV. to some sovereign, which had fallen upon evil days. Securing the twin at a considerable price, he thought out the trick which so astonished the Sultan, and which, though it cost the conjurer a good sum, brought in a very handsome profit in the shape of increased imperial favour and the benefits resulting therefrom.

As a girl travelling on the Continent with my father I was taken to several theatres, which as a rule were terribly stuffy and uncomfortable. I remember, for instance, going to a theatre at Rome in 1845 with Lady Pellew, and there seeing a play which was really very amusing, though it left one with no desire to make a second visit.

The length was the same as an English play of those days—that is, from seven till past eleven—a melodrama, a pantomime, and a farce. The latter amused us mightily ; it was a quiz upon the English, more laughable than fair, for it satirised their riding, an art in which our nation is not behind the Italians. The hero, an immensely corpulent John Bull, with a pert booby of a son, who answered "Yes, papa," to everything, and walked about with his thumbs in the armholes of his waistcoat, was seen mounting a horse for the first time. This he accomplished by means of a crane which lifted him up, with his legs spread out, a good height into the air, and then let him drop on the horse's back. After this followed a lesson in riding, in which John Bull fell off, as did his son, and then they ran against each other, boxing and fighting all the time, till eventually the son went on his knees and craved forgiveness from his daddy, who graciously held out his hand to be kissed. At the end the riding-master introduced a number of tumblers, who threw somersaults over four horses standing side by side and performed other feats of activity, in all of which they were immediately imitated and even surpassed by old and young John. It was great nonsense, but very funny. The audience was so filthy, and the smells so overpowering, that it gave us an idea of what we had heard used to happen in some American theatres, for many of the men took off their coats and sat in shirt sleeves which for colour would have shamed an Irish labourer. The upper ranks of Roman society went at that time only to the opera, and the audience of this theatre consisted entirely of shopkeepers and tradesmen, very different to an English audience of the same class, which behaves in a respectable and gentlemanlike way. These people were dirty to a degree, and might well have been old Westminster or St. Giles turned into the pit and boxes.

On a previous occasion some years before, at Töplitz, in 1838, we all went to a Jewish marriage. We had bought glass and garnets in some quantity, the latter being considered superior to the Oriental ones ; indeed, a mania for buying had seized us all. We had thus been good customers of the Jews, who at that time lived in a quarter of their own and were very numerous there. In gratitude they invited us to their synagogue "to hear the pure worship of One God," upon which I daresay they especially prided themselves in that image-adoring land ; and one day a pretty Jewess ran after us in the street, and invited us to come and see a wedding. My father not only urged us to go but went with us himself. They had very beautiful music, and a sort of marriage song was sung by a single voice, with a chorus that would not have disgraced Braham, so full, so clear, and so sweet was it. The Hebrew chanting, of course, we could make nothing of, but the sermon or address to the newly married pair who stood up before the preacher was in perfectly intelligible Deutsch, and affected both bride and bridegroom to tears. It was a very pathetic homily, and alluded feelingly, though very delicately and distantly, to the present degraded state of the Israelites, urging them to seek their happiness all the more in the "heilige Himmelreich." There was a certain degree of elevation about the whole ceremony, the only drawback being that we were sadly devoured by fleas, which my father somewhat flippantly declared to be of the true Jerusalem breed.

During our stay at Töplitz, a Germa. ws-paper was brought to my dear governess, Redgrave, to translate, on account of its contai. a libellous description of Queen Victoria's habits, which were represented as being sadly gormandis-ing. It purported to be copied from the English Court Journal, and pretended to detail all she ate and drank from rising until going to bed. This statement was denounced to the Minister in Dresden as a libel on Her Majesty, and accord-ingly he inquired into the matter, intending to complain of it, should it appear to be scandalous, but finding that it was only a simple statement of facts copied from an English newspaper he could say nothing to it. The German editor thought it necessary to explain the meaning of several words, particularly toast, "slices of bread roasted on the

coals and buttered hot"; of these he declared
the Queen habitually ate an uncounted number,
whilst three helpings of turtle soup were said
to have cooled the admiration of the Duke of
Nemours!

XIV

WITHIN the last hundred years the changes
wrought by steam and electricity have completely
transformed the world, whilst making it, no doubt,
a very much more comfortable planet to live in
than it ever was before. Nevertheless, much that
was picturesque and curious has disappeared; few
old customs survive, though in certain places they
are still (perhaps somewhat artificially) preserved.
The practice of beating the bounds, for instance,
is, I believe, still occasionally, in a very modified
form, carried out in certain towns; but the serious
necessity for it having passed away, it is more of a
holiday pastime than anything else.

As late as the 'fifties the old custom of wassailing
the orchards was still to some extent preserved in
Sussex, where it was known as "apple-howling."

A troop of boys used to go round to the different orchards, and, surrounding the apple trees, repeat some quaint rhymes and shout in chorus, the leader of the band meanwhile producing some strange sounds from a cow's horn. Part of the ceremony consisted in rapping the apple trees with sticks. At the present day this apple-tree superstition, to which Herrick makes allusion in his *Hesperides*, appears to be extinct.

Wassailing at Christmas time was, of course, a totally different thing altogether, of which possibly some vestige has survived to the present day, though in a very modified form. In the days, not so very long ago, when Sussex labourers could not read, they were absolutely dependent upon tradition for their songs, which, in many cases, were exceedingly quaint. Two favourite ones were the " Blind Beggar's Daughter of Bethnal Green " and the well-known " Bailiff's Daughter of Islington." Others were " Lord Bateman was a Noble Lord " and " A Sweet Country Life." These old songs used to be sung by parties of carol singers who went from house to house, well assured of receiving a warm and hearty welcome.

Formerly, of course, people who lived in the country were much more dependent upon the shops in the local village than is now the case, when everything can be got down from London with the greatest ease. Most country houses of any size had a large brew-house attached to them, where home-made beer was brewed for the labourers and servants; this was at all events exceedingly wholesome, being quite free from all adulteration. Country households were also more or less self-dependent in other ways, and many articles of domestic use were made at home, which in these days are purchased from the huge emporiums with which London abounds. Those were the days of feather-beds, and the feathers of chickens and of game-birds were not thrown away as to-day, but carefully preserved and picked in order that they might be utilised as stuffing for this somewhat hot and uncomfortable sort of couch.

At my old home in Norfolk two women were kept constantly employed at this work. I can still see in my mind's eye old Phœbe Barwick, as she was called, picking away together with another aged character—they never seemed to stop from morning to night, a room being specially set aside for their use. Phœbe's companion has ever lived in my recollection by reason of the fact that when she heard the news of my brother's election, as member for East Norfolk, in 1835, she rushed downstairs, seized a huge dinner-bell, and rang a pæan of exultant triumph on the lawn in front of the house. My brother himself was imbued with but little political fervour even at that time, and in his later years his efforts on behalf of the Conservative party were limited to sending on one occasion a cartload of hares into his market town as presents for the Tory electors. The Liberals, however, having made the driver drunk, proceeded to distribute the hares amongst their own supporters, a proceeding which my brother ever afterwards declared had thoroughly disgusted him with all political propaganda.

In my early childhood there were still men living who had not abandoned the eighteenth-century fashion of wearing a wig. This custom, indeed, did not entirely die out with the coming in of the nineteenth century, some old-fashioned people continuing to wear these head-coverings as late as the early 'thirties. The last man to wear a pigtail is said to have been one of the Cambridge dons, who retained it as late as the year 1835. The higher clergy did not abandon their wigs till a somewhat later date. As recently as 1848 Bishop Monk wore a wig whilst officiating at an ordination at St. Margaret's, Westminster. Archbishop Sumner, however, is said to have been the very last ecclesiastic to discard this head-covering, which Bishops Bagot and Blomfield had been the first to lay aside. Bishop Blomfield was a divine who was noted for his wit, and his sayings were sometimes very amusing. He was once engaged in a controversy with a learned man as to the mental superiority of the East over the West, and after much argument his opponent as a parting shot said, "Well, at any rate the wise men came from the East—you can't dispute that." "Surely," retorted the Bishop, "that was the wisest thing they could do."

On another occasion, at a party where a lady

in an extremely *decolleté* gown excited a good deal of attention, some one remarked to him: "Her appearance is really quite scandalous. Did you ever see anything like it?" "Never," replied the Bishop; "at least, not since I was weaned."

When wigs were first abandoned the new fashion of wearing the hair was not by any means universally popular, and in some country districts old-fashioned parishioners were by no means enamoured of the change in their pastor's appearance. A certain clergyman, for instance, who at the beginning of the last century determined to follow the new fashion, and having discarded his wig, appeared in the village street with a cropped head, was severely snubbed by a lady parishioner whom he had consulted as to the effect of this change in his personal appearance. Her remark was, "Once a man, twice a child." For many years, indeed, people of the old school considered this innovation a most undignified change.

Nightcaps, which were once universally worn, have now pretty well gone the same way as wigs; in old days every one, not only men, but also women, wore them, and they were considered as indispensable as any other article of ordinary attire. There is a well-known story relating to the celebrated Dr. Burney which illustrates this.

Dr. Burney, whilst staying with Nelson at Merton, discovered that he had omitted to bring any nightcaps with him, and so borrowed one from the great admiral. Sitting up to study before retiring to bed, the cap somehow caught fire in a candle, the end portion of it being consumed, upon which Dr. Burney wrote out the following lines, which he sent with the remains of the cap to his host on the following morning :—

> Take your nightcap again, my good Lord, I desire,
>   I would not detain it a minute ;
> What belongs to a Nelson, where'er there's a fire,
>   Is sure to be instantly in it.

Amongst many relics of other days and ways I have several of those old-fashioned wedding and betrothal rings which almost invariably contained a motto inscribed upon their inner surface—posy rings as they were called. The word "posy," it may be added, is simply an abbreviated form of "poesy," which Richardson, in his *Dictionary of Derivatives*, defines as "a brief poetical sentiment," especially one inscribed on a ring. The custom of inscribing a motto or posy upon brooches survived in Scotland up to comparatively modern times. Those known as Luckenbooth brooches were sold in the "Luckenbooths" round St. Giles' church in Edinburgh, and were used as love-tokens and betrothal gifts. On them were inscriptions such as—

> While lyfe is myne my heart is thyne,
> Of earthly joys thou art my choise ;

lines which also occur on many old English rings. Some ladies on the death of their husbands used to convert their wedding or posy ring into a mourning one. This was effected by engraving an elongated skeleton outside the ring, its bones being brought into prominence by a background of black enamel.   Occasionally a death's-head alone was engraved outside.

Another kind of ring which is now obsolete was the Serjeant's ring.   It was an old legal custom for a Serjeant - at - law, on his appointment, to present a ring to the Crown, and also a ring of lesser weight than the royal ring to each of his brother Serjeants.   This custom was only abolished in 1873, when the office of Serjeant-at-Law was done away with.   At Windsor Castle there are said to be candlesticks formed entirely of Serjeants' rings placed one above the other. Unlike the posy rings, the inscription upon the Serjeants' rings (a flat band of gold with a moulding at top and bottom) is placed upon the exterior surface—the motto being, as a rule, in Latin and very seldom in English.   *Vivat Rex et Lex* and *Lex regis præsidium* are two to be found upon ancient rings of this kind.

Posy rings, though usually of gold, are sometimes found to be made of silver, and even of brass. For the most part quite plain, some few have decorative patterns on the outside.   Besides betrothal and wedding rings, there were also posy rings made to be given as presents on St. Valentine's Day ; a certain number of these engraved with suitable inscriptions were, in all probability, always kept in stock by the goldsmiths of other days.

A curious motto found on a posy ring is—

Fare God and lye abed till Noone;
whilst
Like this my love shall endless prove

is one of the prettiest.

Lady Cathcart, on marrying her fourth husband in 1713, had "If I survive I will have five" engraved upon her wedding ring.

Since my young days the prices of many things have changed very considerably indeed. On the whole the necessaries of life have certainly become cheaper, and its minor luxuries have been brought well within the reach of those boasting but a slender purse. When I was a child we used to burn mutton-fat candles in our nursery, and it was only in 1835, as I find from a letter of my dear old governess, that we abandoned this form of illumination for a little lamp trimmed with the best sperm oil. In still older days candles made of deer-fat used, I believe, to be burnt in country houses, where the whole problem of lighting was no easy matter.

The cumbersome oil lamps of pre-electric light days were a great source of trouble and expense, apart from the danger of fire which they sometimes caused owing to careless handling. In large houses men had to be specially told off to attend to the lamps. I remember the uncle of the present Duke of Rutland showing me the lamp-room at Belvoir full of gigantic barrels of oil; at the same time he told me that no less than six men were

kept constantly employed at nothing else but
looking after the lamps. This Duke of Rutland
was very much devoted to hunting and had several
very severe falls. My husband and myself used
often to go to Belvoir, and I remember that on
two occasions, when going to visit there, we
turned back at Grantham, it being there reported
to us that the Duke, having had a terrible fall, was
hovering between life and death; nevertheless he
survived both these accidents. The late Duke
(Lord John Manners) I always considered one
of the most high-bred-looking men I ever saw
in my life. I knew him in youth and in old
age, and in both he was ever the typical English
aristocrat; his polished and courteous address—the
heritage of his race still preserved in the present
generation—will always linger pleasantly in my
memory.

There was naturally something much more
picturesque about old country life than is the case
to-day, when, owing to railways and motor cars,
people are kept in constant and close touch with
town. The poacher, perhaps, is now the sole
anachronism, and even he, I fancy, has discarded his
old-world raiding ways in favour of more calculating
and scientific methods. Poaching in old days was
regarded by the country-folk much as smuggling
had been by their forebears—that is, with a certain
sneaking feeling of sympathetic toleration.

Many years ago, when I lived in Sussex, stories
of the smugglers who formerly abounded along the

T

coast were still told by those who had actually
witnessed and, in some cases, taken part in their
operations.   Smuggling, as a matter of fact, hurting
as it did no one but the Revenue, was not regarded
with any particular horror, and the long trains of
heavily loaded carts escorted by the smugglers
were generally interfered with by no one except
the Revenue officers and the coastguardsmen.
One of the favourite haunts of the " Free Traders "
was in Parham Park, and old Baroness de la
Zouche used to say that, when she was a little girl,
walking one day in the park with her governess,
some smugglers had made her open a gate in order
to facilitate the passage of a long train of pack-
horses loaded with kegs, then on its way to a remote
part of the park near the heronry.   In Eridge
Park, also, caves still exist where smugglers used to
store their bales of goods.   During the eighteenth
century the house was not inhabited, and the surrounding park was practically a wilderness, so that
these caves formed a most excellent and secure
retreat.   There runs beneath the present Eridge
Castle a long passage, the entrance to which is far
distant from the house, and as its existence has
never been accounted for it is not improbable that
smugglers may have had something to do with its
construction ; it is almost certain, at least, that
they knew of it and kept it in repair.

The officers of the Customs, who were called
"riding officers," though sometimes assisted by
dragoons, could do but little against the smugglers,

who sometimes indulged in very savage reprisals. The last occasion when life was lost in a smuggling affray was in 1838 at Camber Castle, but it was some time before that date that the last great party of smugglers passed through Petworth—sixty well-armed men, pistols in their belts and cutlasses by their sides. They escorted two carts and a number of horses loaded with tubs of brandy and hollands, whilst a few of them also had bales of silk slung across their backs. This picturesque procession— the funeral cortège, as it were, of smuggling—came into the old town on a Sunday morning, whilst the inhabitants were at church, and made its way through the streets in a very leisurely fashion, some of the smugglers even halting at the inns to have a drink, for it was in the days when licensing reform was as yet a thing of the future. The last of the smugglers were armed chiefly with "bats"—thick ash poles about six feet long. An old smuggler, Smithurst by name, killed in a fight at Bexhill in 1828, was found with his bat almost hacked to pieces but still grasped tightly in his hands.

A particularly ferocious murder committed by smugglers was that of some Custom House officers in 1749, when five men actually robbed the Custom House at Poole. The criminals were eventually caught, hung, and gibbeted in chains, one only escaping this fate through dying of fright whilst being measured for his irons. One of the leg-irons of William Carter, a member of this gang, who was hung in chains near Rake on the Ports-

mouth Road, came into my possession, and this I
still retain.

The last example of hanging in chains took
place when I was a child in 1834, in which year a
man named Cook, a bookbinder, who had murdered
a Mr. Paas at Leicester, was hung and gibbeted
in Saffron Lane outside the town. So much disorder
and rioting, however, prevailed that the body was
very soon removed, and in the same year hanging
in chains was finally abolished.

It has been sometimes declared that criminals
were at one time actually hung alive in chains, but
this is pure fiction. Before being hung, a criminal,
it is true, was measured for his irons—an ordeal
under which many completely broke down. After
the hanging, the body was taken down and thrown
into a cauldron of boiling pitch, on being taken out
of which it was placed in the chains, which were
riveted around it, and then slung up upon a gibbet,
where it swung in the wind as long as the chains
held together. In some instances sacks took the
place of chains.

At the last public execution in England, which
took place in 1852 at Northampton, the crowd
which had assembled was exceedingly incensed at
finding that the day had been changed. Some of
them, indeed, loudly declared that if they could
only get at the Under-Sheriff "they would let him
know what it was to keep honest folk in suspense,"
whilst one old lady, who was especially vociferous
in her denunciation, announced that she should

certainly claim her expenses from the authorities. It was also at Northampton in 1818 that the governor proudly described the new drop set up at the county gaol as being admirably suited for the hanging of twelve persons comfortably.

It may be observed that pictures of gibbets are exceedingly rarely to be found, the greatest number, oddly enough, being in works illustrated by Thomas Bewick. There are several gibbets in the tailpieces of his *British Birds*, and also one or two in his *Quadrupeds*. I may add that some sixteen years ago a very interesting little volume on the subject of *Hanging in Chains* was written by Mr. Albert Hartshorne, a gentleman well known for his knowledge of old English glass and general love of research into the past. The book in question, however, which is fully illustrated, has now, unfortunately, become somewhat difficult to procure.

On North Heath, north of Midhurst, a gallows once stood. From this, some hundred and eight years ago, swung in chains the brothers Drewitt, convicted of having robbed the mail on that spot. Their guilt, nevertheless, does not appear to have been thoroughly proved, the real criminal, it was thought by some, having been their father, who after the execution used to be seen sitting at the foot of the gallows beneath the bodies of his sons. A curious old Sussex tradition declared that a dead man's hand would cure any affection of the throat, and people would walk great distances to put this cure to the test. Whilst the body of the younger of the two Drewitts swung in the wind (which it did for a long time, a further proof, it was pointed out, of his innocence), children were brought from far away and held up in the air in order that the dead man's hand might swing across their throat. The younger Drewitt, who to his last breath maintained that he was quite unconnected with the robbery, was generally considered a martyr in the district, and the tale of his unjust fate, together with numerous details of his capture, "in a new pair of buckskin breeches," was told at many a cottage fireside long years after hanging in chains had become but a memory of the past.

A far more barbarous method of punishment than hanging in chains was "pressing to death," the last recorded infliction of which took place in Sussex, at Horsham gaol, in 1736. When a man, for no matter what reason, refused to plead, he was ordered to be laid naked on his back on the bare floor of a low dark chamber, and as great a weight of iron as he could bear—and more—put upon him. From time to time he was questioned, and should he continue to refuse to answer, heavier weights were added. As the victims of this torture some-times survived for days, the law very humanely provided that on the first day they were to be allowed three morsels of the "worst bread pro-curable," whilst on the second three draughts of "standing water" were allowed. This alternation of food and drink was to continue from day

to day till the prisoners answered or till they died.
The last man to suffer this horrible punishment was
one who was charged with robbery and with murdering a woman at Bognor, and who refused to plead,
not uttering a word. Many endeavours were made
to induce him to speak, but all of them proving
useless, he was taken back to Horsham gaol to be
pressed to death. The weight which finally killed
him was some four hundred pounds, in addition to
which the executioner, a man turning the scale at
sixteen stone, jumped upon the board and thus
administered the *coup de grâce*.

Executions in quite modern times were horrible
affairs. Within my own lifetime the skin of more
than one murderer has been taken from his body,
tanned, and used to bind a book. Such a thing
happened after the execution of William Corder,
who was hung at Bury St. Edmunds in the year
1828, having been found guilty of murdering Maria
Martin. On this occasion the Bury coach on its
way to London was stopped in order that the
passengers might witness the execution. Macready
used to say that during the performance of *Macbeth*
the same evening at Drury Lane the actor who
impersonated Duncan was interrupted at the words,
"Is execution done on Cawdor?" by a man in the
gallery who shouted out, "Yes! He was hung
this morning at Bury." In connection with books
bound in human skin it may be mentioned that a
copy of the Poetical Works of John Milton in the
Exeter Museum is said to be bound in the skin of

George Cudmore, a Devonshire murderer executed in 1830, whilst I believe there is also a large quarto volume preserved at Bristol which is bound in the skin of a murderer executed as recently as 1843.

During the Reign of Terror in France, it has been stated, several pairs of ladies' white kid gloves were made from the same gruesome material.

In my childhood also, "resurrection men," as those who stole dead bodies for sale to the surgeons were called, were much dreaded, extraordinary methods of protecting corpses from being carried away being often employed. Such things seem quite of another age to-day, but the evil in question was only ended in 1832 when the Anatomy Act was passed.

In the eighteenth century the Sussex roads were notorious for their bad condition, and little effort was made to improve them, partly owing to an idea that better means of communication would bring many cut-throats, pickpockets, and other undesirable folk down from London. Indeed, when the road to Brighton through Cuckfield was first made, the inhabitants of Hurstpierpoint became so alarmed at the proposal to run it through that place that they petitioned Parliament, and were successful in having it diverted. So bad were some of these Sussex roads that there are records of people having habitually used oxen to draw their coaches. Defoe, for instance, travelling in Sussex in the eighteenth century, came upon a lady, whom he describes as "of very good quality," being drawn to church in a village near Lewes by six oxen.

It was largely owing to the isolation produced by faulty means of travel that Sussex villages, up to comparatively recent times, retained so much of old-world quaintness and charm. Many of the labourers of a past generation never moved out of their own district during the whole of their lives. A story used to be told of a Heathfield labourer who, after a quarrel with his wife, deserted his home and went to another village a few miles away. Home sickness, however, soon overcame him, and, coming back to his family, he declared that he had had quite enough of "furrin parts"— nothing like Old England after all! An old lady of the village of Ditchling, who was going up to London, being asked what sort of place she thought she was about to see, replied that she expected it would be "about like the bustling part of Ditchling."

The old cottages in the villages were formerly full of Sussex ironwork, and of this I made a collection, which includes some very good specimens —fire-dogs and backs, rush-light holders, tongs, and the like—of this extinct industry. At that time I lived in the very centre of what was formerly a great iron-producing district, for near Heathfield were many furnaces which at one time kept half the population in full employ. Many Sussex families owed their fortunes to the ironworks, amongst them the Fullers, one grateful member of

which set up the inscription "Carbone et Forci-
pibus" on the house.   The old hammer ponds still
existing are extremely picturesque, in many cases
having clear rippling streams, containing brook trout,
flowing out of them.   The last furnace in Sussex—
Ashburnham Furnace—was only finally blown out
in 1825, having been worked by Lord Ashburnham
up to that time ; the iron produced there was at one
time said to be the best in the world.   As the iron
industry decayed hop - growing was introduced,
which gave some measure of employment to the
population which began to find its old occupation
gone.

Some time before I began collecting Sussex
ironwork I used to live in quite another part of the
county bordering upon Hampshire, and here also
I found much of great antiquarian interest.   Not
many miles distant from our house, for instance,
stood the crumbling walls of Cowdray, the beautiful
seat which once belonged to the Brownes, and
was destroyed by fire in 1793.   I have several
relics and pictures of this old mansion.   At the
time of the fire the young owner, Lord Montague,
was away on the Continent, and the house
was being renovated in view of his return.
In the disastrous conflagration perished many
valuable relics of art and pictures, for the house
being under repair at the time, everything had
been stored in the north gallery, which was
difficult of access.   A picture of Charles I. at
Woburn is said to have been one of the few saved,

another being a painting of the two brothers Fitz-william lying dead in armour. Many relics from Battle Abbey were also destroyed, among them, it is said, the sword of the Conqueror, his coronation robe ornamented with gold and rare gems, and, most interesting perhaps of all, the Roll of Battle Abbey. These had been removed to Cowdray when the seventh Lord Montague sold Battle Abbey in 1717.

After the burning of Cowdray no care appears to have been taken to safeguard any of the contents which remained undamaged. Things, indeed, saved from the fire were taken away to Midhurst by any one who cared to take the trouble, the whole neighbourhood being allowed to roam through the ruins. I myself, indeed, as has been said, possess some relics of Cowdray—several good pieces of carved woodwork (the decoration of the salon) which I purchased near Midhurst from a man whose grandfather, I am very much afraid, had in all probability annexed them without leave.

It was in the Abbots' Hall at Battle that the curse of fire and water was pronounced against Sir Anthony Browne, who was holding his first great feast there after the spoliation of the monasteries by Henry VIII., the abbey having been granted to him by that king, in whose favour he stood very high. Striding through the crowd of guests and re-tainers, a monk is said to have made his way to the daïs where Sir Anthony sat, and, raising his voice, to have solemnly cursed him and his posterity.

"By fire and water thy line shall come to an
end ; thus shall it perish out of the land."

The fact that the eighth Lord Montague was
drowned when attempting to shoot the falls of
Laufenburg at the very time that Cowdray (then
being renovated in view of his coming of age) was
consumed by fire has been regarded by many as
the fulfilment of the curse, but it must not be
forgotten that Sir Anthony Browne himself and his
descendants lived quite free from misfortune for
some two hundred years. As is well known, the
two sons of Lord Montague's only sister, Mrs.
Poyntz, were drowned in the very flower of their
youth, before the eyes of their parents, in a boating
accident at Bognor in 1815—another sad catastrophe also attributed to the curse. On the death
of Mr. Poyntz the Cowdray estate passed out of
the Browne family, being divided amongst his
sisters, and in 1843 it was sold to the sixth Earl
of Egmont for some three hundred thousand
pounds. The new possessors of the place made
no attempt to restore the ruins of the noble old
mansion, a splendid example of domestic architecture, but built a new house on the site of the
keeper's lodge which was pulled down.

In West Sussex we had many pleasant neighbours, amongst them the Rev. Mr. Knox, a most
amusing man and a great authority on birds. He
lived in an ancient manor-house which belonged to
my husband—Trotton Place, a quaint old house still
the property of my eldest son. Trotton, a small

village on the Petersfield Road, possesses some
claim to attention in having been the birthplace
of the unfortunate Otway, who was the son of
the rector of the adjacent parish of Woolbeding.
Educated at Winchester and Oxford, Otway, when
twenty years old, betook himself to London and
became an actor, and, some five years later, a
playwright. Obtaining a cornet's commission in
a regiment about to proceed to Flanders, his
military career was short and unfortunate, lasting
only about a year. The force to which he was
attached never reached its destination, the money
voted for transport having been diverted by
King Charles II., who preferred the worship
of Venus to that of Mars, to more peaceful
and congenial purposes. In his comedy of *The
Soldier's Fortune* Otway clearly alludes to his
disappointment :—

Fortune made me a soldier, a rogue in red (the grievance
of the nation). Fortune made the peace—just as we were
on the brink of war; then Fortune disbanded us and lost us
two months' pay. Fortune gave us debentures instead of
ready money; and by very good fortune I sold mine and
lost heartily by it, in hopes the grinding, ill-natur'd dog
that bought it may never get a shilling for't.

After his retirement from the army the young
poet wrote several plays, amongst them *The
Orphan*, and in 1685 the powerful and beautiful
Venice Preserved, which, as Dr. Johnson wrote,
though the work of a man not attentive to
decency or zealous for virtue, yet shows that the

author was a man of great force and originality, and had consulted nature in his own breast.

At thirty-four years of age Otway died, choked, it is said, by a roll which he too hastily swallowed after a long fast. The unfortunate poet, almost naked, starving, and fearfully harassed by creditors, was given a guinea by a friendly gentleman in a coffee-house where he had asked for a shilling. Out of this guinea he purchased the piece of bread which caused his death. Another account declares that Otway, desirous of avenging the death of a friend who had been shot in the street, pursued the assassin as far as Dover on foot, which brought on a fever from which he died in the " Bull Inn " on Tower Hill. Pope corroborates this version of Otway's death, but says his friend had been merely robbed and not murdered.

A brass affixed to the wall of Trotton church within comparatively recent years commemorates the memory of the unfortunate young man, but Otway himself lies in a vault under the church of St. Clement Danes.

Trotton church is an interesting old building, which contains a tomb of great archæological interest—the sarcophagus of Sir John Camoys and the Lady Elizabeth, his wife. This church has, like many village churches, suffered more or less from the restorations to which it has been subjected. One alteration which particularly annoyed me was the removal of an old door which bore the mark of many a Cromwellian bullet upon

its exterior side. Within the last few years, however, some attempt has been made to repair the
ravages of the restorer—the old wooden altar-rails
having been replaced in their original position,
whilst certain very curious mural paintings have
been once more exposed to view. In the 'sixties
and 'seventies the fiend of restoration may be said
to have stalked rampant through the land, and
rectors vied with one another in renovating and
vulgarising the sacred edifices committed to their
charge. At a Sussex church in a village quite
close to where we lived, great indignation was, I
remember, aroused by workshops being erected all
over the churchyard, in which workmen fashioned
modern Gothic pinnacles and other architectural
gewgaws wherewith to decorate the stately old
church. Tombstones were temporarily taken up,
no particular attention being paid to their exact
position, and in consequence no one felt at all
certain that they were ever replaced in their old
position—the tombstone of "John Smith" being
in many cases placed over the grave of "Thomas
Brown," and *vice versa*, a proceeding not entirely
satisfactory to their families, some of whom were
very annoyed. The rector, however, who was
delighted at his vulgarised church, thought little of
such a trifle as this, and organised an ornate service
of reopening at which his parishioners somewhat
ruefully returned thanks for the blessings of the
restoration.

Not very far from Trotton is the town of

Midhurst, for which Charles James Fox, when only nineteen years of age, was returned in 1768. He actually had two encounters in debate with Burke before he attained his majority. On one of these occasions, it is said, when Fox had set the Treasury Bench in a roar of laughter at Burke's expense, the latter was much nettled, and turning on the youthful member, exclaimed, "You may speak if you like, but being a minor you have no right to vote."

At one time Midhurst was a great place for the manufacture of quilts, and from this, no doubt, originated the weaver's shuttle which was stamped on the town pieces or tokens about 1670. These were known as Midhurst farthings, issued, as the legend on one side of them said, "For ye use of ye Poor."

Midhurst and Rye were the only two places in Sussex which issued town tokens, that is, one token struck for the use of the whole town. The custom of striking tokens—small coins of the value of farthings, halfpennies, and pennies—only prevailed from about 1648 till 1672. As a rule, these were issued by tradesmen, but in some cases towns struck them. In Somersetshire, for instance, there were thirteen town tokens; in Dorsetshire, eight; in Devonshire, five; in Kent, one; and in Sussex the two which have just been mentioned. In Yorkshire there were none at all.

Midhurst has more than once been somewhat closely associated with great political orators, for

not far away, at Dunford, lived Mr. Cobden, whom
I often used to go and hear speak in the House of
Commons, where his oratory never failed to secure
the appreciation which it deserved. In West
Sussex, however, he did not excite any extraordinary attention either as an orator or politician,
many regarding his political views with extreme
distrust, whilst others did not understand them.
Very often it is the case that politicians of quite
European reputation are but lightly esteemed in
their own part of the country, a state of affairs
which is sometimes caused by their talking over
the heads of the audiences whom they address.
Country-folk as a rule do not (or did not) appreciate highly cultured oratorical efforts, but prefer
speeches, not devoid of humour, dealing with
matters of local interest.

I once heard a peculiarly apt criticism of a
speech made by a politician of profound learning
and knowledge, but one not very much in sympathy with the more frivolous side of life. This
orator, having to address a meeting in a country
town, had beforehand been begged to remember
that his audience was not remarkable for any
great intellectual culture, and was consequently unlikely to appreciate historical allusions or erudite
criticism—a chatty, sparkling speech judiciously
peppered with anecdote and chaff would be the
sort of thing to arouse enthusiasm and capture its
sympathies. The evening having come, the speaker,
determined to profit by these hints, attempted to

U

enliven his discourse by here and there interpolating remarks of a less serious kind than those which his speeches usually contained.   Well satisfied with the result, and driving away with an old friend, he said to him : " Well, I hope that suited you ; at any rate no one could say I spoke too seriously."   " It was a capital speech," came the reply, "only, to tell you the truth, it rather reminded me of an article from the *Quarterly Review* out for a lark."

XV

Retrospection—The first train from Norwich—Disappearance of
coaches—Railway mania of the 'forties—Hudson and his house—
Steam carriages of the past—Letter franking—Society and its
love of pleasure—Bridge—Decrease of betting and increase of
speculation—Changes in Parliament—The late Mr. Bradlaugh—
An unfortunate speech—Growth of the Press—Lady Seymour and
the cook—Louis Napoleon—His witty criticism—The Franco-
German War—*Paris Herself Again*—Mr. Mackenzie Grieves—The
overflow of London—Disappearance of nursery gardens—Modern
villagers—Folklore—Friends who have passed away.

LOOKING back to old days in the 'thirties and
'forties, what gigantic changes come into view!
Nearly everything was on a different footing from
to - day, and things which are now permanent
institutions were at that time either at their very
beginning or not dreamt of at all.

The majority of modern inventions were unknown, or in their infancy, whilst life in general
went on very much in the happy-go-lucky fashion
characteristic of another age. Law and order, it is
true, exercised a sort of sway, but the former, if just,
was often terribly cruel, whilst the latter was, by
comparison with to-day, only indifferently maintained. Three years after I was born our excellent
modern police had been established by Sir Robert

Peel, but the county police in Norfolk were only constituted some ten years later—a salutary innovation which, strangely enough, was not greeted with universal approbation. In 1842, indeed, when the new guardians of law and order had already done duty for three years, my father, at a meeting of the county magistrates at Norwich, presented a petition, signed by himself and a large number of other landowners, praying for some reduction or even the abolition of the police force, on the ground that it produced nothing but expense, and caused people to be prosecuted for offences of a very trivial nature.

My father, of course, disliked the new police force principally on account of its being an innovation, for, a staunch Conservative, he opposed changes of any kind whatever, including railroads, which were his special abomination. The advent of the railway in Norfolk was, I remember, a depressing blow to him, and he did all he could to keep the line outside the borders of his property so that he might forget its existence. Direct railway communication between London and Norwich was not established till 1845, the first through train starting from Trowse on the morning of June 30 of that year. In January 1846 all the coaches between Norwich and London had ceased to run, the last of them to go being the mail through Bury St. Edmunds.

In the 'forties came the railway mania, when many of a speculative disposition were completely carried away by dreams of immediate and colossal wealth.   Within a year or two, however, a dreadful awakening was the lot of those who had gambled in railway shares, which went down faster than they had risen, a large number of people being completely ruined, amongst them the great Hudson himself.   During the time when things were going well, flattery and praise were heaped upon him and he was the recipient of several public testimonials; but after the disastrous fall in railway shares he at once became the principal object of an outburst of widespread popular indignation.

Hudson, to whom Carlyle once alluded as "the big swollen gambler," lived on to the early 'seventies, an annuity having been purchased for his benefit by some friends only a few years before. In his prosperous days the "railway king" used to entertain very lavishly at his house at Albert Gate. This mansion, together with the one opposite to it, was built by Cubitt, and the two houses used to be called the "two Gibraltars," it being prophesied that they never would or could be taken; however, as has been said, Mr. Hudson soon falsified this prediction.   The house is now the French Embassy.

Previous to the construction of the railway between London and Norwich, several experiments had been made in Norfolk with steam carriages to run upon the roads—the precursors of our modern motor cars.   As early, indeed, as 1842, a Mr. Parr had patented a steam carriage to run for hire between Norwich and Yarmouth, whilst in the following year a steam coach was experimentally put upon the Yarmouth road. This vehicle, however, did not answer its inventor's expectations, as its wheels refused to revolve unless lifted up from the road, when, as a contemporary somewhat quaintly put it, they at once flew round with alarming velocity.

As far back as 1831 a Parliamentary Committee had decided that carriages weighing three tons, propelled by steam and carrying fourteen passengers, could travel on the ordinary roads at an average speed of ten miles an hour with perfect safety. The first steam omnibus, constructed by Mr. Hancock, ran from the Bank at Paddington in April 1833; it could attain a speed of from ten to fifteen miles an hour, carrying some twenty-five passengers, and consumed a sack of coke every eight miles. Two years later Mr. Hancock ran what was called a "steam-engine coach" between Whitechapel and his house at Stratford. Colonel Macirone and Sir Charles Dance also ran steam cars, as did Mr. Gurney, whose coaches averaged about nine miles an hour. Though these early motor cars were by no means inefficient, they were for some reason or other put down by legislative interference, and a great industry was thus held in abeyance for some forty or fifty years.

Prints of the old steam carriages have now become difficult to obtain, as they are eagerly snapped up by votaries of the motor car, many of whom make a hobby of collecting the records con-

nected with the early infancy of their favourite
sport.   One of the most curious of these prints
represents an accident which happened to a Scotch
steam carriage in the summer of 1834.   Designed
by an eye-witness of the catastrophe, it shows the
unlucky passengers, several of whom were killed,
being shot into the air, the boiler of the car having
burst owing to an overstrain.   It is said that this
accident was really caused by the trustees of the
road between Paisley and Glasgow who were very
much opposed to the new method of locomotion,
and therefore purposely kept the surface of the
highway in such a condition as to impede its progress as much as possible.   The remains of the
wrecked steam carriage are still preserved in a
museum at Glasgow.   Its maker was John Scott
Russell, the builder of the *Great Eastern* steam-
ship, which at the time it was launched was considered one of the wonders of the world.

The spirit of what we call Progress made its
influence felt in the 'thirties and 'forties, and in the
course of a few years, after the passing of the great
Reform Bill, quite a new England began to come
into existence.   Old customs and ways gradually
lost their hold upon the people and another order
of things arose, whilst such privileges as the upper
classes enjoyed became subjects of comment and
criticism, with the eventual result that most of
them were voluntarily relinquished.

Amongst minor changes of this sort was the
abolition of the practice of franking letters.   Up

to the year 1840, when uniform penny postage was introduced, Peers and members of the House of Commons were entitled to have their letters conveyed free of any charge, and I still treasure a few of these frank-marked envelopes—faded souvenirs of a bygone age. In the course of the same year appeared the artistic Mulready envelope, which has now become somewhat scarce, specimens in good condition being much prized by stamp collectors.

Many of the older people shook their heads at what they called new-fangled schemes and inventions, and some, like my father, indiscriminately denounced all reforms and reformers of every kind. My father, as I have before said, hated all innovations, and would hardly consider any merits which they might possess. He was, however, by no means alone in taking up this standpoint, which to-day, when all the world eagerly grasps at anything new, seems almost inconceivable. Men of his generation viewed things from a curious point of view, being firmly imbued with the idea that the acceptance of new methods would send England to the dogs. Their outlook upon life was in reality that of the eighteenth century, and in addition to this they would appear to have vaguely realised that new ways meant the annihilation of their power as a dominant class. Even at that time there were many who foresaw the rise of democracy, a development which they regarded with feelings of the utmost alarm, as tending to bring about the ruin of England. Nor did the wonderful new

inventions please pessimists of this sort, who
declined to welcome them with enthusiasm, and
predicted that in the end they would make for
unhappiness and discontentment. As a matter of
fact these vaticinations, ridiculous as they seemed,
have not proved so fallacious after all, for modern inventions have produced the commercialism which is
undoubtedly one of the chief causes of that curious
creed—Socialism—which, deliberately ignoring the
immutable instincts of human nature, holds out the
prospect of a visionary Utopia, and promises everything to every one at somebody else's expense.

In another chapter I have spoken of the great
changes which have taken place in the constitution
of what is known as " Society," but since I first knew
it there is one respect in which there has in reality
been no alteration at all—I refer to its love of
amusement and pleasure. True it is, perhaps, that
in past days these were indulged in with a certain
reserve and dignity—qualities which to-day seem
to be considered as being of small account. True
it is also that seldom did the passing fancies and
follies of its leaders find their way into the public
Press. Nevertheless they existed, though perhaps
in a more modified form than to-day, when publicity
is too often welcomed rather than shunned. Society,
which is after all but a collection of quite ordinary
individuals—many with more money than brains,—
naturally contains (as it always has done) a certain
number of people whose wealth prompts them to
gratify many a costly caprice. There is nothing

very astonishing about this, nor is it likely that any effect will be produced by the fulminations of those critics whose ideal society would appear to consist of a collection of prigs, faddists, and cranks, perpetually interfering in other people's business as well as lecturing and boring the world in general. In all probability London society is no better or worse than it was in the past, though certainly more stupid. Clever people seem rarer than in former days, whilst an undue importance is attached to wealth, no matter how uninteresting may be its possessor.

Nevertheless, considering all things, society might be a great deal worse, and it certainly does not deserve the indiscriminate censure which is frequently passed upon it, there being, after all, a large measure of real kindliness and generous feeling to be found hidden beneath its veneer of frivolity. Society, however, is always an easy and attractive subject for attack, the British public being apparently never tired of hearing of its crimes. Sometimes it is blamed for the vast sums expended in entertaining, which, after all, circulates money and is good for trade ; nor is it clear why people in a position to do so should not entertain their friends, or even their enemies for that matter. By the austere it is upbraided for its bridge playing, and here, perhaps, is a more legitimate reason for censure, the game in question (which I do not play, disliking all card games) having utterly destroyed much pleasant conversation. At the same time

it seems to amuse a great number who would
otherwise be bored, and many people welcome the
game as a pleasant change from the exchange of
empty and commonplace remarks.

The question of gambling is another and a
graver matter, though I personally have never
heard of any young lady being dragged into playing for stakes which she could ill afford, and, indeed,
I wonder very much what sort of host or hostess
it could be who would allow such proceedings under
his or her roof. Society is to-day a very wide
term, covering as it does a great number of
different sets which gradually fade away into an
almost imperceptible outer fringe ; but even in the
most remote of its confines, surely any man who
deliberately laid himself out to win money from a
young girl (as has been alleged) would be visited
with the censure he deserved. As a matter
of fact good bridge players, as is perfectly well
known, dislike nothing more than the intrusion
of a novice whose errors must of necessity ruin
their game.

Gambling on the Turf has without question
decreased. Where are the plungers of to-day?
Non-existent. Modern youth, except in a few
rare instances, knows better than to risk a fortune
on a racehorse—an act of folly which in former
days was very often committed. On the other hand,
the insidious craze for speculating in stocks and
shares has an almost unlimited number of votaries
—women as well as men—whose one thought is to

obtain information (as a rule unreliable) as to the chances of a rise or fall. This is an entirely new development. The great ladies of the past would as soon have thought of dabbling in City matters as of witnessing a prize fight; in fact, of the two I think they would have given the preference to the latter as being the more select. Those, however, were the days before the City had conquered the West End, and when the jargon of the Stock Exchange was as yet unfamiliar to aristocratic ears.

Finance in these latter days has become as much the appanage of society as politics were in the past, whilst all doors fly open at the advent of a successful speculator or financier. Politics, of course, which in old days were something of an engrossing pastime for the leisured classes, have now become a much more serious affair altogether.

Since the days of my childhood many and great changes have occurred in Parliament in the method of electing its members, and in the admission of others than Protestants to sit in the House of Commons. The first Roman Catholic to take his seat since the downfall of the Stewarts was Daniel O'Connell, who, elected member for Clare County in 1828, was admitted to Westminster in the following year, when the Catholic Emancipation Act having been passed, the Duke of Norfolk, Lord Dormer, and Lord Clifford also took their seats in the House of Lords. The first English Roman Catholic member of the House of Commons was

Lord Surrey, who was returned for Horsham at the same time.

Though Mr. Joseph Pease had been admitted as an M.P. on making an affirmation in 1833, the objection of the late Mr. Bradlaugh as a Free-thinker to taking the Parliamentary oath created a very great sensation some forty - seven years later. In May 1880 the member for Northampton was refused permission to affirm, and it was only some two months later that a resolution moved by Mr. Gladstone allowed him to do so. Much acrimonious controversy ensued as to the legality of such an act, Mr. Bradlaugh being on one occasion prevented from entering the House of Commons by the police. Finally, in 1886, Mr. Bradlaugh was permitted to take the oath, further intervention being stopped by the Speaker. A thoroughly sincere man, the member for North-ampton lived to gain the goodwill and respect of the House of Commons, and when he died in 1891, worn out by hard work and worry, universal regret was expressed at his demise. A pronounced individualist, he was quite uncompromising in his denunciation of anything which he deemed to be false or untrue, and in the debates in which he indulged with certain ministers of religion was very outspoken as to his views on the Christian faith. This not unnaturally caused him to be regarded as a monster of iniquity by many who had no opportunity of realising the splendid qualities which he in reality possessed, and many

were the absurd stories circulated about him—
generally, I fear, to his discredit.

It was declared, for instance, that on more than
one occasion he had defied Heaven itself, by taking
out his watch at public meetings and saying, "If
there be a God, let Him strike me dead within
the next five minutes."

I do not know what truth there may have been
in this story, but some of the Russian revolutionary agitators (so I hear) have actually uttered
this blasphemous challenge—their idea being to
emancipate the peasants from the thraldom of
their priests. It is said that an agitator of this
sort came one day to an out-of-the-way village,
and proceeded to address the peasants thus :
"The God whom you fear so much does not exist,
and I will prove it to you ; for if I am not
speaking the truth let Him kill me within the next
five minutes !" Four minutes passed and the
orator, more defiant than ever, jubilantly exclaimed,
"You see I am right ; there is no God, for I am
still alive." The headman of the village, however,
stepping to the front, altogether changed the aspect
of affairs. "You have proved nothing," said he.
"God exists, and you are going to die. God has
not chosen to kill you, for He knew we should do
so for Him," after which statement the unfortunate
apostle of Atheism was duly despatched.

One of the most striking features of the last
seventy years is the prodigious growth of the
Press. In 1836 there were only about a hundred

and sixty newspapers published in England, whilst all the daily papers put together had only an average of 12,000 copies a day. At that time there were, I believe, but five hundred and fifty newspapers in the United States, of which fifty were dailies. The London morning papers were, of course, few in number, and as a rule not more than sixty to eighty persons were employed upon their production. None of the illustrated papers now issued were then in existence, the *Illustrated London News* only making its appearance in the 'forties. Newspapers were considered quite precious things in old days, being frequently treasured up to be sent on to friends—a very different state of affairs from to-day, when edition succeeds edition with lightning rapidity, and a paper a day old is never looked at again.

In the way of provincial journalism Norfolk was early in the field, for the *Norfolk Chronicle* was founded in 1761, whilst the *Norwich Postman* is said to have been the first local newspaper published in England. It has frequently been stated that the oldest provincial newspaper is the *Worcester Journal*, the first copy of which appeared in 1709; but as a matter of fact, I believe that the *Norwich Postman* appeared some three years earlier, being first published in 1706 by T. Goddard, a bookseller of the town. It was sold for a penny, unless that sum could not be obtained, when, it is rather amusing to learn, a halfpenny would generally be accepted.

The *Newcastle-upon-Tyne Courant* is another paper which can lay claim to a very respectable antiquity, dating as it does from 1711. Many people, in consequence, have stoutly declared that the organ in question, and not the *Worcester Journal* (or *Worcester Postman*, as it was originally called), was in reality the first provincial newspaper; but, as I have said, it is now pretty well authenticated that from Norwich issued the first beginning of what has now become the great and influential Provincial Press.

John Bull, a daily paper which has long ceased to exist, was a great favourite with my father, and we children used to look upon its columns with a sort of respectful awe. In 1855 began a new era in journalism with the foundation of the *Daily Telegraph* and the *Saturday Review*, the latter of which for many years exercised such a remarkable influence by reason of the able writers who at different times were members of its staff. Ten years later, in 1865, was founded the *Pall Mall Gazette*, which still flourishes under the very able editorship of my friend Sir Douglas Straight. It may not, perhaps, be generally known that the word " Gazette " is derived from the name of a small Venetian coin which was the price asked for the first newspaper sold in the city of Venice.

One of the most curious advertisements which has ever appeared was that inserted in the *Times* of 10th March 1858. This stated that the secretary of the Army and Navy Club would pay the sum of

£50 on the due conviction and punishment of the
offender who had sent the *Punch* cartoon of "The
Crowing Colonel" (a picture very unflattering to
the French army, it is hardly necessary to say),
accompanied by a forged message from the club
to an officer in command of a French regiment.
Notwithstanding this liberal reward, the culprit
was, I believe, never discovered.

Although so - called society journalism, as it
exists to-day, was unheard of, the newspapers of
the past occasionally inserted scraps of gossip dealing with well-known scandals and the like. In
1840 was published a somewhat amusing correspondence between Lady Seymour, the Queen of
Beauty at the Eglinton tournament (to whom
reference has before been made—she was afterwards Duchess of Somerset), and Lady Shuckburgh. Lady Seymour, having written to the
latter to ask the character of a servant named
Stedman, and whether she was a good plain cook,
received the reply that Lady Shuckburgh, having
a professed cook and housekeeper, knew nothing
about the under-servants. Upon this, Lady Seymour wrote again to explain that she understood
that Stedman, in addition to her other talents, had
had some practice in cooking for the little Shuck-
burghs. Lady Shuckburgh instructed her house-
maid to answer this as follows :—" Stedman informs
me that your ladyship does not keep either a cook
or a housekeeper, and that you only require a girl
who can cook a mutton chop ; if so, Stedman or any

other scullion will be found fully equal to cook for or manage the establishment of the Queen of Beauty."

At the Eglinton tournament, which had taken place just a year before, Prince Louis Napoleon appeared in a broadsword encounter with a Mr. Lamb, who enacted the part of the Knight of the White Rose.

Prince Napoleon's pretensions to the throne of France were not at that time regarded as being serious, though he himself ever entertained a fixed idea that he would one day succeed in obtaining the Imperial Crown. This conviction, which was firmly implanted in his mind, no doubt had a good deal to do with his ultimate success.

I remember him perfectly well, and suppose that I am about the last living of the partners who danced with him in the London ballrooms of some sixty years ago. An agreeable and clever talker, he could be amusing when he chose, and in later years, when Emperor, many stories were current as to his witty sayings. Perhaps the most amusing of these was the remark which he is supposed to have made at a fancy dress ball at the Tuileries, to which a certain lady had come attired in a costume which was an adornment rather than a covering. In the course of the evening the Imperial host approached this lady and, congratulating her upon her beautiful dress, at the same time inquired what it might be intended to represent. "L'Afrique, Sire," was the reply. "Très bien," said the Emperor, "I

ust then again congratulate you on the accuracy
with which you have followed the progress of geo-
graphical exploration; for of your dress, as of the
Dark Continent, it may truthfully be said que
c'est seulement la partie centrale qui n'est pas
encore découverte."

I was little in Paris during the second Empire,
but after the disastrous war of 1870 I paid a visit
to France and collected a few relics of that dreadful struggle.   Amongst other things I purchased a
number of very amusing caricatures, some of them
dealing with the humours of underground life in
the cellars during the siege of Paris; in others the
(very) irregular forces improvised by the so-called
Government of the Commune, such as the "Volti-
geurs de la Villette" and the "Chasseurs de Belle-
ville," were held up to ridicule.

English sympathies during the Franco-German
war were very generally given to the French,
and a good deal of sarcastic comment was passed
upon the pious utterances of the old Emperor
William, whose piety was nevertheless quite sincere.
Amongst other skits were published some very
ribald verses supposed to be written in imitation
of the Prussian King's letters to his Queen after
a victory.   They began, as far as I remember :—

> By Heaven's aid, my dear Augusta,
> We've gone another awful buster ;
> Ten thousand Frenchmen gone below,
> Praise God from whom all blessings flow.

At the time of the French reverses it was

thought that France could scarcely recover from
the effect of the terrible catastrophe which had
overtaken her, but to the astonishment of the
world this gloomy estimate was completely falsified, and in 1878 Europe, flocking to see the Great
Exhibition, found to its surprise and delight that
Paris, but a few years before bombarded and be-
leaguered, was, as the late George Augustus Sala
wrote, "comelier, richer, gayer, and more fascinating than ever." These words occurred in a very
well written and interesting book which Mr. Sala
produced after a visit to the Exhibition. It was
entitled *Paris Herself Again*, and though it is now
some twenty-nine years old it may still be read
with pleasure. Besides containing interesting information about Paris and the ways of its inhabitants, the volume is also full of amusing illustrations
by clever artists and caricaturists such as Bertall,
Cham and Grévin,—names now but memories
to survivors of the generation which admired a
verve almost amounting to genius.

Mr. Sala was a very clever draughtsman; I
rather think that it was he who drew a pano-
ramic roll illustrating the funeral procession which
accompanied the Iron Duke to his grave; this has
now become scarce, and when in good condition
is somewhat valuable. Mr. Sala's knowledge of
Paris was very thorough, and he had seen the
pleasure - loving city under many different conditions—during the Revolution of 1848, the *coup
d'état* of 1851 (when he was nearly shot), and

in addition he was all but murdered as a Prussian spy on the 4th of September 1870. Having received his early education in France he spoke French just as well as his native tongue, and was as much at home in that country as in England.

In former days there were certain well-known Englishmen who made their home in Paris, Lord Hertford and his brother, Lord Henry Seymour, and later on Sir Richard Wallace, being conspicuous examples. The last of those, however, whom I remember was Mr. Mackenzie Grieves, a gentleman of the old school who in early life had been an officer in the " Blues," and who died not a great number of years ago. Whenever he came to England he rarely failed to pay a visit to Strathfieldsaye, and there I frequently used to meet this polished representative of all that was best in the French society of the past. Possessing the most charming manners, there was something about him which vividly recalled what one had heard of the best days of the old régime ; his costume, for instance, though of extreme simplicity, had a particular note of distinction which has now totally disappeared from men's dress. A remarkable judge of horse flesh, especially of the great Norman horses known as *percherons,* he was also well known as a perfect master of the *haute école.* His judgment in Turf matters was also held in very great respect in Paris, and his immaculate frock-coat and voluminous tie were seldom absent from Long-

champs, where he had something to do with the
direction of the races.

One of the principal reasons given by Mr.
Mackenzie Grieves for his love of Paris was the
delightful nature of its environs, as well as the
charm of the Bois de Boulogne, an ideal spot for
a morning ride.   London, alas! has nothing to
equal this, and in these days one has to go many
miles out before reaching the real country.

One of the greatest changes which I have witnessed, indeed, has been the overflow of London
into the pleasant fields which formerly lay quite
close to what are now the inner line of suburbs.
Streets and streets of uninteresting and depressing-
looking little houses now cover districts which not
so very long ago were quite rural.   About the
time I was married people used very often to
drive out to the market gardens, which were then
quite close, and eat fruit there.   The strawberry
season was the great time for these excursions.
In 1840 quite large nursery gardens existed at
Paddington, whilst some hundreds of acres near
what is now Battersea Park were utilised for the
same purpose up to much more recent times.   The
gardens here were especially noted for the early
fruit and vegetables which they produced, as also
for their asparagus, said to be the best grown in the
neighbourhood of London.

Hammersmith, on the other hand, was famous
for its fruit,—strawberries, raspberries, and the
like, being grown in great perfection.   Fulham also

formerly produced a great quantity of fruit and vegetables, and though several acres of land which had previously served for this purpose were put to other uses in 1865, the ground stretching towards Hammersmith and North End was pretty well covered with market gardens as late as the 'seventies. In my childhood, of course, Chelsea and Hammersmith were considered quite in the country. As an instance of this, it may be mentioned that in the Royal Blue Book for 1826 Chelsea Farm is given as the "country residence" of Lady Cremorne. The ground occupied by this lady's house, after being utilised for the celebrated Cremorne Gardens, has now been covered with streets.

Every year London grows bigger and bigger, and the day now seems to be not far distant when the road to southern watering-places, such as Brighton, will run through an almost unbroken line of villas. Of late there seems to be a tendency to live more and more out of London, City men and others making a practice of travelling up and down every day, journeys which can now be made in perfect comfort and convenience. Luxury in travelling, as in most other things, has much increased.

Marvellous it is how, within my lifetime, the general standard of comfort amongst all classes has been raised, though not, I fear, with any particular increase of contentment. The so-called necessaries of life have become very

much multiplied, and there is now a universal
craving for amusement which was quite unknown
in old days.   Everything is comparative, and
the luxury of to-day becomes the necessity of
to-morrow.   The life of the poorer classes living
in the country, notwithstanding the fact that wages
were lower than at present, was certainly not an
unhappy one in old days, when there was a bond
of sympathy existing between landlord and tenantry
which is now, except in some few cases, a thing of
the past.   Classes were then more strictly defined,
and the farmers, the majority of them sturdy
yeomen of far more distinguished descent than
most of the brand-new Peers of to-day, would
have laughed to scorn any idea of calling themselves gentlemen; now, however, it would seem
that every one is a gentleman or a lady.

Universal and, as many think, misdirected
education has completely destroyed the picturesque
side of village life, and in the place of the quaint
old traditions and picturesque beliefs handed down
by their forefathers, modern villagers possess a
rudimentary smattering of all sorts of useless
knowledge, which, imperfectly assimilated, serves
but to render them loutish copies of the townsmen
whom it is their ambition to imitate.

Students and archæologists, it is true, do their
best to preserve some record of the old country
traditions and ways which have been so ruthlessly
destroyed.   How dignified and spiritual was the
idea which many of them conveyed!   Take, for

instance, the old belief which formerly prevailed amongst Norfolk fisher-folk, that deaths mostly occurred at the falling of the tide. From this East Anglian legend was it that Dickens drew his beautiful picture of the death of Barkis. "People can't die along the coast," said Mr. Peggotty, "except when the tide's pretty nigh out. They can't be born unless it's pretty nigh in—not properly born till flood. He's agoing out with the tide—he's agoing out with the tide." And so Peggotty and David Copperfield watched by Barkis's bed till, it being low water, the latter went out with the tide.

At rural weddings in some parts of Norfolk it was formerly the custom to strew the path of the happy couple with fern leaves, and to greet them on their exit from church with wedding peals rung on all the handbells of the village, whilst in more remote times an elder sister was by an old custom obliged to dance in a hog's trough should her younger sister marry before her. Country maidens in Norfolk who were desirous of a swain used also to recite the following spell, " a clover of two "— that is, a piece of clover with but two leaves— being supposed to possess much magical power :—

A clover, a clover of two, put in your right shoe,
The first young man you meet in field, street, or lane
You'll have him or one of his name.

As has been said, the advent of the school board rang the death-knell of rural tradition and legend, and the rustic of to-day considers himself far above any such superstitions.   Strange old tales and folk-lore handed down from long-dead generations have little interest for the villager of to-day, who seems to spend a good part of his time lolling about the village street, and flattening his nose against the shop windows, which seem mostly to be filled with those brilliantly coloured tins of foreign preserved meats and provisions which our ancestors, happily for themselves, never knew.   The countryman takes his pleasures more sadly than of yore.   His rough old amusements and sports are gone; about the only excitement which penetrates into rural life being furnished by some realistically dished-up tragedy or *cause célèbre* imbibed through the medium of a halfpenny paper.

The folklore of East Anglia has been very thoroughly recorded in various publications, amongst them the *East Anglian Magazine*, which for some time was edited by the late Miss Mary Henniker, who for so many years lived in the little house in Berkeley Street, familiar to a large circle as the residence of her universally popular younger sister. Her death, which occurred but a few months ago, was the cause of much sincere and genuine regret to all her friends.   Miss Helen Henniker, though in latter years labouring under considerable physical disability, ever retained an extraordinary amount of good-natured vitality.   She was, indeed, one of those people whom it is difficult to realise as being dead.   Bright, vivacious, and good-natured to a quite unusual degree, " Helen," as she was affectionately called, possessed a most comprehensive knowledge of all the different types which make up that motley crowd known as London society. She was welcome everywhere, and the disappearance of this kindly and original pesonality called forth many a sincere expression of real grief.

Within the last few years death has robbed me of many valued friends, some, like that most kindly of men, Lord Haliburton, dying after severe illness, and others, like my dear cousin Sir Spencer Walpole, suddenly struck down in the apparent fulness of health and strength. Sir Spencer, who attained a position of some eminence as a painstaking and accurate writer of contemporary history, was by nature a man of most judicial and well-balanced mind, and was an almost unique instance, as he himself would admit, of what I may call a serious Walpole, for the majority of my family, since the days of Sir Robert, have never been conspicuous for any particular mental stability. Mayhap some of the southern blood of old Pierre Lombard, a native of Nîmes, whose daughter was our ancestress, is the cause of this. Sir Spencer himself used to say that this erratic and impulsive temperament had in his case been modified by the marriage of his great-grand-father to a lady of Dutch nationality, and his even temper and calm mental outlook would certainly seem to have justified such a supposition.

Erratic, and sometimes lacking balance to the

verge of eccentricity, the Walpoles were ever a somewhat curious race, their chief characteristic, perhaps, being an intense love of frivolity combined with a real liking for literature and art.   For music, however, few of us have cared at all, whilst most have positively hated its more serious side.   As a rule, too indolent to grasp the political laurels which their intellects were in several cases easily capable of winning, and not by nature fitted for a public career, the Walpoles have now for many generations scarcely attempted to emerge from the humdrum backwaters of private life, the founder of our fortunes, Sir Robert, remaining the first and last great politician which the family has produced. Nevertheless, there is a compensation in that very nature which has rendered serious effort so unattractive to us, for with something of the child's dislike of order and restraint, we have also the counterbalancing advantage of the child's buoyancy of disposition and easy forgetfulness of trouble, retained in some cases to an age when others of more serious temperament have long ceased to take an interest in anything at all.   And now, with these somewhat egotistical reflections, I will take leave of my readers, only hoping that their patience will not have been overtaxed by the perusal of these Notes, Memories, and Recollections.

APPENDIX

APPENDIX

SOME SECRET NEGOTIATIONS OF THE PRETENDER WITH SIR ROBERT WALPOLE

SOME little time ago my nephew, Lord Orford, discovered in his library at Wolterton some rather interesting old papers dealing with certain negotiations which appear to have at one time been afoot between the Pretender and Sir Robert Walpole. It is said that a picture formerly existed at Houghton in which both Sir Robert (as a youth) and his father were shown wearing the Stuart tartan, but notwithstanding this my ancestor has always been regarded as an uncompromising upholder of the Hanoverian succession. Nevertheless, it would appear from the correspondence which he discovered that at one time Sir Robert was not altogether disinclined to learn the Pretender's proposals, though of course he may have only done this from diplomatic reasons. The principal portion of the documents in question consists of a memorandum drawn up by a certain Mr. Thomas Carte, whose name is well known to historical students. A nonjuring clergyman, he had strong Jacobite leanings, and is known to have been much interested in the Stuart cause. My nephew's father, Mr. Frederick Walpole, appears to have made some inquiries about him of his friend Mr. Whitwell Elwin, the well-known editor of the *Quarterly Review*, for the following letter was found appended to the correspondence :—

BOOTON RECTORY, NORWICH,
March 18, 1865.

DEAR MR. WALPOLE—I have been an age in answering your letter owing to my reading the name of Thomas Carte as Thomas

319

Lart. I could not remember that I had ever heard of the name of the latter gentleman, and I searched books and indexes in vain in order to discover what my memory would not supply. Five minutes ago I took up your note, and again scrutinised the word, when all of a sudden it flashed upon me that the name was Carte, though your C is very indistinct. You will find an account of him in any English Biographical Dictionary. If you want any details beyond what an ordinary book of reference will supply you must come to me again. Andrew Stone was sub-preceptor to George 3. when Prince of Wales. There are stories of him in Horace Walpole, Mahon's History, and other books. He was chiefly noted, I think, for his supposed Jacobite bias in early days. You must not assume that I shall be always as dilatory in answering questions. I should have written at once if I could have solved your problem.

Two or three months, I presume, will bring an election which will carry you into Parliament, and long may you flourish there. I do not hear a word of East Norfolk. If Stracey is goose enough to stand it will only end in a fall. He will have no support worth the name. I was delighted to hear that you and Lord O. were one again.—Believe me, ever sincerely yours,

W. Elwin.

At the beginning of the memorandum is the following note in Sir Robert Walpole's handwriting :—

This Paper was delivered to me, the 15th of Sept. 1739, at nine o'clock at night at my house at Chelsea,[1] by Mr. Tho. Cart, a non-jurying Clergyman, as a Copy of Heads, etc., drawn up by Him, by order of the Pretender, as explanatory of some conferences held by Him at Rome upon the subject of the security of the Church of England and delivered to the Pretender by Him in July last. R. Walpole.

The memorandum itself, which is somewhat lengthy, appears to have been drawn up with a view to satisfying Sir Robert that in the event of the Pretender being placed upon the throne of England no attempt would be made to interfere with the privileges of the Protestant Church. It begins :—

---

[1] The site of Sir Robert's house in Chelsea is now covered by Walpole Street, which traverses the ground upon which his mansion stood.

Heads Offered to Consideration in Relation to the Security and Advantage of the Church of England

When in the year 1721 I looked over Archbp. Sancroft's manuscripts and papers, I found among them one containing a scheme for the government of the Church of England under a R.C. Prince; which I thought exceeding well drawn, as well for preserving a just prerogative in the Crown, as for providing a reasonable security for the Church. It appeared to me to be drawn at the time of the Bill of Exclusion, when the late K. Charles offered to come into any scheme of that nature, though he was resolved never to passe that Bill, as conceiving it to be contrary to honour, justice and conscience. I laid that scheme aside, with some curious discourses of the Archbps. and abundance of valuable letters which I selected in order to write his life. But being to passe into Leicestershire and spend 3 or four months before I got to London, I left them at Fresingfield, intending to send for them to town, as soon as I got thither. But being forced to come abroad not long after in 1722, they still remained at Fresingfield, and were swept away by Dr. Tanner, then Chancellor of Norwich, with the rest of the ArchBps. manuscripts, which he bought in the beginning of 1728, about a quarter of a year before I returned to England. Dr. Tanner dying about 3 years ago and leaving all his MSS. to the University of Oxford, I made two journeys thither last year to search for this scheme: but though I looked over every individual paper of his that had been delivered to the University, I could not find what I searched for. This makes me conclude that the Drs. Executors did not deliver to the University all the MSS. that were bequeathed them; and the rather because I did not observe among them half even of the most curious MSS. of the ArchBps. which I had taken a short catalogue of for my own use.

In defect of this scheme, I venture to draw up my own thoughts on the subject, and to mention some particulars which I conceive may be either for the security or for the advantage of the Church of England.

First, that which I imagine would be a very good and perhaps a better security to it than any other privilege, is the restoring

Y

to the Clergy their ancient right of taxing themselves; a right enjoyed by the Clergy in all parts of Europe, and never enjoyed by the English till 3 years after King Charles the Second's restoration; when the Convocation then sitting gave it up by a Solemn Act, without ever consulting their Constituents, reserving, however, to themselves by an express clause a power to resume it whenever they should think fitting.   It would be against all law, justice, and equity to deny them such a resumption whenever they demand it; which they are now universally desirous of doing, having seen the Sitting of Convocations interrupted, and that representative Body and chief judicature of the Church rendered useless, almost ever since they gave up this right.   The House of Commons, fond of allocations of extending their power, and grasping at everything that will aggrandize themselves, may not perhaps care to part with this new branch of their power; but it is not the interest of the Crown that the Commons should grow too great, and the experience of 1641 ought for ever to make a Prince, and indeed all orders of men, jealous of every accession of power which accrews to that Body : and if ever they are to be prevailed with to part with this additional branch thereof, it is most likely to be done on the account here mentioned, viz. for the security of religion.   For by the constant and regular sitting of the Convocation concurrent with every Parliament (which will be fully provided for by restoring to the Clergy this right of taxing themselves), it will be scarce possible for any material steps to be taken for the introducing of another religion, when there is a body of men sitting and on the watch against all measures of that kind, and ready to oppose them by their weighty and prudent remonstrances.   There is no method so proper for redressing grievances as by returning to the old ways of our Constitution; all deviations from which have ever been found of mischievous consequence.   The inconveniences of new institutions are seldom thought of till they are felt; but we have the experience of ages to shew us the wisdom and advantages of ancient usages : and as no inconvenience ever yet attended this right of taxation during the many hundreds of years that the Clergy enjoyed it, it cannot with the least pretence to reason be surmised that any should now attend the restoring it to them.   I knew not whether I need observe that the only reason why the Convocations

grants of subsidies were inserted in Acts of Parliament was that
the Collectors thereof might have a power of distraining on the
glebe and goods of the Clergy; which could not be given by any
Ecclesiastical authority.

2. Another thing that would contribute greatly to the
security of the Church, and be as much for its benefit, is a
repeal of the Act of Submission passed in the time of Henry 8,
which hinders ArchBps. and Bps. from holding provincial
and diocesan synods, to which they were obliged by the old
canons of the Church, but are deterred from doing so by the
dread of a Praemunire, which in such case they would incur
according to the terms of that Act. The right of holding such
synods in provinces and dioceses, for the due ordering of Ecclesiastical affairs and the better execution of the Canons, is as
ancient as the institution of Christianity, and is enjoyed in all
Christian countries upon earth, except in England. For the Act
of Submission having never taken place in Ireland (where as
there had been no exercise of the Legative power, so there had
been no obedience paid to it, and consequently no penalties
thereby incurred), the Clergy in that Island still enjoy the
right of meeting in provincial and diocesan synods. ArchBp.
King of Dublin lately held one of the first sort, and the Acts of
one of the latter kind held by Bedell, Bp. of Kidmore, are
published in the life of that prelate: which are sufficient
evidences of this right of the Church of Ireland. It was in this
manner that the Primitive Church was governed, and it is fit
that every National Church in times posteriour to their should
be governed in the same manner; as that of England indeed
ever was till the Act of Submission. These Synods will be a
great security to the Church of England in the intervals of
Parliaments and Convocations.

They will be likewise of great use in other respects, and
contribute much to the ends of religion. They may restore the
just discipline of the Church, and correct abundance of grievances, as well as in regard of the scandalous corruption of the
spiritual Courts, as of the shameful oppression of the Clergy by
some Bps. in many cases. Bishops in France and other countries
abroad, tho' obliged by the Canons to hold diocesan Synods
every year, are yet not very fond of holding them, because they
are a curb upon their authority. For tho' they can put a

negative upon the resolutions of the majority, yet being often ashamed of dissenting from truth and reason, the Presbyters or incumbents of livings are still found to have the greatest weight in such Synods. And possibly for the same reason they may be as little agreeable to our English Bishops, who having in a manner quite lost the power of exercising any part of their authority over the Laity, endeavour continually to make themselves amends by lording it over other Clergy ; insisting (as their Archdeacons also, after their example and in virtue of their delegated authority, have done) upon the oath of canonical obedience, which they pretend obliges the Clergy to obey them in everything whatever that they enjoin which is not absolutely unlawfull ; an interpretation of that oath contrary to the sense of all Canonists abroad, who agree that it only obliges to obedience in such things as are prescribed by the Canons. But the fonder they are of power, the more necessary is it that their power should be restrained to the ancient bounds, and that institutions of such great use as Diocesan and Provincial Synods should be restored.

It was in such provincial Synods, that all disputes about matters of faith were determined and heresies condemned during the 3 first centuries of Christianity. It is in these that the authority and jurisdiction of the Church has in all ages been chiefly and most usefully exerted. Tis a hardship peculiar to the Church of England to be deprived of a benefit which all other Churches upon earth enjoy, and therefore it is much to be wished this right of holding provincial Synods were restored. There would then be no want of visible judge of doctrine and controversies, such as served to direct the primitive Christians and martyrs in the first ages of the Gospel in the way of salvation. There would not then be any want either of a ready antidote against any heretical or irreligious books that are published nowadays with encouragement rather than impunity, or of power to censure them and punch the authors thereof if they should prove to be Clergymen. There would not then, if any Bp. or other Ecclesiastick should preach and maintain any heretical tenets or assert any of the new erroneous doctrines which the Court or Church of Rome have grafted upon the ancient faith of the Church, or be guilty of any other crime the Canons have decreed to be punished with deprivation, be any want of canonical authority to take cognisance of the cause, and pronounce sentence in a regular manner. For it is in these provincial Synods that Bishops have in all ages of the Church been ever judged and deprived in such cases: and if the same method had been established in England in Q. Mary's time, the church would not then have been ruined. For none of the Edwards Bps. were deprived canonically by a Synod of their comprovincial Bps., but by a few persons, some of them Laicks, empowered by a particular commission from Her Majesty. The High Commission Court has indeed been since put down by an Act of Parliament, which provides that neither that Court nor any like it shall ever be erected for the future. But lawyers may possible dispute whether that Act extends to such particular commission as Q. Mary issued (which perhaps were not thought of in 1690 when this Act passed); so that it is highly to be wished that Provincial Synods might be restored, and the offences of Bps. and Clergymen inferring deprivation, subject to their cognisance.

Diocesan Synods never intermeddled in matters of faith. Their business was confined to points of mere discipline, and their chief care was to make proper regulations for inforcing the practise of that discipline, and to provide for the due observance of the Canons within their district. Offences against these were also within their cognisance, and whatever else was under the jurisdiction of the Bp. in his single capacity, came also before him when at the head of these Synods; which may be composed either of all incumbents in his Diocese, or of the Chapter of the Cathedral, the Archdeacons, Rural Deans, and two Proctors chosen by the Clergy of each Deanery. And if in the interval of these Synods a Bp. was obliged to consult with the Chapter of his Church, and the Rural Deans of his Diocese before he gave judgment in any cause, and to use them as his co-assessors in hearing it, this would add much to the dignity and effect of such sentence, and would probably reconcile abundance to Episcopary, that are at present disaffected to that kind of government.

There was in the last Sitting Convocation in 1713/4 a proposal made and an intention formed or reviving the institution of Rural Deans, and it would probably have taken place in the next, had there not happened a change of government which has ever since put an end to the Sitting of Convocations. But were that old institution revived, and such a method of episcopal and synodical jurisdiction settled, it might easily be so adjusted, as to reform abundance of shameful practices in the spiritual Courts to prevent any false doctrines either heretical or Roman from being instilled into the people. For whilst there is so short and easy a method of calling those who reach them to an accompt before their brethren of the Clergy in their own neighbourhood, scarce anybody will dare to attempt such an innocation, when he must expect a censure to be immediately passed upon him by his Bp. not alone, but assisted by a venerable Council of Rural Deans recommended for their merit by the body of the Clergy, and antecedent to his crime approved of and constituted by their Diocesan.

There was at the same time another proposal made of reviving also the charge of Suffragan Bps. as anciently used in the Church of England, or as at last regulated in the reign of Henry, and continued to that of Q. Elizabeth. And as some Dioceses in England are too large, they might be very useful for the due exercise of discipline, as well as for reforming the corruptions and lessening the power of Spiritual Courts.

It might be observed that the corruption of those Courts is not owing to the Bishops. Some of these have endeavoured to reform them, but in vain, they have put limiting clauses into the patents, and they have granted to Vicars general, Chancellors and Commissaries, but still to no purpose, even with regard to the granting of licenses to preach, which being, by the Rubrick of the Common Prayer book established by Act of Parliament, reserved expressly to Bps. they naturally thought they might very well restrain their deputies from granting them. But these deputies, distinguished by the several titles before mentioned, pretend that a Bp. having constituted them Vicars general, Chancellors or Commissaries by patent, they are in virtue thereof actually invested with all the power usually annexed to such office, and that all restraining clauses are null by common Law : and so they continue to exercise a power in those cases wherein by the express terms of the patent they are debarred the exercise thereof. Our Common Law is in truth but too favourable to such iniquities, and it is highly reasonable that an Act should pass to restrain the power of these officers to the terms of their patent; or perhaps it may not be amiss to provide that such offices should be held only for the life or incumbency of the person that grants them; or if allowed to be granted to persons quamdice bene se gesserint, certain cases may be specified wherein these officers shall be removable by the judgment of the Bp. in conjunction with the Chapter and Rural Deans of the Diocese, from whose sentence there should lye no appeal to Common Law.

The Courts of Common Law, however they have intrenches on the jurisdiction of the Spiritual Courts, do yet give countenance and protection to all their iniquities, which serve to bring them in business; and this makes the Common Lawyers so loath to see them reformed, and so ready to baffle all attempts of that nature. The judges thereof have stuck to no maxim so constantly as to that scandalous one of St. Edw. Cokes, A Boni judicies est ampliare jurisdictionem curice suce, and have by monstrous fictions, and by the help of numberless querks and pretences swallowed up in a manner all the jurisdiction of other Courts, as the Lord Constable and Marshals, Admiralty, etc. in order to draw all business to themselves. Thus also as often as they please they call by prohibitions (for which they never want pretences) all causes before them from Spiritual Courts and other Ecclesiastical or Visitatorical jurisdictions: and when a cause is once brought into their Courts, where they can invent and start an hundred points and issues to be argued, there is no end of the expense or no hopes of a decision, so that it must drop at last after several years continuance without any determination as the late affair of Dr. Bentley. It is very fit there should be prohibitions in many cases, as there are appels d'abus in France; but it is as fair that those cases should be settled fixed and determinate. There was in the time of K. James I. a judgment given upon this subject by the King in his Privy Council (to whose judicature it properly belongs to decide of the just authority of different Courts when they quarrel about their jurisdiction) and proper bounds were fixed to the authority, as well of Spiritual Courts as of those of Common Law, which were tolerably well observed till the troubles of 1641 threw all government into confusion, and Episcopacy being destroyed and the jurisdiction of Bps. suppressed with their Order, the Common Law carried all before it, swallowed up the Ecclesiastical authority, and has ever since kept a great part of what it then invaded.

This is now grown to so intolerable an height, that at present there is not any Ecclesiastical authority in England to call a Clergyman to an accompt, and punish him for preaching or printing any heretical doctrine or any erroneous tenets of the Court of Rome : so that unless the Common Law be restrained in this respect, and the use and authority of provincial and diocesan Synods be revived, I do not see how it can be practicable to secure the Church of England from being overrun with false doctrines. For unless there be a short and easy way of punishing those that vent them, many will be induced to do so, when temptations shall be offered and encouragements given for the attempt : and this power can be vested nowhere so properly, so safely and so unexceptionally as in provincial and diocesan Synods, agreeable to the constitution of the Primitive Church.

If it be apprehended that these Synods may be apt to assume too great a power (not to say that such an apprehension is groundless) it is a very easy matter to prevent their doing so by restraining their jurisdiction to the crimes of heresy, false doctrine and Simony and to the persons of the Clergy, leaving all Laicks who are guilty of the like offences to the cognisance of the Civil Courts.

3. Another method for the security of religion is, to distinguish between *Legatine,* and the *Archiepiscopal* power of the ArchBp. of Canterbury, and to reduce that exorbitant power he possesses at present to what it was before the year 1400, when he enjoyed only his Archiepiscopal authority, not being made *legaties natus* till after that year. These two powers are compounded at present, and the ArchBp, though he enjoys the legatine, only in virtue of the exercise thereof by his predecessors, derived originally from a Papal grant of no force in England, does yet continue to exercise it, tho' he hereby encroaches upon the jurisdiction and rights of all the Bishops and the Kingdom in several cases, and by the abuse thereof may ruin the established church when he pleases. It was in virtue of this Legatine power, which is as yet affirmed by no law, that Dr. Tennison deprived Watson Bp. of St. Davids by his single authority ; tho' according to the ancient Canons and constitution of the Christian Church, no Bp.

can be regularly condemned, but by the sentence of a Provincial Synod, in which twelve Bps. are present. Tis easy to see how fatal such a claim of power, now supported by the seeming countenance of an House of Lords, may be in its consequence to the Church of England.

There was in the time of Henry 8 (when the Papal power was abolished in England) an authority vested in the ArchBp. of Canterbury to grant faculties and dispensations in all cases where the Pope used before to dispense. Under pretext of this general grant Archbishops have taken upon themselves to grant dispensations in cases where the Pope himself could not effectually dispense. Such particularly is the power of qualifying persons for living and dignities annexed by Law to certain degrees in our Universities. The Pope had certainly long used to confer honorary degrees on such as he saw fit, but these degrees never qualified persons in France or other countries abroad for benefices and dignities appropriated to Graduates in their Universities. This is so settled a point that even in the Pope's own territory of the Comtat de Venagsein about Avignon, tho' he confess such benefices on those who are not graduates, yet he always in his bulls obliges them to take their degree requisite in the Universities. Yet in England ArchBps. of Canterbury have of late exerted their power in numberless instances to the great discouragement of learning and prejudice of our Universities. This is a point that well deserves to be corrected.

4. As the Universities are a nursery for the Church, and a great support of the established religion, there cannot be too great an assurance given of the preservation of their privileges, their statutes and rights of election ; which should not be liable to be invaded, by any Ecclesiastical Commission for the extraordinary visitation of particular Colleges or of the Universities in general, or by writs of Mandamus for putting in Heads or Fellows of Colleges, contrary to their Statutes and right of election ; or in fine, by appeals from the sentence of Visitors to the Courts of Common Law, where they have been controverted of late ; particularly in Dr. Bentley's case ; tho' such sentences were ever deemed unappealable and have been so declared in the House of Lords in the case of Exeter College, wherein they gave judgment against their own jurisdiction in this point.

But if it should be apprehended that an unlimited restraint

from all relief at Common Law, may in some cases be hard on a sufferer by a Visitor's sentence, the absolute prohibition of an appeal may be thus limited, "unless the body of the University assembled in a Convocation (whereof, and as well of the occasion of its being called as the day and time when it is to be held, publick notice shall be given a month before) shall within a year or 6 months after such sentence petition the King for a revision thereof; and then his Majesty may issue out a Commission of Delegates, composed of the Chancellor of the University, the Visitors of all the Colleges therein, and an equal number of Drs. of Civil Law, to review the process and give a final decision." If University causes come into Common Law Courts, there is no end of them, and no supporting the expense : and our ancestors wisely provided they should never come there : but those Courts are hardly ever at a loss for pretexts to draw all causes to the Bar, and to break through all regulations. Their power is now grown to an exorbitant height, and with it their oppression is extended ; so that since the Chancery, by being put almost ever since the Reformation into the hands of Common Lawyers, is become in a manner a Common Law Court where equity is little considered, they are become one of the greatest grievances of the Nation.

5. Whereas Deans and Chapters of Cathedral Churches in England do at present retain an empty shadow of the privilege they formerly had of choosing their own Bps. in that a Conge d'Elire is constantly upon the vacancy of a see, sent to them and requiring them to proceed to such election ; but they are obliged to choose the person named to them by the King in a letter missive sent at the same time, under the pain of incurring a Praemunire and subjecting themselves to the penalties of the Act of Henry 8 regulating the election and confirmation of Bishops. It were to be wished that a better regulation might be made in this respect, and that Deans and Chapters may, in the case of a person whom they cannot in conscience contribute by any act of theirs to advance to a See of which he is unworthy (by having preached or published heretical and false doctrines, or by being guilty of Simony or other crimes punishable by deprivation), be allowed the liberty of declining their choice and approbation without being liable to the said penalties. It may not perhaps be fit to make them judges in the case any further

than relates to their own conduct, and therefore upon their signifying the crime of which the person named in the letter missive is accused and on account whereof they cannot choose him, and of the grounds they have to presume of his guilt, till he is judicially cleared, the cognisance thereof may in the case of a Bp. be taken by a Provincial Synod, and in the case of a Presbyter, by a Synod of the Diocese, wherein he has usually resided; and if the person be acquitted therein, the Chapter then to be obliged to choose him under all the penalties of the aforesaid Act, but, if he be condemned, to be justified in their rejecting him, and a better to be named in his stead.

There are some other regulations of a like kind, that would be useful with regard to the inferior Clergy, viz. : that every Certificate of good behaviour and right principles in religion, usually brought to a Bp. by every person that comes for Ordination or for Institution to a Living, be signed by the Rural Dean of the district wherein he has resided for the time mentioned therein; (unless such person hath been constantly resident in the University, in which case the Certificate of his College may serve as at present) otherwise the Bp. to be at liberty to reject him. And if a Bp. upon examining a person presented to a benefice shall find him illiterate and unqualified for the Cure, he shall appoint such person to attend him another day, when he shall likewise summon the Rural Deans of his Diocese to appear and shall in their presence examine the pretentee ; and if upon the concurrent judgment of all or of the major part, or of two thirds of them, he shall be declared illiterate and insufficent for the charge of a cure of Souls, the Bp. shall be justified in refusing him institution without being aliable to any suit in law, or other prosecution whatever.

Such expedients as these afford undoubtedly a very rational security to the Church of England, and yet none of them really intrench on the just prerogative of the Crown, unless the redeeming of the Church from the slavist part of the Letter missive put upon it contrary to the first article of Magna Charta be deemed to do so, tho' it does not infringe the Kings right of naming the Sees but only provides against the ill consequences of his being deceived and drawing into the naming of unworthy prelates; or unless it be in the waving of the claim of right to make writs of Mandamus for putting Heads and

Fellows upon Colleges in the University; which if it was a right of the Crown, has been exercised very rarely and never without great odium, and which seems only to be founded upon a notion, that the incorporation of Colleges and establishment of Status for electing the Heads and members thereof, as well as for regulating their conduct, tho' made at the request of the Founders who endowed them, yet derived their force from the authority of the Crown, which might therefore dispense with Statuts of their own creating and rights of their own granting, whenever there was occasion or it was thought proper to exert the unlimitedness of the prerogative. But if this maxim were good and would hold in Law, it would hold as well in regard to Corporations as Colleges; and yet it was never used in the case of the former, unless upon some crime and forfeiture of their privileges, or at least on a pretence thereof, and even then when advantage was taken of such forfeiture (as was the case a little before the Revolution) it raised a terrible ferment in the nation.

There are some other things which tho' not immediately relating to the security of the Church of England, yet being much for the benefit, dignity, and credit of the Clergy, will contribute not a little to its support.

The English being naturally a serious and devout people ran eagerly in all ages into all the modes of religion then in vogue. Hence an infinite number of Monasteries of all kinds were erected in the Kingdom, and the Religious thereof being by their institution more attached to the Pope than the secular Clergy were, it came to pass that when the Papal power was first introduced into England in the reign of Henry the First (in whose time the Cardinal de Crema came over the first Legate of the See of Rome, and appeals to that Court began to be introduced), they soon got the Pope to exert the plentitude of his power, and the sovereignty he claimed over all the possessions of the Spirituality (tho' originally the grant of our Kings) and to appropriate the tythes glebe and revenues of livings to Monasteries. This was done generally between the years 1120 and 1250. Hereupon the Religious of these Monasteries, keeping all the great tythes and sometimes the small ones also, and even the oblations (which in those days were very considerable) to themselves either supplied the cures by one of their own body,

or endowed a resident vicar either with a slender portion of the
small tythes, or with a stipend in money, which, whatever it was
in those days, is now very inconsiderable, and insufficient for his
maintenance.   When Monasteries were dissolved, and their
lands given to Henry 8, the tythes and revenues of Livings thus
appropriated to religious houses were given to him at the same
time, and were alienated by that Prince together with the
Abbey lands.   Thus was the Church miserably impoverished,
and even to the time of the Rebellion in 1642 there were left
6000 Vicarages in England under £30 a year, 4000 under £20
and 2000 not worth £10 a year.   The Bishops upon the
Restoration having abundance of leases, particularly of Tythes
(for Q. Elizabeth had forced their predecessors to exchange
their manners of their Sees for the tythes then remaining in the
Crown which she could not keep in conscience as she alledged)
that were either expired during the troubles or were near
expiring, took care in the renewal thereof to augment great
numbers of these poor vicarages.   Private persons have since
made them considerable benefactions and many Vicarages have
been of late augmented out of the revenue of the First fruits
and Tenths : yet still there are some thousands so meanly provided for that they do not afford a competent subsistence to a
Minister.

Of all Livings throughout the Kingdom none suffered so
much in the general alienation of Church revenues as those in
Cities and great Towns ; for scarce any of these were without
one or more Monasteries, the Monks whereof supplying the cure
of those Livings, had only a small stipend for their pains.
Hence these Livings are the most provided for of any in
England, two or three of them being often united together to
make up about £30 a year for an Incumbent, whose poverty
neither allows him to buy books to increase his stock of learning,
nor to live with a dignity suitable to his character, not to do
that good or speak with that authority in his parish which a
better income would enable him to do, and generally speaking
worthless Livings will be filled with worthless Clergymen.   This
hath proved as much to the disservice of the Crown as of the
Church.   For these great Towns being sorrily supplied with
Ministers, and being many of them thronged with Calvinists
that came out of the Low countries, Germany and other foreign

countries and settled there for the sake of trade, the Puritan party in the reigns of K. James and K. Charles took care to send Lecturers thither (to whom they gave large stipends) to propagate Sedition and disaffection to the Church and Crown among the inhabitants of those great Towns, which by that means generally sided with the Parliament against the King in the rebellion of 1641, and by their wealth contributed greatly to the neine of His Majesties affairs. Had these Towns been duly supplied with a learned and well affected Clergy, the rebellion would probably have been prevented or the event of the war have proved more favourable to the royal cause. There are few things would be more serviceable to the interests both of the Church and Crown than a proper endowment of the Livings in such great Towns and Cities: and if any forfeited houses therein, or forfeited lands and tythes of lands adjoining thereto were applied thereto, the benefit to both would be great, and the Clergy in such Cities would by their interests as well as principle be obliged to support the Crown from which they desire such benefactions.

K. Charles the First gave all the Tythes remaining in his time to the Crown throughout Ireland to the Churches whereunto they originally belonged, as often as Leases of Crown lands were to be renewed or grants thereof expired. K. Charles the Second after the Restoration gave all the forfeited tythes in that Kingdom to the Church. Many grants of lands in England, with tythes annexed thereto or part thereof, may probably be now expired or are continually dropping in to the Crown; and forfeitures of a like nature will according to the course of human affairs be making from time to time and afford opportunities of the like benefactions; for if tythes were exempted as well in the renewal of such grants as in the remission of forfeitures, they might be very usefully applied for the better endowment of churches in popular Cities. In this or the like manner may that great inconvenience be in a good measure removed.

A noble grant hath been made of the First Fruits, and Tenths for the augmentation of small Livings, which will in a course of years be a considerable, though slow remedy for this evil. But it is still a question whether the Church will gain more by that benefaction, than it will lose in the same term of years, by the late change of the maxims of the Court of

Exchequer in relation to tythes by the great encouragement which the Judges thereof give to pretended and unreasonable moduses (or certain trifling payments of money in lieu of tythes of 20, 30 or fifty times their value) and by the continual multiplying of such moduses all over the Kingdom; which Gentlemen are labouring by all ways to find pretexts to create, and corrupt patrons have too great opportunities of effecting with regard to livings in their Advowson, so that the evil is not unlikely in some years to grow universal.

The case of the Clergy is certainly very hard in this respect. They come to a Living generally Strangers to the place and ignorant of the rights and dues belonging to the Church. It is the interest and commonly the business of every one in their parish to impose upon them with false accounts of the value of their tythes, and to draw them into agreements much below the real value thereof. Their predecessor being dead, his papers neglected or carried off by his executors, they derive little knowledge from either. After long waiting for some equivalent to the large expense of a University education, coming at last into a benefice, they are glad to take the first offer that will make them easy, being either by their former manner of life and attachment to their studies, indisposed to have their time and thoughts taken up in the collecting of tythes, or by the ignorance of country affairs utterly unqualified to manage so new and troublesome an affair as the gathering of them in kind, not caring to oppress or disoblige their parishioners, or to go to law upon a footing they do not fully understand, and at an expense they are not able to bear; especially since they have only a life interest in the Living, and if they can but be easy for their own time, they are willing to leave the burden of asserting the rights of the Church to their next successor. These circumstances and this temper of mind induce the Clergy too often to afford those who have a mind to make a prey of the revenue of the Church, means of effecting their dishonourable purpose; in which they are not a little favoured by the proceedings of the Courts of Westminster Hall.

Great care had been taken in ancient times to preserve the revenue of the church, but it was by methods adapted to the nature and circumstances of those times. Terriers or particular accounts of the rights of each benefice in a Diocese, have been for many ages given in at every Bps. triennial visitation; and these being drawn up by the joint consent of the Incumbent and Parishioners, and signed by the Minister and Churchwardens were used to be looked upon, and in all reason and equity ought to be deemed exceptionable evidences of such rights.   They were accordingly received as such in the spiritual Courts where all suits for Tythes and other dues of the Clergy were carried on, and being Ecclesiastical causes and only of their cognisance. But since the Reformation the Common Lawyers have found out querks in law to draw these causes into their Courts, and particularly whenever a modus is pretended, that pretence is a sufficient reason for a Judge to issue out a prohibition ordering the Spiritual Court to proceed no further in such a cause.   It being thus brought into the Common Law Courts, the next thing is to set aside all the evidences against such pretence of a modus, arising from the agreement of these Terriers for hundreds of years together; which is done on a pretext that these Terriers were taken by direction from Bps. and not in virtue of any special commission from the Crown, the result of which alone is all the evidence allowed in these Courts.

The Clergy thus stripped of all the evidences wherein they confided, and had been ever safe before, were forced to have recourse to other methods for opposing such pretences of a modus.   Now by Law a Modus must have been from time immemorial, and this was judged to be the time of Richard I. higher than whose reign none of our Records relating to this subject go; and indeed none are ancienter except the Piperolls and Domesday book.   When therefore a Modus of sixpence an acre for land now set at twenty shillings an acre and the Crop whereof is probably worth considerably more was pretended, they thought it a sufficient refutation of such Modus, to shew by records of the Tax rolls in the resigns of the Successors of that King, and by Inquisitions taken in virtue of commissions from the Crown, that the very land in question was set in later reigns than Richards but at three pence an acre, and therefore six pence an acre could never be then paid for the tythe thereof.   This proof was indeed allowed till Baron Pryse was removed from the Exchequer Court; since which it has been rejected and all the maxims formerly received there in favour of tythes laid aside ; so that the decision of the

For my part, I readily profess that in all cases I am disposed to have recourse to the old ways of our constitution for the redress of any pressing grievance. There was formerly a reasonable proportion between the representatives of Counties which were about 90, and those of Cities and great Towns which amounted to about 100, and those of lesser burroughs which returned about 70 deputies, these making in all about 256 members of Parliament. This proportion of representation lasted till the time of Q. Elizabeth: but since the beginning of her reign, it has been gradually destroying, and is now so entirely overturned, that the smaller burroughs, though they do not possess the thousandth part of the others property, can outvote them both in the House of Commons, there having been as many representatives for these paltry burroughs added to the Parliament, as it consisted of before that time. In one Session of Parliament in that Queen's reign eight small burroughs in Cornwall were called upon to send Deputies, and the humour went on till the Parliament of 1641 made up the disproportion now complained of with so much reason. There does not therefore appear to me any means of rectifying this abuse and of restoring the ancient ballance of our Constitution, so natural as the disfranchising at once of all those late created Parliamentary burroughs, whose constant corruption and bribery of late years so well known and so easy to be proved, call loudly for such a method to be taken.

If this should be thought too great a change, and the disfranchising of these burroughs should be deemed improper, their corruption may probably be prevented by allowing all the freeholders of 40s. a year within the hundred, in which such burrough is situated, to vote equally with the present electors or inhabitants in the burrough for the representatives thereof: and in case this method be taken, such Freeholders being allowed a right of voting for representatives, no wrong would be done them, if the right of voting in elections of Knights of the Shire were restrained to Freeholders that pay for 10£ a year to the land tax: which would render County elections much more easy and less expensive.

If neither of these methods should be approved, it may be considered whether all these burroughs should not be limited to one representative, and the choice of the other transferred to the several Counties of the kingdom in proportion to their payments towards the Land Tax; by which means the present number of representatives may be preserved. One or other of these methods seems necessary to be taken, or else the corruption, being grown so general and barefaced in these burroughs, will not admit of a cure: and unless it be cured, Parliaments that should naturally be the guardians of all our rights and liberties, will prove the worst of our grievances, and such an one as will make all the rest irremediable. If these great points, of the proportion of our representation, and the unbiassed freedome of elections were once secured, everything else will easily be secured by Parliament.

To establish this freedom and put a stop to the corruption or violence that destroy it, nothing appears at first sight more proper than the putting of Parliaments upon their ancient foot, allowing them to sit but one Session, and never to continue above a year. In such a case foreigners or strangers who have no merit or interest in a burrough but what their bribes and money purchase them, will never be able to carry elections against the Gentlemen of the neighbourhood, who have a natural interest in the place. For as the present circumstances of the Crown and Nation, so different from what they formerly were, require Parliament to be annually held for the granting of new supplies, no private purse can hold out for any length of time in furnishing those immense sums that are now squandered away by strangers in the expences of disputed elections: and as this evill is grown very rife, and all laws made to remedy it have hitherto proved ineffectual, it is scarce possible to be cured by any other method.

There is another practice in the House of Commons itself, that helps to destroy the freedome of Parliaments: I mean the method taken by the stronger party of thinning the House, and expelling such as are of different sentiments from themselves, however duely chosen; altering the rights of electors as they see fit and as will best furnish them a pretence for that purpose. Some method should therefore be taken in fixing the right of voting in elections on an invariable foot, so as not to be violated or altered by any determination of the House of Commons. If this were done by an Act of Parliament, and every person whose vote is refused by the returning officer, or whose right is infringed by the intrusion of a wrong member, had power to bring an action and to recover very great damages, from both of these, this scandalous and mischievous evill might possibly be prevented.

The iniquities of these late times suggest some other measures to be taken; such as the limiting of the number of officers and pensioners that sit in the House of Commons; and the disabling of all Excise men, Custom house officers, and soldiers, that are under command and consequently not free to vote according to their own inclinations and real sentiments, from having voices in elections, unless on account of their freeholds, when they have any.

In former times the Civil and Military power of the Nation lay entirely in the hands of Gentlemen of estates, and was incident to their tenures; but that face of things is now changed, and the exercise of the Civil power is at present vested in the Justices of the peace, as that of the military is in the Lord and Deputy Lieutenants. Very inconsiderable persons have of late years been put into both these commissions; and very ill conse-quences have either been found or are daily apprehended, to arise from thence. This makes it generally wished that none should be qualified for the office of a Deputy Lieutenant who has not £500 a year, or for that of a Justice of peace in any county, who has not £300 or at least £200 a year in such County. These methods for restoring in some degree such con-siderable branches of our old Constitution would at the same time advance the security of the Church.

There are penal laws enough already made, and I do not see any occasion there can be of adding to them unless that instead of receiving the Sacrament occasionally, the cinstant conformity of a person to the established Church, be made the qualification for any government, command or office of rank or profit: and that instead of a Certificate of a persons having received the Sacrament, another of his being a constant communicant with the Church of England be insisted on and given by the Minister and Churchwardens of the parish where such person usually resides six months at least in the year, before he shall be allowed to enter upon the exercise of his office.

Some such regulations as these, (which are but too much wanted at present,) would contribute equally to the security of the Church, and the happiness of the Nation.

At the end of this Memorandum there is appended the following autograph letter from the Pretender, which would seem to show that Sir Robert Walpole had personally authorised Mr. Carte to obtain a statement of his views. It runs as follows:—

ROME, *July* 17, 1739.

The Message you bring could not but appear verry singular and extraordinary to me because you deliver it only from second hand and that I have no sort of proof of your being authorised by the person in question, who cannot but feel that it is natural for me to mistrust what may come from him. It may be and I hope it is the case that he wishes me and my cause well, and I am sensible it may be greatly in his power to serve both.

If he hath realy my interest at heart, lett him send to me some trusty friend and confident of his to explain to me his sentiments and viewes; and if he pursues measures which manifestly tend to my Restoration, I shall be persuaded of his sincerity, and shall consider and reward him after my restoration proportionably to the share he may have had in bringing it about. But whatever may or may not be in this matter, I have no difficulty in putting it in your power to satisfy him authoritically on the two articles about which he is sollicitous, since independant of his desire, I am fully resolved to protect and secure the Church of England according to the reiterated promises I have made to that effect, and shall be ready after my restoration to give all reasonable security which a first Parliament can ask of me for that end. As for ye Princes of the House of Hannover I thank God I have no ressentment against them, nor against any one living; I shall never repine at their living happily in their own Country after I am in possession of my Kingdomes and should they fall into my power upon any attempt for my restoration, I shall certainly not touch a hair of their heads.

I thought it proper to explain in this manner my sentiments on these heads not absolutely to neglect an overture which may be of great importance if well grounded, and if otherwayes no inconvenience can arise from what I have here said.

JAMES R.

At the back of this letter is written in Sir Robert Walpole's writing—

This original letter wrote to Mr. Tho. Cart when at Rome, and given Him by the Pretender was deliver'd to me by the said Mr. Tho. Cart Sept. 15th. 1739 together with the Heads &c.

Whilst this correspondence would seem to show that Sir Robert was not altogether disinclined to enter into secret negotiations with the Pretender, it must be remembered that up to comparatively recent times statesmen at the head of affairs were much given to employing secret agents for the purpose of obtaining information—very often without the knowledge of the Government over which they presided. Cavour, I believe, was about the last to employ these methods, and it is said that though he was very much given to this sort of thing, he never obtained any good by it, as the agents he employed never reported anything of the slightest value, most of their communications being absolutely unreliable and untrue. Mr. Carte, however, appears to have really enjoyed the confidence of the Pretender, and the whole correspondence is somewhat interesting as showing the great amount of intrigue and love of secret negotiation which prevailed at the period of the eighteenth century when this memorandum was drawn up.

INDEX

345

THE END

Printed by R. & R. CLARK, LIMITED, *Edinburgh.*